Eastern European Capitalism in the Making

This book examines the relationship between governments, labor, and business in Central and Eastern Europe as capitalism develops. The tripartite forums for social dialogue in Bulgaria and Poland are described as "tripartism," a new postcommunist species of state-society interaction and a brand of capitalism distinct from American neoliberalism, Western European neocorporatism, and Japanese statism. These forums are understood as institutionalizing of conflict among postcommunist social actors in the industrial arena and consist of three specific elements: political negotiations, civic participation, and multilevel bargaining. The emergence and development of postcommunist tripartism are significantly shaped by the twin domestic necessities to preserve social peace and legitimate and consolidate the social actors. The book explains variations in the establishment and functioning of tripartite institutions across Central and Eastern European countries, industries, and regions, with corporatist legacies and legacies of extrication paths from state socialism, on the one hand, and, on the other, with social partners' strategic commitment to concerted action. Integration into the international economy and polity, especially European integration, has somewhat diminished differences and, in the long run, is helping to preserve and maintain social dialogue structures in the Central and Eastern European region.

Professor Elena A. Iankova is a research fellow at the Institute for European Studies, Cornell University, and a visiting scholar at the Johnson Graduate School of Management, Cornell University. Originally from Bulgaria, she has traveled extensively in Central and Eastern Europe, doing field work in Bulgaria, Poland, and Hungary.

Eastern European Capitalism in the Making

ELENA A. IANKOVA
Cornell University

CAMBRIDGE
UNIVERSITY PRESS

CAMBRIDGE UNIVERSITY PRESS
Cambridge, New York, Melbourne, Madrid, Cape Town,
Singapore, São Paulo, Delhi, Tokyo, Mexico City

Cambridge University Press
The Edinburgh Building, Cambridge CB2 8RU, UK

Published in the United States of America by
Cambridge University Press, New York

www.cambridge.org
Information on this title: www.cambridge.org/9780521813143

First published 2002

A catalogue record for this publication is available from the British Library

Library of Congress Cataloguing in Publication data

Iankova, Elena A. (Elena Atanassova)
Between extrication and integration : Eastern European capitalism in the making / Elena A. Iankova.
p. cm.
Includes bibliographical references and index.
ISBN 0-521-81314-X
1. Europe, Eastern – Economic conditions – 1989– 2. Capitalism – Europe, Eastern. 3. Post-communism – Europe, Eastern. 4. Social conflict – Europe, Eastern. I. Title: Eastern European capitalism in the making. II. Title.

HC244 .I24 2002
330.9438–dc21 2002066514

ISBN 978-0-521-81314-3 Hardback

For my parents
Nadka and Atanas

and to the memory of my grandparents
Elena and Teofil, Riska and Dimiter

with gratitude and love

Contents

Acknowledgments

The project that ends with this book's publication had its beginning eleven years ago, at the very start of the postcommunist transition. In Sofia, Bulgaria, a debate with Derek Jones over the meaning of Bulgarian "tripartism" stimulated me to think analytically about the turbulent events of which I was then a part, with particular reference to government–labor–business relations in Bulgaria and throughout the central and eastern European region.

The book could not have been completed without financial support from a variety of sources: the World Bank Graduate Scholarship Program, the Institute for the Study of World Politics Dissertation Fellowship Program, the National Council for Eurasian and East European Research, the German Marshall Fund of the United States, and a variety of Cornell University sources, notably, the International Political Economy Program, the Peace Studies Program and the Carpenter Chair of the Mario Einaudi Center for International Studies, the Michelle Sicca Fellowship Program of the Institute for European Studies, and the research grant programs of the Institute of Collective Bargaining and the Center for Advanced Human Resource Studies at Cornell's School of Industrial and Labor Relations.

I am thankful to all the government, labor, and business officials and experts from Bulgaria and Poland who provided organizational information. I greatly appreciate the help of their representatives with whom I held interviews. So legion were those who aided my research that the following listing is unavoidably incomplete.

On the Bulgarian government side, I thank three Ministers of Labor and Social Policy: Evgeni Matinchev, Mincho Koralski, and Ivan Neikov; Chavdar Savov, the major of Vratza; Bulgarian Parliament members Blagovest Sendov, Svetlana Djankova, Edward Klein, Nikola Kojchev, Anastasija Mozer, Elena Poptodorova, and Remzi Osman; and, in addition, Vladimir Kissjov, Teodor Dechev, Nikolai Nikolaev, Milcho Dimitrov,

Goran Bankov, Oleg Chulev, Hristina Stojcheva, Raimond Saparev, Stoimen Velev, Valentin Gruev, Dojcho Dinev, Georgi Vankov, Emil Mingov, and Emilia Krysteva.

On the Bulgarian union side, I am indebted to Professor Krustyo Petkov, Ivan Neikov, Yuri Aroyo, Georgi Georgiev, Emilian Abadziev, Elena Vassileva, Ekaterina Ribarova, Nedka Koleva, Nikola Simeonov, Bero Berov, Licho Lichev, Georgi Bochev, Jordan Vassilev, and Haralampi Hristov, of the Confederation of Independent Trade Unions in Bulgaria; Dr. Konstantin Trenchev, Dimiter Manolov, Evgenia Kosseva, Vladimir Bojadziev, Todor Radev, Zdravcho Zdravchev, Aleksander Shalamanov, Krum Krumov, and Alexander Uzunov, of the Podkrepa Confederation of Labor; and Assen Chaushev, of the OSSOB trade unions.

On the Bulgarian business side, I am very thankful to Bozhidar Danev, Georgi Shivarov, Vikran Tebeian, and Dimiter Gadev, of the Bulgarian Industrial Association; Bozhidar Dimitrov, of the Bulgarian Chamber of Commerce and Industry; Rumen Bjandov, of the Vazrazhdane Union of Private Producers; Iliana Derilova, of the Bulgarian International Business Association; and Mincho Koralski, of the Union of Private Economic Enterprising.

I am very thankful also to the Polish social partners. On the government side, these include Labor Ministers Jerzy Kropiwnicki, Michal Boni, and Longin Komolowski; Polish Parliament members Ewa Tomaszewska, Tadeusz Syryjczyk, Maciej Manicki, Pawel Jankiewicz, Zbigniew Kaniewski, and Zdzislawa Janowska; and government officials and experts Elzbieta Sobotka, Zbigniew Zegarski, Zygmunt Gadaj, Henryka Odachowska, and Krzysztof Raczka.

On the union side, I thank Ewa Lewicka, Janusz Tomaszewski, Bogdan Osinski, Henryk Formicki, Maria Borucka, and Dariusz Kucharski, of Solidarity, and Rychard Lepik, Rychard Konrad, Bogdan Grzybowski, Boleslaw Bartnik, and Waldemar Chyczewski, of the OPZZ.

My thanks also go to representatives of the Confederation of Polish Employers: Andrzej Wilk, Henryk Wilk, Jerzy Straszynski, Janusz Tunia, and Marian Osuch.

I especially thank former Lodz governors Waldemar Bohdanowicz and Andrzej Peczak, as well as Lodz government officials and experts Elzbieta Hybner, Mieczyslaw Mik, Wlodzimierz Mielczarek, and Krzysztof Kaczmarek.

My numerous interviews in Poland would have been difficult or impossible without the institutional support of the Institute of Sociology at the University of Lodz and its director, Professor Jolanta Kulpinska, as well as the Department of Sociology at the University of Warsaw and its head, Professor Witold Morawski.

Many scholars, colleagues, and friends have commented on numerous drafts of this book. I am first of all particularly thankful to Lowell Turner,

Peter Katzenstein, Valerie Bunce, and David Stark, my Ph.D. committee members at Cornell, for their helpful comments, their patience, and their understanding and support, as well as for their high expectations, which inspired me to strive for academic rigor. Their searching, critical comments on thousands of manuscript pages were essential to the book's completion, and the professional dedication and integrity they exemplified helped make the endeavor seem worthwhile and rewarding.

I am also thankful to Sarosh Kuruvilla, Harry Katz, Derek Jones, Sidney Tarrow, Peter Auer, Hans Slomp, and Ronald Linden for their thorough comments on separate chapters of the manuscript. For their insightful suggestions during numerous discussions of postcommunist transition issues and social dialogue in the postcommunist region in particular, I am thankful to Linda Gasser, Michael Belzer, Jean Clifton, Alex Colvin, Owen Darbishire, David Dornisch, Elena Gjurova, Mira Yanova, Zhivko Georgiev, Grisha Gradev, Krastyo Petkov, John Thirkell, Jolanta Kulpinska, Witold Morawski, Michal Sewerynski, Jerzy Hausner, Grazyna Chorazykiewicz, Lajos Hethy, Zdenka Mansfeldova, Alfred Pankert, Guiseppe Casale, and Vladislav Egorov.

I am also thankful to the participants in several seminars and conference meetings, at which parts of the book design and results were presented: the Collective Bargaining Workshop at Cornell; the Institute for European Studies Lecture Series at Cornell; the 1997 and 1999 annual meetings of the American Political Science Association; the 1998 and 2000 meetings of the International Conference of Europeanists, organized by the Council for European Studies; the 1998 annual meeting of the American Industrial Relations Research Association; the 1998 meeting of the International Industrial Relations Association; the 1999 convention of the American Association for the Advancement of Slavic Studies; the 1994 meeting of the International Sociological Association; and the November 1997 Harvard Workshop on New Directions in the Study of East European State Socialism.

I owe special thanks to Brian Keeling for his excellent editorial work on various drafts of the manuscript.

The Institute for European Studies and the Johnson Graduate School of Management at Cornell provided all the institutional support I needed to bring this project to its final stage.

Special appreciation is due to the Cambridge University Press team of editors and production staff who made the final stage of the book project a pleasurable experience: Lewis Bateman, Stephanie Sakson, and Marielle Poss. I further appreciate the very helpful comments provided by two anonymous reviewers at Cambridge.

I am thankful to Princeton University Press for allowing the reprint of parts of Wislawa Szymborska's poem "Autotomy" originally published in *Sounds, Feelings, Thoughts: Seventy Poems by Wislawa Szymborska*, translated and introduced by Magnus J. Krynski and Robert A. Maguire (Princeton University Press, 1981).

This project's enormous challenges would have defeated me without the unfailing warm support, encouragement, and love of my family. My son Atanas deserves special thanks for his patience and understanding. My sister Hristina, my brother-in-law Dimiter, and my niece Nadka have always supported me, in joy and sorrow. My parents Nadka and Atanas, and my grandparents – Elena and Teofil, and Riska and Dimiter – have taught me the value of love and caring. I dedicate this book to them.

April 2002
Ithaca, New York

Elena Iankova

Abbreviations

AWS	Solidarity Electoral Action
BIA	Bulgarian Industrial Association
BIBA	Bulgarian International Business Association
BSP	Bulgarian Socialist Party
BTC	Bulgarian Telecommunications Company
CEE	Central and Eastern Europe
CESA	Council for Economic and Social Agreement
CITUB	Confederation of Independent Trade Unions in Bulgaria
(Podkrepa) CL	Confederation of Labor
CMEA	Council for Mutual Economic Assistance
CMKOS	Czech Trade Union Confederation
DDR	German Democratic Republic
EBRD	European Bank for Reconstruction and Development
ELPEM	Sofia-based company, producer of electrical equipment
EMU	Economic and Monetary Union
ESC	Economic and Social Committee
ETUC	European Trade Union Confederation
EU	European Union
GDP	Gross domestic product
GDR	German Democratic Republic
GWTU	General Workers' Trade Union
HAIC	Hungarian Association of International Companies
ICFTU	International Confederation of Free Trade Unions
ILO	International Labor Organization
IMF	International Monetary Fund
INTEX	Lodz-based company, producer of cloth

JCC	Joint Consultative Committee
KCZZ	Central Trade Union Commission
KLD	Liberal Democratic Congress
KOR-KSS	Committee for Social Self-Defense
KPN	Confederation of Independent Poland
KPP	Confederation of Polish Employers
KPPP	Confederation of Polish Private Employers
KSR	Conference of Workers' Self-Management
MAOSZ	National Association of Hungarian Employers
MRF	Movement for Rights and Freedoms
MSZOSZ	National Confederation of Hungarian Trade Unions
NCCI	National Commission for Coordination of Interests
NCTC	National Council for Tripartite Cooperation
NEP	New Economic Policy
NGO	Nongovernmental organization
NTU	National Trade Union
NUEM	National Union of Economic Managers
ODS	Civic Democratic Party
OECD	Organization for Economic Cooperation and Development
OPZZ	All-Poland Trade Union Alliance
OSSOB	Alliance of Free Trade Union Organizations in Bulgaria
PC	Center Civic Alliance
PHARE	Poland-Hungary Assistance for Economic Restructuring
PKWN	Committee of National Liberation
PPR	Polish Workers' Party
PPS	Polish Socialist Party
PSL	Polish Peasant Party
ROPCiO	Movement for the Defense of Human and Civil Rights
SLD	Democratic Left Alliance
SPD	Social Democratic Party
UDF	Union of Democratic Forces
UP	Labor Union
UW	Freedom Union
VSNKH or Vesenka	Supreme Economic Council
ZChN	National and Christian Union
ZPGWK	Association of Stone Coal Mining Employers

1

Hybrid Capitalism in the Making

1.1. On the Transformation Track: Varieties of Capitalism and Tripartite Coordination

With the collapse of state socialism in 1989, the formerly communist countries of Eastern Europe initiated dramatic changes in their political and economic settings and state-society relations, in an attempt to claim a new place in a world characterized by globalization and increased regional integration within three economic blocs: the United States, Europe, and Japan/Asia. Ten years after the dramatic breakthrough of 1989, the nations of Central and Eastern Europe (hereafter CEE) are actively preparing for membership in the European Union (EU). Accession negotiations for the "fast-track" countries (Poland, Hungary, the Czech Republic, Slovenia, and Estonia) started in spring 1998, and those for the "slow-track" countries (Bulgaria, Slovakia, Romania, Latvia, and Lithuania) opened in February 2000.

The accelerated preparations for accession to full EU membership are cause for reflection on some old questions and consideration of some completely new ones. What is the direction of change in CEE, and what conditions frame and shape emerging capitalism in the region? Have the legacies of state socialism and postcommunist transformation brought into being a new form of capitalism? Alternatively, under the pressures of increased globalization and regional integration, could the nations of CEE be moving toward already established capitalist variants?

Mainstream political and economic analyses on the transition from socialism to capitalism that have emerged in the ten years of transformation deal largely with domestic factors of path dependence and transformation.[1] The bulk of this literature analyzes the pros and cons of political

[1] See in Haggard and Kaufman 1995; Dawisha and Parrott 1997; Holmes 1997; Elster et al. 1998; Stark and Bruszt 1998; Tismaneanu 1999.

and economic reforms, of democratization and property transformation.[2] Emphasizing the organizational metamorphosis of state ownership during the privatization process and the "recombinant" character of postcommunist property relations, D. Stark has argued for the emergence of "recombinant" capitalism in CEE. He discovers the existence of networks of firms characterized by decentralized reorganization of assets and centralized management of liabilities, and asserts that this "viable public-private hybrid" "will differ as much from West European capitalisms as do contemporary East Asian variants" (Stark 1996: 993).

This book brings a different perspective to the CEE variant of capitalism. Its analysis focuses on the new roles and interrelationships of social actors such as the state, labor, and emerging business. An interpretive framework that gives them a central place is well suited to analyzing state socialism and its transformation into capitalist democracy. That the harbinger of state socialist collapse – Poland's Solidarity – was a labor union cannot, in my view, be coincidence. The broad reference in the literature to Solidarity as a "social movement" or a "political party" overstates its domestic support – immense though that certainly was, allowing Solidarity to absorb practically all of Polish civil society – and fails to recognize its narrower essence as a vehicle for organized *worker* protest directed at specific failures of state socialism. Since state socialism – at least as an ideology – was largely about the "dictatorship" of labor, the transitions away from it have a lot to do with labor's changing position in politics, economics, and society. With the collapse of the regime, the underlying question of transition was thus path-dependent: What is the nature of the new type of relationship we see emerging in CEE, with a democratizing postcommunist state on one side and, on the other, a dramatically mutating working society in the throes of economic restructuring? The particular types of democratization and democracy, of ownership transformation and markets, to be adopted were matters of secondary contention, compared with the particular roles of the state, labor, and private employers in the emerging capitalist order. The parts played by those actors and their relative prominence would determine most of the other details of the future capitalist societies.

This book investigates the nature of the new type of relationship between the state and the working society in CEE, as a defining characteristic of the emerging new capitalist order. Comparing the Polish and Bulgarian new state-society configurations, the book inquires into the interaction of domestic and international effects in shaping that relationship. Are the emerging new state-society arrangements purely path-dependent and transformation-driven, or they are also significantly influenced by well-established foreign models and, accordingly, the foreign aid conditionality of various international organizations?

[2] See in Commisso 1991; Bartlett 1992; Stark 1992, 1996.

An interpretive framework that gives government-labor-business relations a central place has distinguished three major variants of contemporary capitalism: corporatism as practiced in most of Western Europe, U.S.-style neoliberalism, and Japanese statism (Katzenstein 1978; Hart 1992). That widely used typology of capitalist variants does not capture the details of, for example, firm or bank organization, or the range of public/private property distributions within capitalist societies. It underscores, instead, how governments, labor, and business are linked differently and can have varying roles in state governance and market processes, with labor marginalized and the state playing only an indirect part in the neoliberal United States, governments actively engineering economic development in Asia, and strong interventionist states incorporating policy inputs from labor and business in most of western Europe.

More particularly, neoliberalism favors individualism, rational self-interest, the primacy of freedom over equality, a minimal state role in the economy, and marginalization of labor by powerful businesses. Neoliberal solutions do not rely on political intervention but treat the interplay of demand and supply in functioning markets as the most efficient and, in the long run, most viable approach to the problems of capitalist evolution. In contrast, Asian statism emphasizes collective interest, social equality, and the merits of extensive government intervention. Corporatism as practiced in Western Europe envisages a similar active role for the state, but in tandem with employers' organizations and trade unions. Thus, corporatist arrangements are based on the view that markets are always socially and politically embedded. Involving the peak associations of business and labor unions in consensual compromisal arrangements, according to this view, will facilitate implementation of the structural and monetary policies the government and central bank choose to adopt and will reduce social inequality. In contrast to the invisible politics that supports neoliberalism, economic policy-making in the Western European social market economies is visibly political.[3]

The early years of transition reveal that most of the formerly communist countries approached global capitalism using corporatist-like institutions on

[3] The work of David Soskice incorporates these variables into a broader typology of political economies. He distinguishes two main types of political economy, which he refers to as "coordinated market economies" (CMEs) and "liberal market economies" (LMEs). CMEs include the Scandinavian countries, along with much of continental Europe (though Italy and France are, according to him, somewhat anomalous). LMEs comprise mostly the Anglo-Saxon economies (the United Kingdom, the United States, Canada, New Zealand, and Australia). See in Soskice (1999). Similarly, Michel Albert (1993) presents a broader typology of capitalist variants – the Rhine (German-Japanese) model and the Anglo-Saxon model – based on two main differences: the role of the government in the economy and the social safety net. He finds the Rhine model in countries such as Germany to be more successful in the long run, due to growing ideological hegemony, increasing capital mobility, and the search for short-term profits that characterize the Anglo-Saxon model.

a large scale and at both national and subnational levels. So-called tripartism, based on the idea of "social partnership" among governments, unions, and employers' organizations, has appeared in all of the postcommunist countries, whether economically devastated or economically struggling but sound, left-wing or right-wing in government, or having strong or weak civil societies.[4] After the 1989 breakthrough, there was a broad social consensus that the society at large should move away from one-party rule, central economic planning, and a central focus on egalitarianism, and should build a new order based on democracy, the rule of law, and a market economy, with a readiness to accept greater social inequality as part of the price for economic prosperity. The transition plan worked out by "tripartite coordination," with government, labor, and emerging business interests as the three main voices in a system of compromise that was, in broad terms, to preserve social peace by distributing the burden and pain of transformation across the population as fairly as possible, with successful political and economic restructuring the anticipated reward.

Hungary was the first to introduce tripartite arrangements that differed qualitatively from the typical state socialist experience. As early as the 1960s and 1970s, the Hungarian communist party, in connection with the preparation of Hungary's Economic Reform (1968), set a precedent by formally recognizing that differences and conflicts of interest existed even under socialism (Hethy 1994b: 1). At the end of 1988 a tripartite National Council for Reconciliation of Interests was set up as part of the party-state's deliberate attempt to soften unpopular economic measures and to incorporate broader social groups in the process of government decision-making. The tripartite National Council for Reconciliation of Interests was revived in 1990, and at present it holds regular sessions on social, economic, and labor issues (Hethy 1994b; Lado 1997).

In Germany, which has what is generally considered a weak and anomalous neocorporatist system (Thelen 1991), the challenges of unification and instability in the east have brought a renaissance of neocorporatism (Webber 1994; Turner 1998). In 1991 the privatization agency THA (Treuhandanstalt), state governments, unions, and employers' associations negotiated an agreement, and a Solidarity Pact was concluded in 1993. The roundtable negotiations on the Solidarity Pact took place between September 1992 and March 1993, and involved the major political and social forces – the federal government, the state governments, the trade unions, the principal business associations, the Social Democratic Party (SPD), and the major opposition party Christian Democratic Union (CDU) – in discussions of measures for coping with the East German crisis and rebuilding the East German economy (Sally and Webber 1994).

[4] See in Thirkell and Tseneva 1992; Freeman 1993; Hausner et al. 1993; Pankert 1994; Hethy 1995; Thirkell et al. 1995.

In Bulgaria, social dialogue emerged in December 1989, and in March 1990 a General Agreement was concluded between the government, the Confederation of Independent Trade Unions in Bulgaria, and the Union of Economic Managers. The agreement was designed to manage the economic crisis and control the social unrest and disaffection that were anticipated in the wake of pending economic reforms. In April 1990 the signatories of the General Agreement became partners in a National Commission for Coordination of Interests. After changing several times its name and scope, finally, in the beginning of 1993 the National Council for Tripartite Cooperation was formed following the adoption of the new Labor Code, which made social partnership mandatory. The council continues to function today (Thirkell and Tseneva 1992; Petkov and Gradev 1995; Iankova 1998, 2000).

In Czechoslovakia the federal tripartite Council for Economic and Social Agreement (CESA) was established in October 1990, and from the beginning of 1993 the republican councils for economic and social agreement of the Czech Republic and of Slovakia continued to function separately. The main task of these councils, which are known broadly as the "Tripartite," is to conclude annual general agreements defining conditions of employment and incomes policy (Cambalikova and Mansfeldova 1997).

In Romania a joint government–trade union commission has existed since the end of 1990, with participation of twelve unions, the government, and emerging employers. It functioned regularly in 1991 and 1992 and concluded annual national labor accords, but failed to conclude an accord for 1993. At present, regular tripartite consultations continue in a national economic and social council on issues such as pay indexation and minimum wages (Stefan 1994).

Similar tripartite negotiation bodies were also created in the states of the former Soviet Union. In Russia a national tripartite commission for the regulation of social and labor relations was set up in January 1992, and each year it negotiates national wage agreements (Kirichenko and Koudyukin 1993; Kubicek 1996; Christensen 1999). National tripartite commissions were also set up in Belarus,[5] Moldova,[6] Ukraine (Kubicek 1996), and Latvia,[7] among others.

In Poland, however, whose civil society was a front-runner in the extrication from state socialism, institutionalized social dialogue emerged only in 1994. Before then, relations among social partners were complicated by Poland's monolithic and "ethical" civil society (Linz and Stepan 1996) or the lack of divisions within the civil monostructure that fought against the

[5] *BBC Summary of World Broadcasts*, 15 March 1994.

[6] *BBC Summary of World Broadcasts*, 2 October 1993.

[7] *RFE/RL Daily Report*, no. 248, 29 December 1993.

communist regime in the 1980s. There was informal bargaining between the unions and the Ministry of Labor, while a tripartite forum – the Main Employment Council – was institutionalized by law only in regard to the most explosive social problem of restructuring, that is, unemployment. A formal tripartite arrangement on broader issues of social and economic restructuring had to wait for the Enterprise Pact, signed in February 1993. In February 1994 a Tripartite Commission on Socio-Economic Issues was formed and became a forum for constant negotiations between the government and the Confederation of Polish Employers, Solidarity, the All-Poland Trade Union Alliance, and seven branch unions (Hausner and Morawski 1994).

At the same time, the postcommunist countries have developed tripartite institutions at lower branch and regional levels. Additional single-issue tripartite forums also were created, mostly at the national level, but some spread to lower levels as well. Each of these forums addressed pressing problems in a particular area: employment and unemployment, vocational training, labor protection and work conditions, health and safety at work, social assistance, social security and social rehabilitation, and social issues of particular professional groups, such as employees in the civil service and budgetary institutions.

These easily observable tripartite-corporatist configurations of state-society relations across the CEE region have prompted, however, a confusing variety of interpretations, from pure neoliberal pluralism to neostatism and corporatism, with multifarious mixtures in between. The problem actually surfaced earlier, with CEE observers' conclusion in the late 1980s that the quickening of civil society, and especially the rise of Solidarity, heralded conflicting outcomes. On the one hand were observers who saw the "demise" of corporatism as a "political project and as an immoral practice in political life," clearing the way for "genuine democratic institutions" (Chirot 1980; Staniszkis 1984). On the other hand were authors such as David Ost, who concluded, on the contrary, that the 1980 Gdansk Agreement between Solidarity and the regime, as well as the agreement signed in the spring of 1989 in Poland that legalized the Polish opposition, point in the direction of an "inevitable" corporatist outcome in Poland (Ost 1989, 1990).

In the early 1990s, the quick institutionalization of tripartite forums for social dialogue across the region has led many observers of the postcommunist transformations to conclude that *corporatist-like* practices have been established in the formerly communist countries, especially in Hungary, the Czech republic, Bulgaria, and Poland (Pedersen et al. 1993; Gradev 1994; Hethy 1994a; Thirkell et al. 1995). Following the initial liberal phases of economic reform, however, some authors argued for the emergence of a typical *neoliberal pluralism* in Poland, Hungary, and

Romania, one that has persisted into later phases (Tatur 1993; Schienstock and Traxler 1994; Millard 1999: 113). The supporters of this view emphasized the impressive organizational pluralism and the weakness of trade unions in these countries.

Other authors, while acknowledging the institutionalization of tripartite forums but also their allegedly "inefficient and meaningless" policy-making outcome, argued for the emergence of *neoliberal tripartism* (see in Thompson and Traxler 1997). Others saw a similar mixture of neoliberal pluralism and corporatist tripartism, but one that was determined by country variation rather than conflicting institutional and policy ensembles. Thus, some observers argued for the emergence of pluralism in Hungary and Romania but the prevalence of tripartite concertation in Poland, as in Bulgaria and, to a less elaborated extent, in Russia. Hungary has qualified as a pluralistic regime on the grounds that its interest reconciliation council "has no rule-making competence" (Morawski 1994; Schienstock and Traxler 1994; Thompson and Traxler 1997). Another observer has concluded, in contrast, that Poland developed a confrontational-pluralist model and Hungary a compromise-corporatist one (Seleny 1999).

And finally, there were authors who emphasized Asian developmental-style practices and outcomes in the postcommunist region. The prevalence of state ownership and the important role played by the state in the process of postcommunist restructuring have moved them to regard postcommunist governance as basically statist in character (Amsden et al. 1994).

The next section attempts not only to sort out the merits and weaknesses of these contrasting interpretations, but also, and more important, to establish a sound basis for analytical explanation and policy responses to existing tripartite arrangements.

1.2. The Institution of Postcommunist Tripartism

It is noteworthy that part of the confusing variety of analytical interpretations listed above reflected the underdeveloped and immature "corporatist" nature of the tripartite arrangements that spread so rapidly across the CEE region in the early 1990s. Confusion also comes, however, from contested meanings of the concepts – and in particular that of corporatism – in the Western literature. As Williamson wrote, "corporatism remains an ambiguous concept in the political vocabulary, encompassing a wide range of all too often imprecise definition" (Williamson 1985: 3). On the one hand, there are political reservations with the usage of the concept. The interwar experience left, regrettably, a confusing mixture of corporatist and fascist ideologies. Despite the genuine revival of the concept in the 1970s as "neo-corporatism" (Schmitter 1974), and particularly as "democratic corporatism" in reference to the postwar experience with western European corporatist settlements (Katzenstein 1984, 1985), it, as Perez-Diaz (1987) notes, can still awaken in Spanish public opinion the echo of the Francoist "Estado Corporativo" (Corporatist State). That burdened historical legacy, despite the addition of prefixes such as "neo-," "societal," "liberal," or "democratic" to corporatism, gives preferences to the usage of terms other than corporatism, such as "concertation" and "tripartite cooperation," "social partnership" (mainly in regard to the Austrian and German examples of corporatism), "negotiated economy" (the Scandinavian case), and "organized" and "coordinated" capitalism.

Most of these terms stem from various segments of the more encompassing analytical concept of corporatism, thus creating confusing conceptual diversities of its meaning. Lehmbruch pointed to three analytically distinct developments of "classic neo-corporatism"[8] that have been labeled as "corporatism": "(i) the development and strengthening of centralized interest organizations or 'peak' associations – which possess a representational monopoly; (ii) the granting to these associations of privileged access to government, and the growth of – more or less institutionalized – linkages between public administration and such interest organizations; (iii) the 'social partnership' of organized labor and business aimed at regulating conflicts between these groups, in coordination with government policy (usually in the form of 'tripartism')" (Lehmbruch 1984: 61).

This study uses the insights of the neocorporatist literature to analyze the emerging tripartite forums for social dialogue in CEE – hereafter referred to as "tripartite coordination" or, interchangeably, "tripartism"[9] – as a new postcommunist species of state-society interaction and a new brand of capitalism that is distinct from the three major variants of contemporary capitalism, including Western European neocorporatism.

[8] It reflects the heyday of corporatist arrangements in Western Europe in the 1960s and 1970s, marked with impressive social and political stability and economic growth, on the basis of centralized negotiations over wages and incomes and social and employment policies.

[9] I have chosen this term, first, for policy and practical convenience. Despite the immature employers' side in tripartite negotiations, the official policy label for these corporatist-like forums in different postcommunist countries contains, in fact, the word "tripartite": the National Council for *Tripartite* Cooperation in Bulgaria, for example, and the National *Tripartite* Commission in Poland. Similarly, the International Labor Organization – which has encouraged the promotion of social dialogue since it was founded in 1919 – has in its numerous conventions and recommendations the notion of *tripartite* cooperation as its ideological thread (Trebilcock 1994: 5–6). Second, the concept of tripartism emphasizes some critical differences with the classic neocorporatist arrangements that peaked in Western Europe in the 1970s. In particular, as a more neutral concept in terms of social purpose and policy outcomes, it emphasizes the political-ideological disentanglement of postcommunist tripartite arrangements from the social-democratic thread that was so typical for the Western European "corporatism" – often used interchangeably with "social democracy" – of the 1960s and 1970s.

Central is the understanding of these forums as the *institutionalization of compromise* among social actors in the industrial arena. I apply an institutionalist perspective to their analysis, as part of what B. Guy Peters called "societal institutionalism" (Peters 1999: 20).[10] Although the early corporatist literature did not explicitly advance an institutional analysis, it clearly delineated a "structural relationship" between government and interest organizations in the society that could be interpreted through all the major institutionalist perspectives, such as historical, rational choice, and sociological (normative) institutionalism (Peters 1999: 117). The relationship between government and interest groups could be viewed as "rational" (the rational choice perspective), but also as aimed at an "appropriate behavior" understood as general consensus (the normative-institutionalist perspective) and as "path-dependent" (the historical-institutionalist perspective).[11] The common methodological theme is the institutionalist one, the recognition that the interests held by individuals are in part organizationally – not individually – determined.

This study emphasizes the importance of the normative-institutional aspects of tripartite coordination, the pursuit of social peace through compromise on the basis of general consensus among all actors involved over commonly desired political and economic outcomes. In its broad sense, tripartite cooperation implies the inclusion of social groups in the political and governmental decision-making process, in order to minimize conflict and maximize growth. This inclusion is grounded in a shared understanding of the necessity to cooperate in the resolution of pressing common problems. Tripartite compromise implies that the state and all interest groups participating in tripartite bargaining moderate their positions and make trade-offs to achieve "second-best" results.

The normative, consensual-compromisal aspects of tripartism have a special meaning for societies undergoing major sociopolitical and economic transformations, such as the CEE countries. While ruling elites, new opposition movements, and the society at large all agreed to disentangle themselves from the old practices of state socialism, successful accomplishment of this strategic goal was largely contingent on their commitment to maintain social peace. This meant a continuous societal effort to balance the

[10] Peters outlined four basic elements of an institution that distinguish the institutionalist approach from other approaches: (1) the existence of a structured feature of the society and/or polity, which could be formal (a legislature, an agency in the public bureaucracy, or a legal framework) or informal (a network of interacting organizations or a set of shared norms); (2) the existence of some stability over time; (3) evidence that individual behavior is affected by the institutional constraints; and (4) the existence of some sense of shared values and meaning among the members of the institution (Peters 1999: 18).

[11] See the review article by Hall and Taylor 1996; also Thelen and Steinmo 1992; March and Olsen 1984, 1989.

dynamic and intensifying conflicts between the "high" public interest in transforming the old social order and the "low" group and individual interest in keeping wages and living standards at high levels. Among the elements of transition on which consensus was reached was the need to construct the three major capitalist institutions: private property, a market, and wage labor.

My institutionalist methodological framework further emphasizes policy procedures rather than policy outcomes. The tripartite institutions and procedures of transition reflect social dialogue arrangements that might have different policy outcomes: Keynesian of a social-democratic type and leading to active interest group involvement in the decision-making process, or austerity-oriented, neoliberal ones which – as inevitable as they were in order to secure the creation of functioning markets in the CEE region – might also lead to the marginalization of interest group input in government policy-making, or some hybrid in between (Iankova and Turner 2000).

Postcommunist tripartism critically differs from the classic neocorporatist arrangements that peaked in Western Europe in the 1970s. CEE's tripartite forums for social dialogue could be regarded as a *transitional* form, an *immature* approximation of classic neocorporatism, with important differences in terms of social purpose and policy functions, participating actors, and organizational-institutional structures.

Noteworthy, however, is that the CEE arrangements seem to be "on track" with the most recent developments of corporatist practice in Western Europe. By the early 1990s, when tripartite corporatist-like arrangements peaked in the postcommunist region, the Western European classic neocorporatist arrangements had declined and "withered away," as a result of increasing flexibilization, internationalization, and globalization of the world economy, combined with the decline of Keynesian economic policies and the rise of neoliberalism. Thus, from the early 1980s, a trend toward an increasingly "disorganized" capitalism ensued in Western Europe (Lash and Urry 1987; Gerlich 1992). From the early 1990s, however, a surprising "renaissance" of Western European corporatist arrangements was observed (Grote and Schmitter 1999). The new forms of corporatism bear clear signs of restructuring and transformation, and point to the emergence of new features such as "decentralization" (Schmitter 1990; Treu 1992), "flexibilization" (Soskice 1988), "segmentation and fragmentation" (Streeck 1984), "less regulation" (Scheuer 1998), and, most important, disengagement with the social-democratic ideology and practice of classic neocorporatism even in the conditions of empowered left-wing governments (Ferner and Hyman 1998). Overall, in an increasingly neoliberal global environment, the Western European corporatist arrangements are still searching for a new identity and role in the domestic political economies of western European countries, with a rethinking and revision of "classic" corporatist theory.

In addition, with a history of development already a decade old, postcommunist tripartism could hardly be regarded as a transitional form and immature approximation of Western European neocorporatism. The tripartite arrangements in the region developed distinct elements, some of which have proven to be transitory, while others have been consolidated and integrated in the new political economies of the CEE nation-states. I trace tripartism's features along three lines: social purpose and policy outcomes, participating actors, and organizational-institutional structures.

In terms of social purpose and policy outcomes, tripartism developed as a dynamic hybrid characterized by *political negotiations* rather than bargaining over purely social and economic conditions that is so typical for the Western European policy-making process. As far as participating actors are concerned, tripartism represents a broader *civic arrangement* rather than a classic tripartite formation for coordination of the interests of labor and business with those of the state. And finally, in terms of institutional structures, tripartism developed as a complex *multilevel bargaining* structure that links together national, regional, and sectoral actors for the resolution of problems with national and local importance. In the course of transition, the purely political traits of postcommunist tripartism have gradually faded away, and have opened the way for more socially and economically embedded negotiations as an integral part of the policy-making process. The other traits of tripartism – namely, its characteristic as a civic arrangement that spans to the third sector, and its multilevel character – have gone beyond the logic of transition and have been integrated in CEE's new political economies. I describe below in a greater detail the three closely interwoven elements of postcommunist tripartism: political negotiations, civic participation, and multilevel bargaining.

Social Purpose and Policy Outcomes: Political Tripartism

The imperatives that gave rise to and shaped the Western European corporatism in the aftermath of World War II were to minimize class conflict and promote social cohesion and solidarity. In addition to this important "social peace" function, during its heyday, Western European practices with "democratic corporatism" focused on centralized wage bargaining and involvement of the interest associations of labor and business in macroeconomic policy-making that could promote growth, dampen inflation, and facilitate industrial adjustment. Williamson (1989) recognized two both linked and distinct usages of corporatist arrangements: interest intermediation as a mode for organizing and controlling conflicting functional interests, and as a mode for making and implementing public policy.

Postcommunist tripartism does not really constitute such a comprehensive social system combining both aspects of Western European classic neocorporatism. The public functions initially performed by the CEE tripartite forums, given the uncertainties of the transition, have largely focused on the preservation of social peace and the legitimation of actors, rather than – as has been so typical for Western Europe – public policy coordination of wages and income. Postcommunist tripartism was originally conceived with a single social purpose: as a temporary safety valve to prevent an explosion of social conflict during the difficult times of economic restructuring and political democratization, and as a legitimating glue for social partners' organizational restructuring.

It does not mean, however, that CEE tripartism is nothing more than "empty institutional shells" that play a minimal role in the course of transition and transformation. In times of transition and transformation with great political and social uncertainties, the "social peace" aspect of tripartite coordination plays a crucial role in keeping the system from a complete breakup and disentanglement of its elements. This is a broader, but, I believe, more precise perspective of tripartism's transformative role and impact on postcommunist transitions (Iankova 1998).

Tripartism's crucial "social peace" function is well matched with its facilitating role in the democratization of political and social life. In this regard, CEE's tripartite coordination, which in Western European political economies is predominantly at play in the industrial-economic arena, has developed prominent *political* traits.

The downfall of state socialism occurred, without exception, in the name of democracy and led to the introduction of the major institutions of democracy, including competitive elections, multiple political parties, an independent judiciary, the legalization of independent organizations, and an end to political censorship. While discussions of democratization in CEE initially focused on these issues, attention gradually turned to broader questions of state-society relations. It became more widely recognized that civil society has played a crucial role in third-wave democratization (Huntington 1991), and that the deepening of democracy depends on the degree of access to the policy-making process by groups representing the interests of different sections of society.[12] The art of associability and association is part of the democratization process, and tripartism contributed to it by legitimating the social partners as independent organizations and by helping them consolidate organizationally.

Furthermore, the emerging tripartite arrangements were a far cry from granting "monopoly of representation" to "privileged" groups, developments that have spurred a lot of analytical controversies and theoretical debates over the "democratic" meaning of Western European

[12] See in Diamond 1992, 1999; Diamond et al. 1995; Fischer 1996; Linz and Stepan 1996; Dahl 1998; Sorensen 1998.

corporatism.[13] In fact, in the initial years of transition, all interested social actors and groups had an access to the tripartite forums, as no specific criteria for representation in tripartism were adopted. A too early selection of the social partners might hinder their organizational restructuring and development and, moreover, might deprive the new organizations of the chance to gain a foothold. Also, in the difficult years of political and economic transition, the broader the social partners' involvement in sharing the burdens of transition, the better were the chances for social peace. Even later on, when criteria for representativeness in tripartism were formulated in Bulgaria, the Czech and the Slovak republics, and Romania, they were based on the same sound basis on which representational democracy is generally based, namely, a satisfactory minimum of membership coverage, and another satisfactory minimum in the organizational articulation of represented interests. Both minimums are jointly agreed upon by the social partners.

Tripartite arrangements also play a potentially important "educational" role in the democratization process. As G. Di Palma argued, democratization and the survival of new democracies depend on the consensus of all powerful elites and important social actors and their commitment and ability to "sign on" (Di Palma 1990). To be stable, democracy must find a balance between a number of competing values: conflict and consensus, participation and passivity, protest and allegiance, consent and effectiveness, elite conciliation and popular mobilization, and representativeness and governability. What better institution than tripartism for developing the art of compromise? Tripartism helps to inculcate norms of tolerance, trust, moderation, and accommodation that facilitate the peaceful, democratic regulation of rifts and conflicts and that link the vigor and dynamism of civil society with the capacity and authority of the state.

Some authors have argued that successful transformation depends on minimizing its social costs and gaining society's tolerance of these costs (Arato 1990; Bruszt 1992). Adam Przeworski modified that thesis with the claim that the road to a market economy that is most likely to reach that

[13] While Philippe Schmitter – who revived the concept in the 1970s after a period of disuse – differentiated between "societal" (in the sense of "democratic") and "state" (in the sense of "authoritarian") corporatism, the rather confusing definition he provided inherently implied a nondemocratic outcome. Schmitter regarded corporatism as an institutional arrangement through which the state grants a deliberate representational monopoly to a "limited number of singular, compulsory, non-competitive, hierarchically ordered and functionally differentiated categories," in exchange for "observing certain controls on their selection of leaders and articulation of demands and supports" (Schmitter 1974). As Grzegorz Ekiert observed, Schmitter's notion of societal corporatism as a democratic variant thus came to contradict his very notion of corporatism itself, because the latter's sine qua non is a strong state able to create and control interest groups (Ekiert 1991: 296).

goal is not the one that minimizes social costs but the radical one that is able to move ahead with economic transformation and *simultaneously generate popular support* (Przeworski 1991: 136–88). Overall, tripartism has served as the chief vehicle for effecting this strategy and as a basis for democratic stability.[14]

Yet in terms of purely policy outcomes, tripartism has some undoubted "failures." Ironically, in the conditions of economic crisis and difficult economic restructuring, the social partners often do not negotiate real wage and income increases but mutually acceptable, reasonable drops in living standards. Where and when tripartism can be successful as a policy-making mechanism during postcommunist restructuring is determined not only by the extent of the threat on social peace but also by the nature of the specific issue to be resolved. Thus, tripartism is obviously well matched to some bands of the policy spectrum. Perhaps least controversially, given the wide acceptance of tripartism as a means to more fairly distribute the social burden of restructuring across the population, it plays a particularly important role in the area of employment policies, and less so in deciding some purely monetary distributions such as wages. Tripartite bodies dealt extensively with policy measures to cushion the unemployed and have incorporated social safety nets into the plan for economic reform. The social safety nets comprised mainly support services, providing, for example, help in finding new jobs, retraining, and benefits for the unemployed or those who are undergoing retraining. The safety nets had, in addition, to guarantee everyone a basic subsistence; minimums were thus defined, based on agreed levels of social need, for wages, income levels for families with children, and old age pensions.

In addition to social and employment policies, minimum wage, and income regulation, tripartite arrangements have dealt with the elaboration of new labor legislation and the consolidation of collective bargaining. Postcommunist tripartism has also included questions of economic reforms, such as restructuring and fiscal and privatization policies. Actually, not wages but ownership transformation issues have been the source of most tensions among the social partners in CEE (Hethy 1994a: 330). Such issues have been avoided in official talks, as when Hungary's government in 1991 did not submit its privatization strategy to the interest reconciliation council, but they have been addressed directly by the social partners, as, for example, in Poland in 1992, on the signing of the State Enterprise Pact, which covered the role of unions during privatization, worker share ownership, and the scope for worker buy-outs.

Overall, tripartism's alleged "failures" in some policy areas are, as this study finds out, attributable less to institutional and procedural failures with

[14] Pollert 1999: 212. See more in Atanassova 1994.

tripartite structures than to the transitional context of historically burdened economies and a general move away from state socialism's solidaristic and egalitarian policies and toward more market-oriented mechanisms, a trend that is also under way in Western Europe, under the pressures of global neoliberalism.

Participating Actors: Civic Tripartism

Some CEE observers have expressed reservations about the use of the term "tripartism" to label state-societal arrangements in which the number of participating social partners is indefinite (Thirkell et al. 1995). Their point about the transmutation of "tri-" into "bi-" in the transitional economies with unfinished privatization goals – and, hence, not clearly identifiable employer organizations – has merit. The literature on Western European corporatism has widely recognized that corporatism is a tripartite relationship that involves state *intervention* in the economy on the basis of state influence over the major producer groups of employers and unions (Lehmbruch 1979, 1984; Schmitter 1979), as well as *integration* of interest organizations in the state decision-making process (Panitch 1979).

The literature has also emphasized, however, classic corporatism's practical mutations into bipartite forms (Maier 1984; Streeck 1984). Usually, the corporatist cases of Austria, Germany, and Switzerland are considered bipartite because of the weak formal involvement of the state in social partnership talks. In Austria the government is largely excluded from the bargaining process; government representatives in the "Paritätische" have only "deliberative voice" in its work (Lehmbruch 1979; Tomandl and Fuerboeck 1986). Incidentally, Japan is also considered a bipartite corporatist case, although on different grounds, that is, the exclusion of labor at the levels above the enterprise (Pempel and Tsunekawa 1979). Overall, corporatism loses its identity and mutates into either neoliberalism or statism only when the state – not a union or an employer organization – completely retreats from tripartite talks. In such cases, the state could either continue its intervention in the economy by other means (thus moving into a form of "statism") or completely withdraw from intervention in the economy (the neoliberal variant).

In the CEE "tripartite" talks, the questionable partner is not the state but the employers who had to undergo most drastic changes of organizational and functional separation from the state. While newly formed employers' organizations were included in social dialogue talks, their participation was weak because of still undifferentiated organizational structures and nonconsolidated programmatic platforms. Yet the corporatist-like character of "tripartite" talks was preserved because the state participated in them with a dual role, not only as an employer in state firms but also, and more importantly, as a policy-maker. Moreover, with the advancement of transformation and consolidation on the business side, the employers' organizations are becoming more and more visible in tripartite talks.

However, in terms of participating actors, there is a more critical difference between the CEE tripartite arrangements and the Western European classic neocorporatism. Namely, in the conditions of political and social uncertainty, marketization, and drastic ownership transformation, the CEE tripartite arrangements have gone beyond the classic corporatist "triangle." As political parties, youth organizations, religious organizations, different social movements, nongovernmental organizations (NGOs), and others became involved in various tripartite structures, the resulting tripartite bargaining in CEE – which bore similarities to the grand political alliances, collectively known as consociationalism, that spread in Austria during the postwar recovery and lasted until 1966 (Gerlich 1992) – acquired multipartite, *civic* traits. While preserving a standard "tripartite" core, tripartite negotiations and institutional arrangements spread to the political spectrum and the society at large, involving multiple participants in popular direct participation for successful exit from state socialism and, later on, the promotion of stable social and economic development.

Institutional Structures: Multilevel Bargaining

Unlike the predominantly national-level, centralized bargaining in Western European corporatist arrangements (especially the Swedish case), with some limited developments at the meso-level (Cawson 1985), tripartite negotiations in the CEE's transforming polities and economies acquired dimensions and features on multiple levels. The literature on economic and political transition has extensively focused on national and/or company-level industrial restructuring, while largely neglecting the intermediate levels of bargaining[15] and remaining almost silent about the existence of any linkages among bargaining levels.

This study finds out that within a transformational context, national tripartite talks spread quickly to lower levels as well. At the regional level, regional employment councils comprising local governments, employers, and trade unions were established to complement the national employment councils, which were trying to tackle the most acute problem of the economic transition, namely, unemployment. Sectoral negotiations emerged especially in sectors where there were acute restructuring problems caused by the collapse of old industries such as textiles and coal mining in Poland (Buchner-Jeziorska and Kulpinska 1994). Collective bargaining to regulate the terms and conditions of employment emerged at the company level, but it was closely interwoven with collective negotiations at upper levels, and

[15] Schienstock and Traxler 1994; Slomp et al. 1996; Mason 1995; Thirkell et al. 1995.

in the more problematic cases representatives of upper bargaining structures became directly involved in company bargaining.

On the one hand, centralization of bargaining structures was necessary, because the state remained the major employer in the still nonprivatized state sector and the most important employer in the public sector. Furthermore, in situations of economic crisis and high uncertainty, some centralization of power is an expedient way to maintain social and political stability; the state's withdrawal from intervention in the economy would have been undesirable, especially for trade unions, since in the absence of a normal market environment, the radical decentralization of employment relations threatened to produce serious negative social consequences and tensions. In short, given both the legacy of a highly centralized state socialist economy and the unavoidable centralization of decision-making during the economic transformation, tripartism was promoted at upper levels, especially at the all-national, confederal level.

On the other hand, however, decentralization of bargaining structures was important for democracy. A move toward decentralization, away from state socialism's highly centralized regulation of the employment relationship, was necessary in order to democratize state governance. Local government that is accountable to local electorates is an important element of the democratic process (Lipset 1981; Diamond et al. 1995: 45–46).

Overall, the move toward multilevel bargaining structures was accompanied with increasing interdependencies and interactions among levels of bargaining. Multilevel tripartism and collective bargaining among committed social partners helped alleviate economic and social problems facing particular companies, regions, and industries, as well as those confronting the transition countries as a whole. These practices eased the transformation away from the state socialist experience and toward a new model based on the principles of democracy, markets, and private property.

1.3. Explaining Tripartite Coordination in Central and Eastern Europe

The overwhelmingly communitarian culture and the basically corporatist character of politics under state socialism, as well as the importance of corporatist settlements in the demise of communist regimes, facilitated but did not directly cause the establishment of tripartite arrangements immediately after the collapse of the regime. Two major factors, I argue, are significantly shaping the emergence and development of postcommunist tripartism. These are the twin domestic necessities to preserve social peace and legitimate and consolidate the social actors in order for political democratization and economic restructuring to occur successfully.

What accounts, however, for clearly observable variations in the establishment and functioning of tripartite institutions across CEE countries, industries, and regions? To answer this question, the book focuses on two postcommunist countries, Bulgaria and Poland. The empirical basis for the analysis presented in this book stems from field research undertaken in these countries between the summer of 1993 and the summer of 1999.[16]

Although Bulgaria and Poland have both suffered economic crises and undergone transformation, the degree of their difficulties and the lengths to which they have gone to alleviate them differ substantially. Poland has produced the most favorable national economic indicators of any country in postcommunist Europe, while Bulgaria still lags behind in economic reforms. Poland was able to recover comparatively early, by 1992, from the "shock therapy" treatment associated with the Balcerowicz Plan of 1990. It was able to sustain high growth rates of 5 percent or more from 1994 to 1998 (with gross domestic product (GDP) growth of 6.5 percent in 1995 and 6.0 percent in 1996) and to attain single-digit inflation in 1998 following the near hyperinflation of the early phase of transition. The budget deficit had been reduced to below 3 percent of GDP by that year. The European Bank for Reconstruction and Development (EBRD) 1998 Transition Report revealed an impressive recovery in Poland compared with other transitional economies, showing GDP in 1997 to be 112 percent of its 1989 level, while all other economies were still on the negative side of growth compared with 1989 levels: the Czech Republic with −2 percent, the Slovak Republic with −5 percent, and Hungary with −10 percent, for example (Faulkner et al. 1999: 1). Despite the much greater severity of the crisis in Poland in 1989 compared with that in all the other countries in the region, Poland's achievements are impressive. Indeed, it is increasingly referred to as the "European Tiger" (Blankert 1997: 303).

For Bulgaria, evident economic recovery did not start before 1997, following a sharp downturn in economic reform in the winter of 1996–97 as

[16] In Bulgaria, I conducted more than 100 interviews with national, sectoral, and local government officials, representatives of political parties, trade unions, and emerging employer associations, parliamentary officials, and academic scholars. I also attended, as an observer, numerous sessions of the National Council for Tripartite Cooperation, as well as sessions of sectoral and regional tripartite councils (in postal services and telecommunications, electronics, metallurgy, light industry, and chemicals; in Vratza, Sofia, Plovdiv, Blagoevgrad, and Dupnitza). I analyzed a variety of government documents, constituting materials and platforms of the major employers' and union organizations, decisions and minutes of tripartite negotiation forums at the national, sectoral, regional, and enterprise levels, and a variety of national, sectoral, regional, and enterprise collective agreements and contracts. In Poland, I conducted more than eighty interviews at the national level, in the Lodz region, and with regard to the textile industry. I interviewed government representatives, representatives of political parties and members of Parliament, representatives of trade unions and employers, and many representatives of Polish academic circles. I also attended two sessions of the Tripartite Commission for Socio-Economic Interests, and analyzed numerous documents and minutes of tripartite councils. In addition, I conducted some forty interviews in Hungary and a dozen interviews in the Czech Republic.

a result of mismanagement by the socialist Videnov cabinet. In 1996, Bulgaria ranked at the bottom of CEE countries in economic development, with a negative growth of −10.9 percent of GDP, hyperinflation of 311 percent, and currency depreciation. With startling speed, however, the new Union of Democratic Forces (UDF) government of Ivan Kostov, backed up by the introduction of a currency board and a three-year agreement with the International Monetary Fund (IMF), stabilized the economy and brought inflation down to 1 percent in 1998. By 1999, Bulgaria ranked third among CEE countries in economic growth, trailing only Poland and Hungary, and had the lowest inflation rate.

Despite the sharp differences in the economic side of their extrication from state socialism and their adaptation to a market economy, however, Poland and Bulgaria have had very similar social problems along the way. Both countries experienced increasing disparities in incomes, high unemployment (in Poland, the official level of 0 percent in 1989 climbed to around 16 percent in 1993 and 1994, then dropped to 10 percent by 1997; in Bulgaria, unemployment reached 15 percent in 1996, but dropped to 12 percent by 1998), disillusionment with the early reform process, and a return to power of the ex-communists (in Poland, 1993–97, in Bulgaria, 1994–97). The transition process in both countries proved to be complex and multidimensional, with winners and losers.

While Poland's and Bulgaria's common need to preserve social peace and legitimate the social actors during generally similar economic crises and transformation processes resulted in the emergence of similar tripartite adjustments, there were distinct accents in the timing, goals, focus, and manifestations of tripartite coordination – a largely informal and parliament-based arrangement in Poland and a legislatively institutionalized one in Bulgaria.

My empirical evidence from Poland and Bulgaria reveals that, on the one hand, corporatist legacies and legacies of extrication paths from state socialism and, on the other, social partners' strategic, long-term commitments to concerted action are what account for marked diversity in tripartism across countries, industries, regions, and time. Integration into the international economy and polity, especially European integration, has, in contrast, somewhat diminished these differences and, in the long run, is helping preserve and maintain social dialogue structures in the CEE region.

The corporatist legacies of state socialism are separately discussed in Chapter 1. Below I outline the remaining factors that shape the emergence, development, and variations of postcommunist tripartism.

Social Peace

Postcommunist tripartism involved a fragile concord, the loss of which might have had explosive consequences. While democratization, which was expected to benefit everybody, was almost universally embraced, privatization, with its accompanying social inequality, was highly controversial. The economic transition's "new social contract" aimed to facilitate the rise of the able and entrepreneurial, creating conditions of "fair play" for the accumulation of wealth (Musil 1991). Those who were really advantaged by the new deal were not always and only the "able," however. A new criminal class, an offspring of corruption, could also prosper. Besides, the great mass of the population – especially those on fixed incomes – far from enjoying the dramatic material improvements foretold by advocates of the transition, have suffered a drastic decline in their standard of living. The more acute and durable such effects appeared to be – unfair accumulation of wealth by a few on the one hand, scarcity for the majority on the other – the less likely was the mass public of the CEE countries to continue accepting the transition.

The 1990 strike of truck and taxi drivers in Hungary, the fall of the Suchocka government in Poland in 1993, and the return of the former communist parties to power in 1993–94, among other events, showed that as the unpopular neoliberal economic reform advanced, there was a growing risk that social and political support for the new democratic regimes would wither away. A critical purpose of tripartite arrangements was to avert potential conflict by distributing the costs and rewards of economic restructuring more equitably, thereby preventing clashes between a new economic elite committed to the full and rapid flowering of the market economy and an enfranchised mass population determined at the very least to moderate the harshness of the transition. The authors of the CEE reforms were aware that "the greatest danger for the reform would be the breaking of the existing social peace" (Musil 1991: 384). Fears of large-scale social conflicts stemming from the economic crisis and the rapidly falling living standards, and political efforts to find mechanisms for dealing with conflicts, provided a major motive for the development of national tripartism across the region (Orenstein 1996).

Related to the preservation of social peace was the adoption throughout the region of laws on strikes and collective labor disputes. In Poland in 1982, Hungary in March 1989, Bulgaria in March 1990, and Czechoslovakia in early 1991, such laws became a salient part of the transition plan, which had to recognize two things: first and foremost, the existence of divergent and conflicting interests between state and society, and within society, and, second, ways to cope with them and channel social unrest to protect the public interest. Tripartism's roots were not, however, all of one cast. In the face of some issues – shock therapy versus gradualism, for example, and neoliberalism versus social markets – that elicited disagreements so fundamental and profound as to be unmanageable by programmatic means, policy concertation was combined with spontaneous and illegal but sometimes internally channeled open conflict.

Occurrence of strike action has been limited in Czechoslovakia and Hungary since 1989–90.[17] Strikes in Hungary have been insignificant because of the country's vast informal economy, which provides to important groups in the work force some compensation for losses caused by government policies. Poland and Bulgaria, in contrast, have experienced more strikes. In Poland, the signing of the Enterprise Pact in February 1993 was preceded by many strikes organized by Solidarity's lower structures, especially in the public sphere (health care, education, and culture), and was almost immediately followed by the collapse of the Solidarity-led government of Hanna Suchocka and the dissolution of the Solidarity-dominated Parliament. In Bulgaria in December 1990, despite the presence of a fully functioning national tripartite forum, the Podkrepa Confederation of Labor initiated a massive national strike wave that led to the resignation of the Lukanov postsocialist government. And from December 1996 to January 1997, although the National Council for Tripartite Cooperation was meeting regularly, massive civil protests and a strike wave throughout the country paved the way for the resignation of Zhan Videnov's Socialist cabinet, the subsequent appointment of a caretaker cabinet by President Peter Stoyanov, and early parliamentary elections in April 1997. Overall, there is a generally low strike level throughout the region. Strikes are infrequent, and where they occur they are generally directed toward the government rather than employers (MacShane 1994).

As crisis management bodies, the tripartite forums generally provided the basis for successful political democratization and economic restructuring.

Legitimation

The government, unions, and emerging employers all faced the need to adapt their organizational structures and platforms to the changing political and economic realities. In sharp contrast to corporatist institutions in established liberal democracies, where the composition of represented interest groups can be modified in the process of concertation but the actors enter negotiations with given organizational identities and sharply articulated interests (Streeck and Schmitter 1985), new identities and interests were emerging and vanishing spontaneously in the initial phases of the postcommunist transformations. Aiming at functional and organizational separation from the state and political parties, trade unions experienced a boom of pluralization and fragmentation in the beginning of the transformation, and then, as it advanced, underwent a period of consolidation and mergers. Superadded to this organizational pluralization were union divisions on ideological bases, for example, between the old, official unions and

[17] According to OECD data, cited in Hethy 1994b: 327.

the newly formed ones that were heavily defined by their anticommunist agenda. Business organizations also experienced varying degrees of pluralization across the region, with pronounced fragmentation in Hungary and Bulgaria and more homogenization in Poland and the Czech Republic, for example. Because of the inapplicability of the existing labor legislation and the difficulties encountered in creating new governing rules, tripartism and collective bargaining became the legitimating and consolidating mechanism for all actors.

For the new trade unions, such as Solidarity in Poland, Hungary's Democratic League, and Bulgaria's Podrkepa, their origin as anticommunist movements created organizational consolidation problems. Once the enemy was defeated, these unions found it hard to shift to a purely syndicalist direction. Participation in tripartite talks helped them make this organizational transition. For the existing "official" unions, participation in tripartite talks facilitated organizational reforms that included their separation from the state institutions and political organizations, a shift toward confederative, decentralized organizational structures and democratization of internal administration, and representation of workers' interests and the defense of workers' rights as a top priority for action.

The legitimating influence of tripartite arrangements has affected emerging employers most strongly. Employers, like the trade unions, deviated for years from their basic functions, and after 1989, unlike wage earners, they were hard to identify and define, given the variety of earlier quasiemployer organizations (such as the chambers of commerce, of industry, and of economy, as well as the associations of cooperatives) and newly emerging employers' organizations. Employers' formation and restructuring picked up considerable speed due to pressure from the other social partners, especially trade unions. Throughout the CEE region, employers were pushed to organize nationally and get involved in national tripartite talks, and subsequently pushed by the other social partners and the rules of the tripartite arrangements to develop lower branch and regional structures.

Tripartism also helped social partners define their new class identities. In the initial years of transition, by giving each "social partner" (the state, unions, and employers) a single voice in the tripartite structures, tripartism became a crucible in which the political and ideological divisions between former communist forces and newer anticommunist, democratic forces that existed within each social partner were broken down. Tripartism thus became a generator of *class* cleavages; it legitimated the social partners as class entities. The importance of this factor is suggested by examples of social partners whose internal rifts have gone unmended: trade union wars between old and new organizations have at times almost silenced the workers' sides of tripartite structures in Hungary (Lado 1996), and the animus between Solidarity and OPZZ has delayed the establishment of tripartism in Poland and pushed the unions to separately lobby for workers' interests in the Polish Sejm, as direct participants in electoral coalitions.

Extrication Paths

Poland was the first country in the Soviet bloc to break from communist rule, and it did so – like Hungary – in a highly compromisal, negotiated way (Karl and Schmitter 1991). Yet after the collapse of the regime, Poland, unlike any other country in the region, did not develop institutionalized tripartism until early 1994, when it established a national tripartite commission as a forum for government-union-employer concertation. One explanation for that lies in the dominance of neoliberal politics (the Balcerowicz "shock therapy" plan) in the initial years of transition. However, the popularity of neoliberal ideas and interest-based politics was evident not only in Poland but all over the region, including Bulgaria, as a natural move toward the market. And it generally played a downgrading role for the development of tripartism not only in Poland but in Bulgaria and the other postcommunist countries as well. Hence the relative weakness of Polish tripartism compared with the rest of the region cannot be solely ascribed to the dominance of neoliberal politics in Poland's first transition years.

What made the Polish tripartite scenario worse was the complex interweaving of neoliberal and interest-based politics with the unique monolithic civil society and ethics-based politics found in Poland. The reason for that politics lies in Poland's painful, decade-old extrication from state socialism. Unlike the other postcommunist countries, Poland has a history of prolonged and painful resistance against the communist regime. While in other countries mass discontent and attempts to reform the system radically erupted once in a while, Poland was regularly shaken by mass outbursts. In 1956, 1968, 1970, 1976, and especially 1980–81, the rationales for Polish communism were challenged by both the masses and increasingly by reformist elites. In a post-1989 era, the "ethos and values" of the Solidarity legacy initially hampered the articulation of interests and the institutionalization of a tripartite compromise of transition, developments that had happened in the early 1990s in all other postcommunist countries. Four governments in quick succession drew their main support from the Solidarity movement. In fact, even the founding members of the Confederation of Polish Employers (KPP) had been Solidarity activists before 1989.

Bulgaria, as well as the rest of the postcommunist countries, did not have a monolithic civil society on the eve of the 1989 breakthrough. Hungary, like Poland, extricated itself from state socialism through a negotiated compromise between reformist elites and the opposition forces, but very much unlike Poland, its civil society comprised the most autonomous and articulated interests in the CEE region. At an "Opposition Round Table" established in Hungary on March 23, 1989, eight groups represented conflicting interests and opinions. They were empowered to reach internal agreement on details of their negotiations with the party, such as a firm commitment to free elections rather than an emphasis on asking for concessions in the social sphere (Bozoki 1993). As Linz and Stepan argue, Hungary's round-table negotiations were unique in the region in the sense that Hungary's ruling elite entered into negotiations with an already well-constituted political society based on mutually recognized conflicts of interests rather than ethical "truth," as in Poland (Linz and Stepan 1996: 293–343). Furthermore, starting in late 1988, the party ideology in Hungary officially recognized the existence of conflicts of interest in society and tried to reconcile them in the industrial arena through tripartite means.

The civil and political societies in the rest of the postcommunist countries ranged between the extremes of Poland's ethical civil society and Hungary's well-constituted political society. In Bulgaria, although independently organized democratic opposition activities emerged as an effective force only by mid-1989, they were closer to the Hungarian model than to the Polish one. As the party initiated a controlled transition through a palace coup d'etat, the opposition first consolidated as a civil society within the UDF umbrella, and as such it held round-table negotiations with the party. Once the communist monopoly of rule was broken, it was much easier for the Bulgarian opposition to constitute a viable political society resting on conflicts of interest and compromise. It is noteworthy that the union Podkrepa – which was a constituting member of the UDF – left the coalition as soon as it gained political power in 1991.

Strategic Commitments

Maintenance of a political system based on tripartite compromise demands a political effort from all participants: government, unions, employers, and, most important, the society at large. Variations in the strategic commitment to social partnership explain diversity and variation in postcommunist tripartism across countries (Poland versus the rest of CEE countries), as well as across regions, industries, and time. Still, it is safe to say that national-level tripartism, by alleviating social tensions during economic and political reform, could have fit into the short-term philosophy and approach of most social partners after 1989 even if their political ideologies had been diametrically opposed to each other.

As part of the negotiated transition plan, conflicting strategic commitments, which can be summed up as "markets versus states," became officially accepted side-by-side, with a wide social consensus in favor of accommodating both as well as practicably possible. Postcommunist countries undergoing transformation have therefore sought to strengthen both markets and states simultaneously. On the one hand, unregulated markets promise efficiency and economic growth; on the other hand, an interventionist state is both economically viable and socially justified. But where markets are nonexistent, as in Eastern Europe prior to 1989, states are inevitably involved in their creation. And since markets are the final goal of such active state intervention, they are tolerated, even when embryonic, as mechanisms of further market expansion.

At the outset of the transition, the Eastern Europeans, especially in Hungary and Czechoslovakia, had a remarkable faith in privatization and market forces, and their devotion to "free market" ideas greatly exceeded that of Ronald Reagan and Margaret Thatcher in their heyday. Favoring the supremacy of free markets and a minimal state role in the economy (Andrain and Apter 1995: 36–48), liberalism was believed to be essential to the establishment of market economies, and it became the official strategy of governments – right- and left-wing alike – and business and employers' formations. In addition, political and market liberalism was backed strongly by international financial institutions, western governments, and private investors in Eastern Europe. Paradoxically, it has also become an accepted strategy among trade unions in the region, both new and reformed. Reluctantly but inevitably, they have accepted the major principles of political and economic liberalism as the "common," necessary guidelines for the creation of a market economy and a liberal political order.

Coexisting with market liberalism is a neostatist strategy imported from east Asia, which emphasizes the merits of government intervention and state building for restructuring politics and the economy (Amsden et al. 1994). Especially when markets are embryonic, state oversight is necessary to ensure that capitalism develops smoothly and fully. In CEE, one task subsidiary to that large responsibility was to restructure the devastated economy.

Despite commitments to different strategies, widely spread among the social partners was some degree of commitment to tripartite compromise, at least as a short-term means to alleviate social tensions during economic restructuring. Even conservative governments recognized early on that it was in their own interest to forestall social upheaval and share the responsibility for major economic sacrifices with "social partners" (Hethy and Kyloh 1995). In Hungary, the conservative Antall-Boross government claimed that its program was to create a "social market economy" in which the negative consequences of the market would be neutralized by an effective social safety net. Later, the socialist-liberal coalition government of the Socialist Party and the Alliance of Free Democrats (1994–98) also advocated tripartite cooperation and adopted an interventionist and social-market approach to the economy. Since 1998, the Orban government has continued the commitment to tripartism, though not with the same strength.

The leftward political shift in 1994–96 illustrates the high price governments have paid when they have chosen to quit "courting" tripartite institutions (Cook and Orenstein 1999). In Poland and Bulgaria, this political shift reestablished the rule of former communist parties. In the Czech Republic, with one of the most firmly rooted free-market transformation agendas in the region, there was also a remarkable shift to the left and a revival of social democracy (Pollert 1996; Rueschemetyer and Wolchik 1999).

The blurring of lines between contrasting ideologies as they have fused in tripartite institutions has also blurred the divide between "right" and "left" political spectra. In most historical circumstances, the definition of the "left" has been associated with societal change shaped by calls for greater economic equality. In postcommunist transformations, however, change meant an increase in social inequality, a traditional "rightist" objective. Hence, those who endorsed change could see themselves as "leftist" inasmuch as they attacked the status quo, or as "rightist" because they welcomed more inequality and market allocation of scarce resources (Kitschelt et al. 1999).

Due to the peculiarities described above, the alliance between corporatism and social democracy that typified Western Europe until the early 1980s is not an absolute rule in postcommunist CEE. There is a wide variation in each country and across the region in the way unions are related to political parties under tripartism. There are cases of union alliances with socialist or social-democratic parties. Most of these are between reformed unions and reformed communist parties; examples include the Democratic Left Alliance (SLD)/All-Poland Trade Union Alliance (OPZZ) match in Poland, and the National Confederation of the Hungarian Trade Unions (MSZOSZ)/Hungarian Socialist Party alliance that won the 1994 Hungarian elections. But there are also serious "deviations" to the right: alliances between trade unions and right-wing parties or coalitions. This is more common among new trade unions – such as Podkrepa in Bulgaria, which was a member of the UDF coalition – and it occurred most frequently during the initial phases of transformation. Finally, there are cases in which unions are not tied to political parties at all. This is most common among reformed old unions, such as the Confederation of Independent Trade Unions in Bulgaria (CITUB). In the Czech Republic and in Slovakia, however, the trade unions have been left out of electoral coalitions (Pollert and Hradecka 1994).

Poland presents a unique case in regard to the variation in the way unions are related to political parties. Poland's political system was dominated by the Solidarity movement, not by parties (Millard 1994). The Solidarity union became directly represented in parliament, as did the OPZZ union, which had allied with the victor in the 1993 Polish elections, the postcommunist Democratic Left Alliance. Four years later, electoral victory was claimed by Solidarity in conjunction with Solidarity Electoral Action (AWS), this time an alliance dominated by a union, not a party.

Unions have generally been wary of forming direct links with political parties. They have also striven to avoid too close an association with policies that have been instrumental in creating large-scale job losses and mass unemployment (Cox and Mason 1999: 158). In general, both successor and independent unions have increasingly advocated policies aimed at minimizing job losses and improving pay and conditions, while political parties have looked toward unions to deliver mass votes. But it has been difficult for both unions and political parties to stick to their parts of the bargain. Unions have been fragmented and have lacked the ability to influence their members during elections. As for political parties, not only have they suffered general weakness and underinstitutionalization since the fall of communism – with the result that they have tended to "float" above society and its interests and cleavages (Zubek 1993; Bielasiak 1997; Grzymala-Busse 1999) – but political parties in coalition governments have also found themselves under enormous pressure from international institutions to push privatization forward irrespective of the social impact (MacShane 1994: 360).

Integration

While international lending institutions have strongly favored neoliberalism as the new creed for states extricating themselves from state socialism, they have also supported the establishment of social dialogue among governments, unions, and employers. In fact, the International Labor Organization (ILO), the World Bank, and the European Community/EU have contributed to the development of tripartism (Hethy 1995). The ILO has packaged its philosophy of tripartism with the practical expert assistance it has delivered all over the region. In Bulgaria, negotiations between the IMF and the government have been broadened to include representatives of trade unions and employers' organizations, and IMF missions have required the conclusion of national social peace agreements as a condition for granting loans. The 1992 revival of tripartism was closely linked to negotiations with the IMF (Thirkell and Tseneva 1992). With the introduction of a currency board in Bulgaria in July 1997 that pegged the Bulgarian currency, the lev, to the German mark, the role of the IMF has become even more important in Bulgarian tripartism.

Most noteworthy, however, is the EU's increasing importance as a regional power. Its Poland-Hungary Assistance for Economic Restructuring (PHARE) Social Dialogue Project, and the launching of its eastward enlargement project, have reinforced tripartite arrangements in the region.

The EU's aid to the social partners dates to the early 1990s, when the EU's PHARE Social Dialogue Project helped reform, strengthen, and extend the structures and processes of social dialogue at various levels. The project's objectives were to professionalize the structures of the social partners in order to ensure the adequate functioning of social dialogue, develop an arbitration and conciliation service and strengthen the structures and processes of the industrial court, and establish an information and resource base to meet the social partners' needs. A major emphasis was on training the trainers, with expert assistance from western Europe. Arrangements were made for representatives of the social partners and governments in both western and eastern Europe to visit one another. The study trips were expected to engender twinning arrangements. To develop social dialogue at branch and regional levels, training became the crucial element of the project. A series of policy seminars was organized, covering the major areas of skill the social partners needed, such as labor and social welfare legislation, privatization and employment contracts, negotiation skills, development of a local economy, conflict management, and general technical skills for use at the base organization. The Social Dialogue Project within the EU's PHARE program contributed to the establishment of institutionalized tripartism in Poland in early 1994, and has significantly strengthened tripartite institutions in postcommunist Europe.

In addition to the Social Dialogue Project, Europe has fostered the development of tripartism in the CEE applicant countries through its accession conditionality. The EU accession criteria (elaborated at the EU Summit in Copenhagen in June 1993) were silent about social factors, including employment issues and social dialogue. The social dimension of accession received greater attention in the contracts for EU membership known as "accession partnerships." As a medium-term goal, the partnerships emphasized such elements of accession as "the development of employment and social policies in harmony with the European social model, further development of active, autonomous social dialogue, and further development of social protection."[18] And finally, governmental and trans-European institutions and networks involving Europe's social groups, on the one hand, and their respective counterparts in the ten applicant countries, on the other, have also fostered the maintenance and development of tripartism in the CEE region.

To conclude, initially tripartism was mostly shaped by the need to secure social peace and legitimate the actors in times of rapidly falling living standards and uncertainty, as a result of economic, political, and legislative reforms. With the speedup of the accession process, however, and the stepped-up harmonization of CEE countries' laws with EU common law, the applicants for EU membership are also subject to the requirement to "establish and maintain social dialogue" as a precondition for their entry. While this EU requirement or norm is not stringent with respect to details,

[18] *Official Journal of the European Communities*, vol. 41, 29 June 1998.

it is nonetheless viewed as important for defending tripartism against potential attempts by neoliberal governments to abolish it, and may as a result boost tripartism's further development.

1.4. Structure of the Book

Chapter 2 focuses separately on the corporatist legacy of state socialism as one important factor influencing the development of postcommunist tripartism in the early 1990s. It pays special attention to state-society relations, interest group politics and other associational developments, and economic and social institutions and policies in the evolution of state socialism. The chapter finds out that while in Western Europe, in the aftermath of World War II, corporatist arrangements developed on new democratic traits, in Eastern Europe these arrangements – in the face of a dominant party-state – acquired strong authoritarian traits, albeit skillfully hidden behind a hypocritical ideological and institutional mask. It describes how authoritarianism and hypocrisy characterize aspects of the species of corporatism found under state socialism. The chapter focuses on three major adjustments made by the party-state to preserve state socialism's hypocritical corporatist deal, adjustments that subverted it in the end: institutional infiltration and takeover, toleration of "moral" (solidarity- and equality-based) and informal-sector activities, and expansion of political opportunities for the opposition.

Chapter 3 looks at the process of political and economic restructuring in Bulgaria with the aim of illustrating the major features of the Bulgarian variant of tripartite adjustments at national level. It first traces the elitist collapse of state socialism in Bulgaria and the political legitimization purposes behind the tripartite arrangements. The chapter further reveals the consolidation of social dialogue with the launch of neoliberal economic reforms in February 1991, its substantial deterioration in 1992 as the newly elected UDF government pursued antiunion policies, the consolidation of tripartism after its legal endorsement in 1993, and the impact of international organizations and the process of accession to the EU on Bulgarian social dialogue.

Chapter 4 addresses the question of why Poland, unlike any other country in the region, did not develop tripartism in the early 1990s, and why in early 1994 it established a national tripartite commission as a forum for government-union-employer concertation. The chapter traces the distinctive features of Poland's tripartism at each significant step in the country's transition away from state socialism. It looks at critical junctures in the processes of Polish reform that shaped distinct variants of tripartism in the years after 1989.

Chapter 5 examines the numerous functions of postcommunist tripartism at the sectoral level of government. Through an in-depth exploration of social dialogue at the Bulgarian Ministry of Industry (the electronics industry, in particular) and the Committee for Communications (the telecommunications industry), as well as in Polish textiles, it reveals the interplay of sectoral actors in the process of postcommunist restructuring in Bulgaria and Poland, and traces the emergence of two distinct paths of sectoral tripartite adjustments: an institutionalized path in Bulgaria and an informal, noninstitutionalized path in Poland.

Chapter 6 traces the interplay of local, regional, and national actors in the process of regional restructuring in Bulgaria and Poland. A critical focus is on the tripartite arrangements in regions with heavy restructuring problems, such as Lodz in Poland, and Vratza and Blagoevgrad in Bulgaria. The chapter examines the various accents and priorities of the regional social dialogues in these countries and regions, and shows that in addition to ad hoc efforts to stem social upheaval, the emerging local social dialogues sought to achieve speedy economic revitalization through regional restructuring.

The concluding chapter compares and analyzes the empirical evidence and findings presented in Chapters 3 to 6. It outlines the purely transitory and more permanent traits of CEE's civic-political species of tripartism. The chapter further analyzes cross-country variation between Bulgarian and Polish tripartism, and across sectors and regions. It finally discusses tripartism's prospects for the future in light of CEE's anticipated accession to the EU.

2

The Corporatist Legacy of State Socialism

> You can always find more than sufficient causes for every great event – after the event. Certainly there were major structural causes of what happened in 1989. Not the least of these was the widening economic gap between East and West, a gap which detente policies did enable ordinary East Europeans to appreciate and resent. But we must beware of what Henri Bergson called "the illusions of retrospective determinism." Interpretations that present the events and outcome of 1989 as inevitable are probably further from the truth than we were at the time, in our heady cloud of unknowing.
>
> Timothy Garton Ash, "Ten Years After,"
> *New York Review of Books*, 18 November 1999

2.1. Introduction

World War II left Europe in economic devastation and ruins, both East and West. The immediate postwar years set the stage for the development, however, of two distinct types of corporatism in Western and Eastern Europe. In the West, the postwar settlements among labor, business, and the state embraced a new, nonfascist, democratic brand of corporatism. They established the foundations of a comprehensive social system that peaked in the 1970s, producing remarkable economic miracles on the basis of internal social cohesion and solidarity. In the East, the postwar years of transition to state socialism also encompassed significant adjustments and compromises between society and the state. Unlike the immediate postwar settlements in Western Europe, however, the Eastern European arrangements in the period 1945–49 were used to establish the dominance of the party-state and embodied both society's adjustments to and its revolt against the emerging party-state rule. While in Western Europe corporatist arrangements developed on new democratic traits, in Eastern Europe these arrangements – in the face of a dominant party-state – acquired strong authoritarian traits, albeit skillfully hidden behind a hypocritical ideological and institutional mask.

This chapter focuses on the corporatist legacy of state socialism as one important factor influencing the development of postcommunist tripartism in the early 1990s. It pays special attention to state-society relations, interest group politics and other associational developments, and economic and social institutions and policies in the evolution of state socialism, and describes how authoritarianism and hypocrisy characterize aspects of the species of corporatism found under state socialism. The rise of open dissent against party-state rule, which produced a series of opposition activities (starting in 1953 in Germany, then spreading to Poland and Hungary in 1956, to Czechoslovakia in 1968, and again to Poland in 1970, 1976, and 1980–81), highlighted the merits of a neocorporatist approach to the analysis of state socialism, in contrast to other analytical devices that had emerged to explain its evolution, such as totalitarian realism, modernization liberalism, and civic opposition analysis.[1]

Developed as a device to analyze the communists' postwar seizure of power and consolidation of their one-party regimes in a Soviet bloc within an emerging Cold War international order, totalitarianism focused on the struggle for power and on power relations, in both domestic and international arenas. It emphasized the explanatory primacy of global ideologies and nation-states, Leninist communist parties, and individual leaders such as Stalin. In the social order it depicted, communist parties exercised total control over citizens; autonomous social institutions and individual freedoms were eliminated; "high politics" eclipsed all other concerns; and state-society relations were discontinued (Mikolajczyk 1948; Seton-Watson 1951; Brzezinski 1967).

In the mid-1960s it became increasingly clear that state socialism could not be evaluated solely in terms of democratic-totalitarian dichotomies. As Ekiert put it, the decline of political terror, increased popular participation at the local level, the inclusion of experts and intellectuals in the decision-making process, the improvement of living standards, and the expansion of social welfare benefits greatly undermined the premises of the totalitarian analytical framework (Ekiert 1991: 291). Economic modernization through rapid industrialization, as well as some political liberalization, were the driving forces behind these new developments. Scholars used the logic of modernization observed in Western societies to explain modernization's effects in state socialist societies and the impact of intellectuals and state bureaucracies on state socialist industrialism (Lowenthal 1970; Field 1976; Bielasiak 1980). Modernization liberalism was particularly interested in human rights and the well-being of individuals rather than in the state's rights and national interests, and in improvements wrought by the

[1] For a review of the different perspectives, see Ekiert 1991; Stark and Nee 1989.

scientific-technical revolution, such as economic growth, the enhancement of social welfare, and a general expansion in culture, education, and political participation (Jowitt 1971; Korbonski 1975).

Like totalitarian realism, however, modernization liberalism's picture of state socialism was not complete. Moreover, it was to some extent misleading. Modernization liberalism assumed that one automatic spillover effect of economic change would be the creation of more democratic institutions. And it focused on intellectuals and professionals, experts of all kinds, as the principal agents of change in state socialist practices, the new dominant elite in alliance with pragmatic party bureaucrats (Konrad and Szelenyi 1979). More fundamentally, as Stark and Nee argued, by projecting an idealized image of Western development onto state socialist nations, modernization liberalism overlooked or distorted some of the distinctive features of the economic institutions of state socialism (Stark and Nee 1989: 7–8).

To the extent that totalitarian realism overemphasized party politics and international politics (Soviet–Eastern European relations, in particular) and modernization liberalism focused too fixedly on economic industrialization and intellectual elites, neither elucidated the regime's goals in regard to society, or the ways in which society responded to communist power.

Scholars who rediscovered the concept of "civil society" in the early 1980s emphasized the conflict between the party-state and civil society, usually by drawing attention to various informal community developments that – within a social order previously characterized as "amorphous" – had persistently waged resistance to the communist regime since 1953, through self-organization and communal and network activities (Tokes 1979; Arato 1981, 1981/82; Havel et al. 1985; Judt 1988; Pelczynski 1988; Skilling 1988; Goodwyn 1991). Other scholars emphasized the importance of informal economic networks: state socialism's "economics of shortage" and soft budget constraints, its self-reproducing institutional mechanisms, informal and second economies, emerging entrepreneurship, networks of subordinate social groups, and rising economic and social inequalities (Gabor 1978; Szelenyi 1978, 1988, 1989; Kornai 1979; Szelenyi and Manchin 1987; Bloch 1989). Like the research associated with totalitarian realism and modernization liberalism, however, the literature on oppositional activities and informal economic networks drew an incomplete picture of state socialist practices. In particular, the view of state-society relations it presented was one-sided, foregrounding either the openly conflictual elements or the purely "clientelistic" ones.

The neocorporatist approach that emerged in the 1970s directly addressed the question of cooperation and conflict between state and society, as well as the links between economics and politics. Moreover, the concept of corporatism was especially applicable to societies marked by fusion between the economic and political realms, such as state socialism (Bunce 1983, 1999). The emphasis on compromise enables the corporatist approach to recognize that in state socialist regimes, communist repression was not the only influence on workers' experience; state socialism was the creature of both societal resistance and societal accommodation to the regime. As a result, as some authors have pointed out, state socialism was essentially characterized by negotiation and "corporatist deals," direct and indirect, between the regime and social groups (Bunce and Echols 1980; Chirot 1980; Pravda 1981; Bunce 1983; Harding 1984; Staniszkis 1984; Hauslohner 1987; Ost 1989; Laba 1991; Kenney 1997).

This chapter explores the essence of corporatist-bargained state socialism by first briefly outlining the corporatist path to a Janus-faced party-state in the transition to state socialism. It then identifies the authoritarian nature of corporatist arrangements under classic state socialism. And finally, the chapter analyzes the three major adjustments made by the party-state to preserve the corporatist deal of state socialism, which in practice unveiled the hypocritical nature of the party-state's policies and led to the collapse of the regime: institutional infiltration and takeover, toleration of "moral" (solidarity- and equality-based) and informal-sector economic activities, and expansion of political opportunities for the opposition.

2.2. Transition to State Socialism: The Corporatist Path to a Janus-Faced Party-State

The Yalta agreements did not directly prescribe the Soviet model for the region, however; they also assigned Western influence in clearly stated proportions (Boll 1984; Max 1985; Toskova 1995). Besides, the Soviet Union was weak at the close of the war and was courting new allies and divergent "national roads" to socialism in Eastern Europe. According to the "Declaration on a Liberated Europe," part of the Yalta agreements, the Eastern European states were to have freely elected governments "responsive to the will of the people." Yalta thus left room for substantial societal negotiation and compromisal arrangements that went beyond political elites to include workers, trade unions, and owners of private enterprise. Western influence thus facilitated the establishment of corporatist "people's democracies" as a transitional form of governance comprising communist parties, antifascist bourgeois parties, peasant parties, and social-democratic parties.

The reformist policies of the coalition governments focused not on the introduction of the Soviet system but on a widely divergent range of interests and issues, such as the purging of fascists, the implementation of social reforms (especially agricultural reforms that distributed the land more widely), the provision of political freedoms and freedom of expression (except for criticism of the Soviet Union), and a foreign policy sympathetic to both the Soviet Union and the West (Ionescu 1964; McCauley 1977; Kovrig 1979; Kaplan 1981; Tomaszewski 1989). Overall, however, the communist parties found themselves in strong strategic positions througout the region, given the collapse of the old society and the Russian presence.

Domestically, a potentially influential factor was societal support for the new regimes in each country, based on the leaders' advocacy of antifascism, issues of modernization long overdue in backward Eastern Europe, and considerable expansion of the social sphere. This support strongly manifested itself in the spontaneous emergence of worker control movements all over the region, the goals of which, however, deviated considerably from the Soviet model.

Compromisal arrangements between the regime of the coalition people's democracies and the publics, including the working class but also private enterprise owners and entrepreneurs, emerged in the first years of transition to state socialism. These arrangements had the basic tripartite (state-union-employer) character typical of postwar settlements in Western Europe. The Eastern European arrangements, however, were turned into an important nexus in an intensive power struggle between the communist parties and antifascist bourgeois parties, and also an instrument for the elimination of rivalry between communists and socialists/social democrats in their bid to represent workers.

In Bulgaria, the September 1944 economic program of the Fatherland Front government envisaged restrictive measures against big capital, a program that accorded with communist views, but also with the traditional views of the agrarians and the social democrats who were members of the coalition. The other member of the coalition, the antifascist bourgeois popular alliance Zveno, acquiesced to these restrictive measures, since the program did not directly advocate abolishing private ownership, which accounted for about 90 percent of industrial enterprises (Bogdanova 1983; Ficorov 1996). One compromise in the early corporatist deal formally inaugurating the transition away from the wartime was the preservation of private property, on the one hand, but with the provisos, on the other, that "unfair distribution of wealth would be abolished" and owners "should have a different attitude towards the direct producers."

Worker stakes and worker institutions thus became important in this early corporatist deal, and in the power struggle that would determine the abolition or preservation of market processes and private property, and hence of the bourgeoisie as a class. In fact, in 1945 all political parties throughout Eastern Europe attached great importance to the trade unions as a means of political power and hoped to influence them (Kenney 1997: 50). Additionally, the communist, socialist, and social democratic parties strove mightily to win the support of the worker control movement, while the bourgeois parties (and, later, communist parties) strove to neutralize the radicalism of works councils.

Genuine support from, but also genuine manipulation of, workers' institutions (trade unions and works councils) inhered in the transition away from wartime that led, by the early 1950s, to the establishment of the Soviet model.

Trade Unions in Power Struggles

Taking their cue from the Soviet experience of the 1930s, Eastern European communist parties went about winning and controlling the working class by creating procommunist trade unions that would be actively incorporated in state policy-making.

In Bulgaria, new trade unions were formed by the communists and the social democrats in September 1944. The influence of the General Workers' Trade Union (GWTU) on the transition occurred in both the "high" and "low" political spheres. On the "high" front, trade unions investigated factory employees and office workers and recommended that many be fired as "fascist enemies." By the terms of a law enacted in May 1946, trade unions were assigned the function of approving appointments of managers and other personnel. Unions were also involved in state administration purges, participating as members of a special government commission, created in October 1947, for the improvement of the work of state administration. The unions were also prominent in the battle over the agrarian party, and in confronting the resistance of the Bulgarian peasantry to collectivization (Migev 1997). Most important, unions were given direct representation on the Supreme Economic Council (similar to Russia's Supreme Economic Council (VSNKH) of 1921), the government, and parliament (*Istorija na profsajuznoto dvizhenie v Bulgaria* 1973: 599).

The "low" politics area in which unions were involved during the transition was economic recovery. A 9 December 1944 decision of the coalition Fatherland Front government "entrusted" trade unions with inspecting production in the enterprises and securing high labor discipline (*Otechestven front*, no. 83, 9 December 1944). First, the unions were charged with disciplining the workers against "idleness, wastefulness, and red tape in enterprises" by implementing and promoting labor "emulation" and "shockwork" (defined as competition modeled closely on the Stakhanovite system in the Soviet Union) in all branches of industry. Second, and more important, the unions were assigned the task of organizing production and distribution within privately owned factories, and, as necessary toward that end, disciplining and controlling private employers.

To strengthen their position in dealing with private owners, the communists put much effort into manipulating workers and trade unions. While Zveno held that industrial development and efficient production could be achieved only by stimulating the private sector, the communists' official position was that economic recovery, the defrayal of huge state expenditures, and the improvement of the lot of workers could be achieved at the financial expense of the private enterprises, through pressure on entrepreneurs to limit their profits. And the workers themselves had to be the "engine" for the fulfillment of this task. The unions, together with works councils, were assigned the task of checking any economic resistance on the part of private owners. Toward that end, they were given oversight not only over the industrialists' behavior, but also over the supply of goods to the factories and their use, the quality of production, and the marketing of output (Zaev 1964).

At the national level, the GWTU actively collaborated with the state apparatus in the preparation and adoption of all important laws and decrees concerning the new regime's economic policy. Unions were also in the front line in implementing the government's social policies (Minchev 1985). The unions also initiated the adoption of several laws, such as a law on labor norms (1946), which required industrialists to adopt standard hours of labor in their enterprises, and to pay workers extra for additional hours of work. The standard hours in each factory had to be jointly decided by the employer and the union committee (Ivanov 1969: 63–64).

The conclusion of general agreements with trade unions further weakened private employers by considerably restricting the scope of their activities. While keeping the right to privately own their factories, the industrialists acquiesced to trade union control over the implementation of the new labor laws, and to union supervision of steps to improve working conditions in the enterprises. Under the provisions of collective agreements, hiring and firing of workers could be carried out only with union consent, and employers were required to discuss all production issues with their workers.

The intense competition between the private sector and the emerging state sector over regulation of work and employment conditions, a contest artificially created with trade unions' help, strengthened the Fatherland Front government's attack on private employers. Under union pressure for better working conditions, the government adopted decrees that improved working conditions in the state sector, and other simultaneous decrees that forced similar changes on employers in the private sector. The regulations were implemented by trade unions, which forced the issue through local collective agreements (Isusov 1971).

Similarly in Poland, reforms in the trade unions began in the summer of 1944. A Central Trade Union Commission (KCZZ) was formed in November of that year. Although the conference establishing the commission had joint representation by the communist and socialist parties (the Polish Workers' Party (PPR) and Polish Socialist Party (PPS), respectively), the communists dominated, with seventeen representatives compared with the socialists' nine (Polonsky and Drukier 1980). In early KCZZ meetings, trade union activists raised radical demands for worker control and participation in management. They argued that revitalizing state industry and normalizing factories' operation was as impossible without the participation of representatives of the working class (that is, the unions) in management as without the participation of specialists.

To strengthen the role of the working class in management, the KCZZ called on trade unions to work with the government in developing economic plans, to monitor the fulfillment of those plans in the factories, and to nominate directors of factories, industrial associations, and so on. As in Bulgaria, the trade unions in Poland, to serve as the foundation for the new economic order, came to be composed of both workers' representatives and politicians (Kenney 1997: 62). The trade unions became the largest bone of contention in the "high" corporatist power battles (*kto kogo*). In the early postwar years the Polish Ministry of Industry and Commerce was in the hands of the communists, and there was a close relationship among the various ministries, the PPR and PPS, and the trade unions (Kenney 1997: 29).

Again as in Bulgaria, the most important tool used to control workers and adapt them to the Stalinist system was socialist emulation. The objective was to improve productivity and labor discipline at a time of falling living standards. The decline in living standards was a foreseeable result of policies designed to hold consumption down in order to provide for the sharply increased investment targets set for 1947, and the pressure on living standards was further intensified with Poland's rejection of Marshall aid in July 1947 at the request of the Soviet Union. The push for socialist emulation drew a more hostile reaction in Poland than in Bulgaria. It provoked a storm of protest that escalated to violent strikes, such as in Lodz in the autumn of 1947.[2] The right to work was transformed into a duty to work, and if employees did not fulfill this duty, the state could assign them to two years' compulsory labor; it could even imprison them for five years. The threat of forced labor became a widely used instrument of persecution to forestall the emergence of any independent leadership in the workers' movement, and it was an especially effective weapon in the campaign to impose socialist emulation.

Works Councils and the Battle for Ownership and Control

In contrast to the trade union bodies with their top-down planning and formation, the spontaneous worker control movement caught the communists by surprise, especially with its demands for worker ownership and direct worker control over the factory. Such demands were much more reminiscent of the industrial conflicts and the worker control movement in Russia between 1917 and 1921 (Kaplan 1968; Shapiro 1977; Malle 1985) than

[2] On the strike in Lodz, see also Kenney 1997.

of the 1930s Soviet model, which was based on state ownership, the principle of democratic centralism, and one-man management.

In their postwar struggle for power, the Eastern European communists faced both an ally and a rival in the independent worker control movement. Initially, the communists tried to legitimate the worker control movement and then use it, as had been done in Russia, to weaken the bourgeois parties and chip away at private property. But it soon became clear that in the struggle for power over the factory and society at large, the communists faced a new and more dangerous rival: the workers themselves. Throughout Eastern Europe, the councils challenged the communists by directly interfering in factory management and by spontaneously nationalizing smaller factories for themselves. Concurrently, the communists were threatened by the growing numerical strength of rival working-class parties – socialist and social democratic – and by their direct interference in the party/workers confrontation. By siding with the workers, these parties were pushing the communists toward greater concessions to the works councils. Accordingly, the communists soon undertook radical measures to limit the influence of works councils in the factories, and to eliminate them completely by merging them with the trade unions.

In Poland, after initial confusion, representatives of the coalition Committee of National Liberation (PKWN) encouraged worker initiatives, and on 2 October 1944 the Communist party issued directives on factory committees' functions. The councils were supposed to be an arm of the state's economic policy. The "great role" they were to play was to exercise social control over the factory's economic activity, a function they were to fill by cooperating with the state organs or with local government; most important, they were to join the director and delegates of the local administration as representatives in the management of the factory. As nationalization of industry in Poland began, a large role was envisaged for the councils, which were officially granted legitimacy by special decree in February 1945. The councils were to monitor working conditions, collective agreements, and factory social and cultural organizations; participate in the establishment of work rules and employment procedures; take part in the distribution of goods to workers; and mediate worker-employer disputes. The director of the enterprise was to decide all matters related to the operation of a factory, including the awarding of bonuses (Reynolds 1978).

In reality, the factory councils often took a very radical line, opposing piece work, organizing strikes in response to food shortages, stressing short-range production goals, demanding equal payment for everyone, and, in general, acting independently. Frequent conflicts arose between the director and his technical staff, on the one hand, and the factory councils representing the manual workers, on the other. Most often the factory councils clashed with management over bonus payments and incentive schemes, the council favoring an egalitarian wage policy, while the factory management often hoped to use differentials to raise productivity. Management also wanted to link incentives and bonuses to productivity and skills, while the councils demanded an equal cut for all (Reynolds 1978). The council movement in Poland further challenged official ideas of factory nationalization; after defending and rebuilding their factories, workers were not likely to hand them over to the Soviets, the government, or a private employer. Taking official pronouncements about the working class literally, factory councils regarded the factory as belonging to the workers, and attempted to nationalize small factories not yet targeted by the state (Kenney 1997: 60). In many cases factory councils even tried to choose their own director from among themselves or from among respected prewar technicians. Stefancic observes that no one knew who precisely was in charge, the councils or the managers (Stefancic 1992).

Council attitudes became closely linked to party politics. Thus, where the majority of council members were socialist members, the council "regarded itself as the only power in the factory." Where communist members dominated, councils tended to be "little interested in factory affairs." Many of the latter surrendered their powers to the factory personnel director, who was usually a communist member. In January 1947 a ministry decree on factory councils mandated the incorporation of factory councils into union bureaucracy.

In Bulgaria, the factory committees were officially legitimated in December 1944 by the National Committee of the Fatherland Front. Together with trade unions, they were granted supervisory functions over the private owners. Their assigned job included supervising the implementation of the new laws and government decrees by the industrialists and controlling the production process, production costs, and price formation – albeit while observing the principle of noninterference with enterprise management. The committees were also responsible for procurement and distribution of supplies. Together with the trade unions, the committees participated in regular production meetings with the private owner and the technical staff, where important production and distribution questions were discussed. They also were deputized to help purge enterprises of "enemies" of the new regime (*Istorija na profsajuznoto dvizhenie v Bulgaria* 1973: 604–7).

The workers' growing maximalist demands for substantial wage increases, a six-hour working day, free food, free clothes, and free housing (*Zname na truda*, vol. 1, 20 October 1944), however, soon challenged the economic policies of the new government, which stressed improving efficiency in order to quickly restore the war-ruined economies. The popular alliance Zveno, representing the interests of the private owners in the coalition government, firmly opposed the workers' committees' interference in enterprise management. Although Zveno acknowledged state and public control of private industry, its general position was that the workers' committees were more harmful than useful; regarding them as one of the basic obstacles to private activity in industry, it held that their powers must be reduced (Ficorov 1996: 72). The communists, siding with Zveno in the power struggle with the socialists, denounced the committees as "instances of economic sabotage in factories that benefit the enemies of the new regime," "instances" that had to be overcome with the help of trade unions (*Istorija na profsajuznoto dvizhenie v Bulgaria* 1973: 589). In a special November 1946 plenum, the communists decided to introduce one-man management to all enterprises, and soon afterward the works councils were incorporated into the union structures.

A common pattern throughout the region was the neutralization of the workers' control movement through the merging of its elements with trade union structures, as the trade unions increasingly reshaped themselves to serve as a "transmission belt" between the Communist party and the masses (Korbel 1959; Ionescu 1964; Nemes 1972; Kovanda 1977; Schopflin 1977; Vago 1977; Bloomfield 1979; Myant 1981). With the merger, the trade unions were given the unaccustomed task of raising productivity. By that time, the trade union apparatus was a centralized body covering virtually the entire labor force.

2.3. State Socialist Corporatism

Although the communists were constrained to work within compromise-based parameters and could not flagrantly infringe on the prerogatives of rival political parties, their deft handling of trade unions and works councils to do their bidding enabled them to seize power relatively quickly, by 1947–48, even before the outbreak of the Cold War, the advent of which would greatly accelerate the pace of change. By the late 1940s and early 1950s, the countries of Eastern Europe had already adopted Stalinist regimes. They had all declared the dictatorship of the proletariat and anointed the workers and peasants as the new ruling class. And they had all introduced democratic centralism and the monolithic party-state political structures through which the communist parties gained ascendance over the state and society.

In its mature form, after nationalization of industry, corporatist-bargained state socialism was not a typical compromisal arrangement between the state and social groups (unions and employers' organizations), as exemplified by postwar regimes in Western Europe. Its fundamental difference lay in the fact that with the liquidation of private property as the reproductive basis of the bourgeoisie and the establishment of state property and one-party rule, the communist parties were able to gradually penetrate the existing state structures, fusing with state administration and economic management (Bunce 1999).

These developments gave rise to a strange transmutation or inversion of the usual power relationships (see Bunce 1999), with the counterpart to workers and trade unions – which in market economies is the employer and/or management – becoming, in corporatist arrangements, the Communist party, which had assumed the functions of both enterprise management and state administration. Thus, although corporatist-bargained state socialism preserved an interface between wage earners and employers ("state enterprises"), on the one hand, and the state, on the other, beneath that superficial configuration lay the principal-agent relationship fundamental to classic state socialism: the interplay between the allegedly "victorious" working class and its political vanguard, the Communist party. In other words, state socialism as fashioned through corporatist bargaining ended up as an official pact between "partisans" and "their" party.

The state socialist variant of corporatism was not a simple matter of concessions between "rulers" and "ruled," regime and public interest groups, in the interest of a modus vivendi (Brown 1988: 23). Rather, like any principal-agent relationship, it was defined primarily by the allocation and disposition of two functions: ownership and control. As the principal of a new regime, the working class could exercise its "dictatorship" and maintain and reproduce its rule either through worker ownership and direct worker control over the factory and the economy or through public/state ownership and the rule of its vanguard political party. The rapid, spontaneous spread of the workers' control movement and workers' spontaneous expropriation of factories all over the region in the first postwar years clearly demonstrate that the workers favored worker/factory or "social" ownership and direct worker control, as they were introduced in Yugoslavia after the breakup between Stalin and Tito (Pasic et al. 1982), rather than anonymous state ownership and rule by political proxy (the Soviet model).

The communist parties, however, once they had consolidated their role as the prime political agent of the working class by absorbing the more popular of the workers' socialist and social-democratic parties, had quite other interests to defend. Both the overall terms of the Yalta accord and the Soviet Union's and Red Army's support put them in a strong position to ensure their own organizational survival and reproduction by gradually imposing the Soviet model of the 1930s. That model had eliminated workers' control in Russia by 1921 and had succeeded in maintaining the "dictatorship of labor" through its by then single political agent, the Communist party. The package was secured economically by the replacement of private property with public/state property, instead of workers' or factory ownership.

The introduction of state property, however, fundamentally blurred the official principal-agent relationship of state socialism, because the instant it fused with state administration, the agent – the Communist party – made itself principal owner. The duality of the "employer's" (party-state's) status gave rise to contradictory imperatives: To satisfy the party-partisan relationship, the communists must give workers (and all those who aligned with the workers, such as the peasants and the technical intelligentsia) as much as possible, and to satisfy the employer-employee relationship, they must give the workers as little as possible. Cynicism, specious reasoning, self-deception (Elster 1996: 1), and hypocrisy regarding the "social compact" (Pravda 1981) or the "social contract" (Hauslohner 1987) of state socialism inevitably resulted.

De jure and in theory, the social compact had to manifest the "victory of the working class." Hence, it could not be admitted that a well-developed social security net came only *in exchange* for the minimization of political liberties (Bunce 1999: 33), or that citizens were allowed to pursue (within limits) private and selfish ends only in exchange for their withdrawal from public life and politics (Ekiert 1991: 301). In its "de jure" essence, corporatism under state socialism had to provide extensive *political and economic* benefits to workers and all party sympathizers, in exchange for political stability and economic growth.

As a party-partisan affair, corporatism under state socialism had both "high" and "low" ends, corresponding to "high politics" and "low politics." Political liberties and extensive state governance and control were at its "high" end. Workers were given extensive governance rights through the interest representation of trade unions, with unions empowered, among other things, to initiate legislation and participate directly in distributive state functions. Some prominent items at the "low" end were tremendous expansion of the social safety net, elimination of unemployment, egalitarian wages, and minimally demanding work norms. Both the "low" and the "high" ends were aimed at securing political stability and economic growth, as well as maintenance of the party's rule. In more general terms, it was toward those goals that the party acquiesced to many of the workers' demands for a "moral economy" – a set of values and ideas colored by egalitarianism, social justice, and basic collective rights – raised in the first years of transition to state socialism.[3]

De facto, the history of state socialism reveals the party-state's dynamic provision of "better positioning" within state socialism's hypocritical deal, and the workers' increasing struggle against this basic arrangement.

2.4. Toward Dehypocritization

At the "high" end of the corporatist deal, a *first step* of de facto "adjustment" that would effect a compromise between the rule of workers and one-party rule was *institutional takeover*, or the interpenetration of party and union elites, which produced state-controlled trade unions conceived as "partners" in a corporatist pact.

[3] The concept of "moral economy" was articulated by Thompson 1991.

The party/state, management, and trade unions were designed and expected to act in "full harmony" on the basis of the "common public interest" as grounded in public/state ownership. The top-level formal interaction (or division of areas of control) between the state and trade unions in regard to the employment relationship was an important component of the corporatist arrangements. This interaction included, first, the social welfare function granted to trade unions. Unions had the role of a one-way transmission belt from the party/state to the workers, but they also performed important distributive functions on behalf of the state, such as allocating health care, child care, recreational facilities, and pension benefits. Second, although under state socialism job grades and pay rates were fixed nationally by "tariff scales" and the existing collective agreements dealt mainly with the fulfillment of the state plan and some social issues, there was some bargaining, in a form harmonizing with the whole political environment. At the national level, normative documents concerning labor and social issues and living standards were jointly prepared and signed by the government and the trade unions. However, all these documents needed preliminary Communist party approval. At the local level, both unions and state managers were controlled by the top monobloc of party, state, and union officials through the principle of "democratic centralism." The etatization of trade unions and their infiltration by officials of the state and the Communist party, processes that occurred at all levels of state socialist structure, blurred the horizontal boundaries between the state/party and the trade unions. Union officials acquired parallel positions within the Communist party and government structures.

Lacking the means for stimulating economic growth and diffusing worker protest that could be found under market economies, the communists relied on mobilizing trade unions to advance their agenda. Even as the living standards of the mass of the population fell during the state socialist years, trade unions, through the system of socialist emulation and collective agreements, exerted continuous pressure on workers to speed up their pace of work and produce more. Enterprise collective agreements were an effective mechanism for "overfulfillment" of the enterprise plan, "over-increases" in labor productivity, and "overplanned" reductions in production costs, and as such they were themselves an "overplan" or "superplan" for the enterprise. Any "super" results that were achieved, however, became the basis for the next year's state-designated targets and thus produced little more, from the workers' perspective, than increased plan parameters (Hristova 1961).

In response to the institutional takeover of their representative organizations, workers became increasingly alienated from the institutional web of the party-state. And each time the workers openly revolted – in East Germany in 1953, in Poland and Hungary in 1956, in Czechoslovakia in 1968, and in Poland in 1968, 1970, 1976, and 1980–81 – they did so not by using the existing trade union structures, but by creating alternative institutions: *works councils.*

In Poland in 1956, workers initially protested against low wages, poor economic conditions, high production norms, strict labor discipline, and the government's periodic attempts to offset its heavy subsidization of basic living costs by raising prices. Later, political demands were added, generally advocating freedom and opposing communism and the Russians. Works councils had no legal status, but they began to function in the open as if they had, and held regular meetings. The councils actively supported the reshuffled reformist party elite, led by Wladislaw Gomulka. At the same time, however, by increasing the powers of the local union organizations, the new party elite held fast to its position as sole power-broker. Although Gomulka proclaimed in May 1957 that the specifically "Polish road to socialism" was characterized by works councils, he attacked the "anarchist utopianism" of those who advocated using them "to replace centralized administration," and he stoutly declared that "the party organization in the factories must remain, as before, the leading political force." The law on works councils adopted in November 1956 set down the basic guidelines for the formation and activities of works councils in industry, manufacturing, construction, and agriculture. The councils were given mostly an advisory position in the management of enterprises. All major decisions related to an enterprise were still controlled by central planning, and work norms, wages, and quotas were set by authorities above the enterprise level.

To bring the workers back under party-state control, the party tried to revive the defensive functions of trade unions and make them more responsive to the needs of workers. Unions were given greater control over working conditions, workers' wages, the drafting of production plans, and the spending of surplus enterprise funds, precisely the areas over which the independent works councils were claiming jurisdiction (Stefancic 1992: 17). Thus, the works councils had already lost much of their autonomy when, in 1958, they were incorporated – alongside factory party and trade union committees, the youth organization, and the technical staff organization – into quarterly Conferences of Workers' Self-Management (KSRs). The conferences themselves, moreover, were given no more than advisory power, while in 1959 the works councils were given the "major task" of mobilizing and disciplining workers for the ostensible purpose of meeting an ambitious new production schedule. This vague assignment appears to have been part of a game plan to phase out the councils by wearing them down; in early 1960, they were abolished.

Similarly in Hungary in 1956, "revolutionary councils" emerged everywhere, and in a great variety. The councils asserted a program of workers' control ("the factory belongs to workers"; "the supreme controlling body of the factory is the workers' council democratically elected by the workers"), but they also took a firm stand against Russian troops, against any return to Stalinism, and against the prewar factory owners (Fowkes 1993: 81). Both the Hungarian works councils and, to a lesser extent, the Hungarian power elites were more radicalized than their counterparts in Poland at that time. Thus, power passed into the hands of the councils at the local level. The Nagy coalition government, which comprised members of the Socialist party, the Smallholders' party, and the Communist party, recognized the councils on 30 October 1956.

In defiance of the Soviet intervention on 4 November 1956, the workers started a strike in the factories. District works councils were formed. Also formed, on 14 November, was a Central Workers' Council of Greater Budapest, which assumed coordinating functions across the country. The council was to start negotiations with the new Kadar government; it even suggested that works councils might, following the example set in Yugoslavia, elect a National Council of Producers. Khrushchev decided, however, that it was not possible to negotiate a Yugoslav-style arrangement, because whereas the Yugoslav works councils remained at the factory level, the Central Workers' Council of Greater Budapest had allegedly advanced a political program and the restoration of the Nagy government. On 22 November 1956, factory councils were banned from discussing political issues, and on 26 November the Central Workers' Council of Greater Budapest was denounced as counterrevolutionary. Workers were granted economic concessions, but all councils above the level of the individual factory were dissolved on 9 December 1956. Local works councils survived for a time, but their powers were greatly reduced by a decree of 5 January 1957, and they were finally abolished on 17 November 1957.

Thus, for the first time since the making of the corporatist deal in eastern Europe in 1944–49, a state socialist country – Hungary – had openly expressed its will not just to reshuffle the hypocritical corporatist arrangements of state socialism but to entirely end them, which would have eradicated the social order of state socialism per se. Unlike Gomulka in Poland, Imre Nagy's government did not restrain the Hungarian workers' revolt, and it actively fostered political pluralism, freedom of the press, and liberal democracy. Nagy even began to negotiate for Hungary's withdrawal from the Warsaw Pact, and on 1 November 1956 he proclaimed Hungary's neutrality, an action that drew Soviet military intervention on 4 November 1956.

The events in Czechoslovakia in 1968, although initiated by intellectuals, also led to the emergence of works councils, and in April 1968 the government officially encouraged their formation. A steady economic decline after 1963 had made the party leadership more reformist, and a decentralizing market-oriented economic reform program had already been implemented in January 1967 (Pravda 1973). The changes in the economic sphere stimulated demands for political liberalization and for freedom of expression and debate. Alexander Dubcek, the new party leader, spoke of "socialism with a human face." The party's April Action Program attacked the concentration of party power and proposed freedom of the press, freedom of assembly, and freedom of travel. Political censorship of the media was abolished, as was control over writers, trade unions, and other organizations.

In April 1968 the government officially encouraged the formation of works councils, which were viewed not only as a means for improving the economy but also as a political weapon for transforming society. The councils were charged with serving the long-term interests of workers qua co-owners and entrepreneurs, with unions serving the immediate interests of workers qua employees. In June 1969, some 300 councils and 150 preparatory committees (bodies for planning and organizing councils) were in operation (Kovanda 1977: 49). They were empowered to decide on two fundamental issues: hiring and remuneration of top-management personnel, and statutory matters such as mergers and subdivisions. In Czechoslovakia in 1968, just as in Hungary in 1956, the hypocritical corporatist arrangement of state socialism would have been rejected had it not been for Soviet direct military intervention. Both the workers and the party-state had agreed on a basic modification – elimination of one-party rule – that would have swept away the basis of the state socialist regime.

As the worker protests proved to be permanent rather than incidental in the 1950s–60s, it became clear that the mechanism of institutional takeover would no longer suffice to keep the corporatist bargain alive; workers were becoming increasingly alienated from the institutional web of the party-state. A *second major adjustment step* was thus necessary for the preservation of state socialism, one that would induce workers to compromise on their hard-core interest in the "moral economy" and the ownership question, and the party to compromise on the inviolability of its rule. Closely related to the achievements of industrialization and the necessity to introduce flexibility and rationality into the economy, this step included increasing toleration and eventual legalization of a variety of *informal economic activities* that were previously forbidden. Hungary was the first to introduce some flexibility and rationality into its economy through decentralization, but the economic reforms it started in the late 1960s were the only successful ones in the region. Overall, the party-states tolerated the emergence of a booming second economy (Szelenyi 1989) and high levels of clientelistic corruption, which could compensate to some extent for the incomplete realization of corporatist state socialism's "low politics" goals (economic growth, enhancement of social welfare, and a general expansion in culture and education) and thus help reconcile society to the regime.

With the expansion of industrialization and the second economy, technical intelligentsia and intellectuals at large sided with workers in demanding overhaul of the regime (Szelenyi 1979). With the rise of an organized mass opposition uniting workers and intellectuals (Solidarity in Poland began this process), the accent on individual/group demands, such as "moral economy" and worker control and ownership through works councils, was combined with and even overshadowed by "high politics" demands for radical restructuring of the state and reconfiguration of its place in the world polity and economy. New, nonhypocritical types of corporatist arrangements emerged in 1980, with the formation of Solidarity and its challenge over the party regime.

The Gdansk accord between the Government Commission and the Interfactory Strike Committee stated that the new trade unions should have a voice in the decision-making process by expressing their opinions in public on the major decisions that affect the living standards of working people. The new unions accepted, however, the constitutional guarantee of the party's "leading role in the state." This trade-off notwithstanding, the Gdansk Agreement was memorable as a corporatist compromise because it provided the basis on which the Solidarity movement could involve itself in the hottest political issues.

In early 1980, simultaneous with the formation of Solidarity, illegal workers' commissions came into being. In April 1981 a "horizontal structure" of self-management was formed, known as the Network of Solidarity Organizations of Leading Workplaces, or the Network (Siec). The works councils movement was much more radical than the Solidarity leadership, and the key to the Siec plan was decentralization of the economy (Stefancic 1992: 79–80). Influenced by the workers' control movement, Solidarity proposed the 3S reform formula for the economy – self-contained (independent), self-financed, and self-managed enterprise – and it pushed for expansion of self-management beyond the factory to the national enterprise that was Poland itself, to establish a Self-Managed and Self-Governed Republic (Jakubowicz 1988).

In a hostile Cold War environment, however, the 1980–81 Polish historical compromise was too high a target for either of the two sides: the old communist regime or the new alternative structure (Solidarity). As in Hungary in 1956 and Czechoslovakia in 1968, the party's declaration of martial law in Poland in December 1981 was partly a Soviet correction to an honest, straightforward attempt by well-meaning elements of the state and the society to democratize nonviolently.

Not every vestige of Poland's new corporatist innovations was demolished, however, and in fact their lingering effects eventually were to lead to dramatic and irreversible changes. The October 1982 law on trade unions prohibited the existence of more than one trade union in a given factory, as well as the creation of regional and national trade union structures. Despite its heavy regulatory and restrictive character, however, the law led to the recognition of collective labor disputes and the right to strike. And a law on self-management, also enacted in 1982, recognized workers' right to have a say in the economic management of their enterprises, through works councils.

In Eastern Europe as a whole, the early 1980s saw an acute energy crisis, which in turn produced shortages of food and manufactured goods. The crisis was deepened by the drying up of Western credit during the same decade, as the East European governments were unable to repay the large amounts they had borrowed in the 1970s. As a result, by the 1980s, the economies of all the East European states and the Soviet Union had GNP growth rates declining to near zero and were burdened by colossal external debts (Mason 1995: 31–32). The deteriorating economic situation and the rapidly decreasing living standards in the region sparked mass protests and consolidated the reformist camp within the party-state.

In a *third major adjustment step*, the party-state, in an act of self-preservation, made a much closer approach to fulfillment of workers' initial 1945 demands for worker control and worker/factory ownership. Echoing, in some key respects, the successful Hungarian economic reforms and Poland's early experience with a revised corporatist arrangement, this new adjustment aimed at somewhat better satisfaction of the "high politics" promises of the corporatist deal through the creation of a *new "political opportunity" structure*. An expansion and reshaping of existing structures rather than a whole-cloth creation, this development consisted in a growing elasticity in the political environment, wherein existing political alignments were disturbed, political access widened, and the policy agenda reordered (Bunce 1999). Contributing to this development were Soviet perestroika and glasnost, which provided a model for reform in Eastern Europe, and the withdrawal of the threat of military intervention, which broadened the possibilities for change.

Official works councils were introduced not only in Poland and the Soviet Union (Slider 1985; Moses 1987), but also in Hungary, Bulgaria, and Romania (Petkov et al. 1987; Petkov and Thirkell 1991). The goal was to increase enterprise autonomy and decentralize administration. In allowing these changes, however, the party-state still was not without ulterior motives. In particular, it hoped to prevent, by half-measures, the rise of an independent trade union, which could significantly weaken party control over workers' actions, as had happened in Poland, and threaten the exclusive role of the party in important political questions, including personnel decisions. Despite the broad rights of self-management, workers did not become genuine masters of their enterprises through the work collectives. The most important questions of production planning, financing, and supply and distribution of the final product remained under state control, and almost all self-management activity was concentrated in distribution.

Moreover, indications are that the fundamental question of ownership was still nonnegotiable to the communists. The general assumption behind the self-management reforms had been that democratization would develop on the basis of state ownership of the means of production. The concept of "property transfer" adopted in Bulgaria in 1987 represented the most radical revision in property relations in Eastern Europe since the early 1950s (when changes adopted in Yugoslavia had made the enterprise "social property"). "Property transfer" was presented as the final step in the process of developing the labor collective as "*stopanin*" (or "sovereign master"). Property was to be transferred initially to the labor collectives of fifty-five selected enterprises through agreements specifying the rights and duties of the state as the owner of socialist property and the labor collective as the "sovereign master" that would manage this property. The essence of the agreements was the transfer of funds and property and of the machinery the workers used. In August 1988, however, the process of transfer was terminated, after a series of accounting problems and other technical difficulties (Petkov and Thirkell 1991: 128).

Overall, after a certain critical juncture, the party-state, when responding to newly emergent autonomous movements, could no longer freely choose between suppressing or incorporating them, having already abandoned the former as an option. Voices calling for democracy and institutional change, finally given official hearing, changed the political agenda. By 1988, the Soviet leadership, schooled by the events in Poland in 1980–81, had cleared the way for major changes in Eastern Europe.

2.5. Conclusions

Fundamental to the collapse of state socialism was the impossibility of continuing to maintain the corporatist deal between the workers and the party. As the one-sided nature of that deal grew more and more apparent, with the party's dictatorial control exposed as an instrument for its own preservation and profit, the workers refused, at all costs, to acquiesce on the question of ownership. They initially rejected a deceptive form of anonymous "public" ownership in the name of "social enterprise" or "worker" ownership. Then, as state-tolerated bureaucratic corruption spawned a maze of privilege and payoffs, resulting in growing inequalities, while newly introduced market mechanisms (as in Hungary in 1968) created inequalities of their own (Szelenyi and Manchin 1987; Dye and Zeigler 1988), workers shifted their focus to private ownership. The burgeoning of informal and second economies had produced new entrepreneurial thinking and a new entrepreneurial elite among the workers, which together were pushing strongly toward reestablishing private property. Dovetailing with this trend, the workers, starting with the Polish works councils experience of 1956, had begun valuing high skills and education in the management of enterprises much more than before, which tended to give them a more nonegalitarian and individualistic attitude toward ownership.

Nor were workers and civil society, at any cost, prepared to concede to the party-state on the questions of control and real political participation. Although the Polish Communist party offered many economic concessions to Solidarity-led workers and society as a whole, throughout the 1980s Solidarity never abandoned or compromised on its basic demand for independent trade unions, whose introduction could easily be seen to spell an end to the one-party regime of state socialism.

The communist parties, in turn, realized that economically inevitable industrial democratization through the transition to self-management directly challenged their leading role. A final attempt to save this highly contested role was their offer to "transform" it from a direct to an indirect one, with no further direct intervention in the running of enterprises or the economy. This concession was in evidence, to a greater or lesser degree, in policy documents adopted in the 1980s by almost all communist parties in state socialist countries (Petkov et al. 1987: 12). And the benevolent neutrality of the party elites during the 1989 revolutions was a major reason for the success of these revolutions.

At its heart, the state socialist historical experiment had a dual nature. On the one hand, it was an unrealized workers' drive for "worker," "social," or "collective" ownership and the *direct* participation of all working people in the resolution of important questions affecting every level of community, all the way up to the level of the nation itself; it thus amounted to a challenge to representative democracy by a vision of "pure" democracy (Donath 1982). On the other hand, the state socialist experiment was a ruthlessly conceived, rational challenge to private ownership and private economic initiative, and to democracy at large, through the creation of anonymous "state" ownership and the establishment of one-party authoritarian regimes. Riddled, in the end, with cynicism and self-deception due to the party's split identity as both agent of and dictator over workers, corporatist-bargained state socialism could be exposed for what it was, denounced, and rejected.

3

Bulgaria's National Tripartism

3.1. Socialist Persistence, Economic Crisis, and Emergence of Social Dialogue

Elitist Extrication from State Socialism

In the 1970s and 1980s, Bulgaria, which arguably had the strongest economy and one of the least liberalized political regimes in Eastern Europe, avoided the ferment against state socialism that troubled other countries in the region. Bulgaria was the only socialist state whose regime never succumbed to the temptation to deviate from Soviet directives in any policy dimension – political, economic, or cultural; domestic or foreign (Brown 1970; Bell 1986; Rothschild and Wingfield 2000: 211–17). Bulgaria's unstrained relationship with the Soviet Union had favored its specialization within the Council for Mutual Economic Assistance (CMEA) in high-tech industries such as computers, electronics, transport, and nuclear energy, and it had eventually earned a reputation as the "Eastern European Japan" and the "Japan of the Balkans" (Ramet 1991: 12). From 1976 through 1980, Bulgaria's rate of growth in national income was 6.1 percent, compared with 1.6 percent in Poland, 3.7 percent in Czechoslovakia, and 3.2 percent in Hungary. Its foreign debt of $6 billion in late 1988 was smaller than that of any other Soviet bloc country. In contrast, Poland owed $32 billion to Western countries and $5 billion in transferable rubles to the CMEA states as of late 1987, and was compelled to use 67 percent of its export earnings to service these debts (Ramet 1991: 15).[1] Bulgaria's success, beyond the growth attributable to cheap Soviet energy and raw materials provided at below world market prices to all CMEA countries, stemmed from the extreme openness of its economy to CMEA, mainly

[1] Thus between 1981 and 1987 food prices in Poland rose 500 percent while wages rose only 100 to 200 percent, and hence about 25 to 30 percent of the Poles were experiencing poverty hardships as early as 1985 (Ramet 1991: 15).

Soviet, markets. Thus in 1989, Bulgarian foreign trade accounted for 90 percent of GDP, and 76 percent of Bulgarian exports went to CMEA markets (mostly in the USSR), as compared with 45 percent for Poland (ILO 1994: 3–40).

The considerable worsening of the economic situation in Bulgaria in the second half of the 1980s, however, precipitated a regime collapse patterned much like those that had already taken place in other Eastern European countries (Crampton 1997: 205–15). In the second half of the 1980s, signs of economic stagnation were clearly noticeable: Growth rates in the major economic sectors sagged; the volume of foreign trade declined; and the foreign debt began to rise uncontrollably. In addition, fuel and consumer goods shortages eroded confidence in the system (Petkov and Gradev 1995: 35–36).

The relatively modest economic deterioration of the 1980s did not, however, lead to Polish-style mass political discontent. Some strikes occurred in late 1985, when workers at a Sofia locomotive factory called for passive resistance to the government's new economic policies and to its exploitation and oppression (Petkov and Gradev 1995: 35–36). But the strikes were not enough to destabilize the government. Parallel to the unorganized workers' protests, dissident organizations began to emerge after 1985. They were stimulated by developments elsewhere in Eastern Europe but were built mainly around ethnic tensions and environmental issues, neither of which significantly challenged the political legitimacy of the party and produced strong demands for the dismantling of the political system.

As of March 1989, nine independent (dissident) organizations were reportedly active in the country, such as the Independent Association for the Defense of Human Rights, the Discussion Club for the Support of Glasnost and Perestroika, the Committee for Religious Rights, Freedom of Conscience and Spiritual Values, the Green Party, and the Ecoglasnost movement (Kiuranov 1991; Ramet 1991: 260). Of them, Ecoglasnost was particularly important (Crampton 1990; Dimitrov 1991). Influenced by the mass protests in the other countries, it made increasingly political demands and gradually broadened its activities to include political opposition to the regime. In October 1989, Ecoglasnost organized mass civil demonstrations in Sofia that drew worldwide media coverage, embarrassing the Zhivkov regime before its final collapse a month later. Other tensions arose on an ethnic basis. Government efforts to assimilate or expel the Turkish minority resulted in a mass exodus of Bulgarian ethnic Turks to Turkey in 1988–89, which created considerable problems for the Bulgarian economy and resulted in increased isolation of the country from the international community. The economic disruption, however, being ethnically based, did not mobilize mass discontent against the Zhivkov regime among the rest of the Bulgarian population.

No independent trade union, which might have channeled economic and political protest, was founded until February 1989. Even then, Bulgaria's first independent trade union, Podkrepa, had only sixty members (Poland's Solidarity, by comparison, had almost 11 million in its heyday).[2] No mass economic discontent comparable to that in Poland existed in Bulgaria, and Podkrepa was made up of only a small group of intellectuals who were not strongly linked with workers. Podkrepa focused exclusively on radical opposition to the existing political order, with the dismantling of the political regime as its exclusive objective, and hardly raised economic demands. In Poland, in contrast, although Solidarity's political demands prevailed over economic ones, the two sets of demands were strongly intertwined.

The weakness of Bulgarian mobilization against the legacies of state socialism also reflected the general weakening of official trade unions during the period from 1986 to 1988. At the enterprise level, unions were reduced to mere administrative instruments of the self-management organs that were established by the 1986 Labor Code. Practical problems and specific rivalries between the two structures of workers' representation – unions and self-management – soon emerged (Petkov et al. 1987; Sotirova et al. 1987; Tseneva 1988; Walliamann and Stojanov 1989). Trade unions were further weakened by changes in the mechanism of collective agreement at the enterprise level. The 1986 Labor Code provided for vertical collective contracts, that is, contracts between the primary collective (the shop-floor brigade) and the basic collective (the enterprise council), an arrangement that contradicted the essence of collective bargaining as a union-management affair. The model did not work at all in practice, and the process of collective bargaining – traditionally, the most important union domain – was effectively blocked in 1987 (Tseneva 1991: 9–10).

Because of its relatively mild economic crisis and the underdevelopment of its dissident elements, Bulgaria's extrication from state socialism was greatly influenced by external events, such as the Gorbachev reforms in Russia and revolts in the other Eastern European states. The Bulgarian revolution was initiated by elites within the Bulgarian Communist party, rather than by opposition groups. It took the form of a palace coup – Zhivkov peacefully resigned on 10 November 1989 – and was not aimed at the deconstruction of socialism. Overall, this "revolution" amounted to a gentle (Raikin 1998: 240–44), controlled transition (Linz and Stepan 1996: 333–43), one that delayed the radical dismantling of the system (Bell 1998: 1–6; Daskalov 1998), since the communist elite involved in the coup attempted not to go beyond the Gorbachev reformist model of glasnost and perestroika.

2 Data from CL Podkrepa Information Department; interview with Konstantin Trenchev, President of Podkrepa, July 1993.

Organizational Restructuring

The political change of November 1989 was followed by spontaneous strikes and other forms of industrial action that facilitated the emergence, restructuring, and consolidation of the Bulgarian social partners (Ararski and Chavdarov 1990). The first "true" collective agreement was signed on 15 December 1989 by Sofia mayor Stefan Ninov and Atanas Stanev, chairman of the Trade Union Federation of Transport Workers. The agreement ended a month-long tension over unpaid wages, overtime, and deteriorating work conditions of the transport workers in Sofia.[3]

After the political change of November 1989, Podkrepa emerged into the open and was formally constituted as Podkrepa Confederation of Labor (CL) at its First Congress in March 1990. By the end of 1990, the confederation consisted of thirty-two labor unions and federations and thirty regional organizations, and claimed 300,000 members.[4] Podkrepa became part of the Bulgarian opposition and was one of the thirteen founders of the Union of Democratic Forces. With only a few thousand members at the time of its formation, Podkrepa operated mainly at the elite level. Despite its small numbers, it was extremely active and powerful as both a political and industrial force. Podkrepa participated in the major political discussions and events of 1989–90, such as the round-table political negotiations, as a part of the UDF. Its priority was the political aim of establishing a movement to overthrow the communist system. Its broader political goals were dismantling the old structures, creating new ownership and new attitudes toward ownership, and supporting its political partners and allies.

The 1989–90 winter strike wave led to workers spontaneously deciding to leave unions. To survive, the official unions had to undertake radical internal reform and begin to defend the immediate interests of workers. In February 1990, the official unions constituted themselves as the Confederation of Independent Trade Unions in Bulgaria (CITUB). Starting with a membership of seventeen big federations and unions, CITUB expanded to forty-one at its first Coordination Council (April 1990); at the Second Extraordinary Congress in February 1992, it reportedly united seventy-two federations and trade unions. CITUB has built twenty-eight regional centers for trade union defense and has territorial structures in 165 municipalities of the country (Tseneva 1990). These organizational reforms were

[3] "Reshitelni dejstvija na Bylgarskite profsyjuzi: Sled mychitelni pregovori rabotnicheskite iskanija sa zadovoleni. Sporazumenie mezhdu Izpylnitelnija Komitet na Stolichnija naroden syvet i Federalnija syvet na Federatsijata na profsyjuznite organizatsii ot transporta" (Decisive Action of the Bulgarian Trade Unions: After Hard Negotiations Workers' Demands Were Satisfied. Agreement between the Executive Committee of the Sofia Municipal Council and the Federal Council of the Federation of Trade Union Organizations in Transport), *Trud*, 16 December 1989.

[4] Data from Podkrepa's Information Department.

accompanied by a steady decrease in membership. At the end of 1990, CITUB claimed 3.72 million members, which decreased to 2.40 million by the end of 1991, and to 1.1 million at the end of 1995. Despite the absolute decline in employment and membership, CITUB's share of all employees has stabilized at 60 to 70 percent.[5]

CITUB's activities at the elite level were initially restricted by its reluctance to collaborate actively with the former Communist party, on the one hand, and, on the other, by the emerging democratic opposition's suspicion that the official unions were covert agents of the communists. To overcome its isolation and gain legitimacy at the elite level, CITUB relied on traditional syndicalist methods, such as consultations and negotiations with the government.[6]

Parallel to these changes on the union side, important changes occurred on the side of managers/employers.[7] The relationship between state enterprise directors and the state was fundamentally altered by the formation of the National Union of Economic Managers (NUEM) in January 1990. In its effort to establish social partnership, CITUB assisted in the formation of the managers' association (Petkov and Gradev 1995: 45). Although NUEM was designed mainly to defend the interests of economic directors as state employees, it played an important role in laying the foundations for an organization of employers. Because privatization was delayed, all Bulgarian employer organizations have lacked clear character or policies and have been linked to the state.

The Bulgarian Industrial Association (BIA) and the Bulgarian Chamber of Commerce were founded under state socialism and played an important role mainly in the creation of small- and medium-sized enterprises. However, as part of the state economic machinery, their status as employers' organizations was artificial, and they were restricted by the command economy. The BIA, founded in 1984, was the first employers' group to reshape itself as an autonomous entity, following the events of November 1989. Uniting 1,808 employers and comprising thirty-seven branch and twenty-eight regional associations, it appears to be the most active employers' organization in the branch and regional structures of social partnership in Bulgaria. The association has made proposals and submitted discussion projects on such matters as wage regulation, unemployment, protection and encouragement of employment, and various projects for the recovery of the national economy.[8]

[5] Materials of the Third Congress of the CITUB, 1993 (in Bulgarian).

[6] "Kolektivnoto dogovarjane – Osnova na sindikalnata dejnost" (Collective Bargaining – The Basis for Trade Union Activity), *Korespondentsko obuchenie* (Sofia: CITUB), no. 6 (November 1990).

[7] For a detailed analysis, see Martin et al. 1996.

[8] Materials of the Sixth General Meeting of the Bulgarian Industrial Association, 1993 (in Bulgarian).

The Bulgarian Chamber of Commerce and Industry, with a hundred-year history, functioned during state socialism to develop international economic cooperation for its members. It completed its reorganization in April 1990, after a General Meeting adopted statutes and other program documents. The chamber has 6,967 member employers from the state and private sectors, united in ten branch and twenty-one regional structures.[9] Although its goals are focused tightly on the defense of the economic interests of its members (individuals, companies, and other organizations), the chamber became involved in the emerging tripartism at national and lower levels.

The main function of the new employers' organizations has apparently been to protect the interests of small private businesses. In December 1989, the Union of Private Economic Enterprising and the Vazrazhdane Union of Private Producers (later renamed Vazrazhdane Union of Private Entrepreneurs) were founded. The Union of Private Economic Enterprising comprises more than 8,000 members, 80 percent of which are small- and medium-sized enterprises. It has eight branch associations and forty-three regional organizations all over the country.[10] The union is oriented toward the defense of the economic interests of its members: entrepreneurs or organizations with less than 50 percent state property. The union became actively involved in tripartite cooperation at national and lower levels. The Vazrazhdane Union of Private Entrepreneurs was founded as an organization of private entrepreneurs in different sectors of the economy. It has more than 800 members in forty-five regional and branch organizations.

Emergence of Social Dialogue

The Atanassov government, as a coalition between the Communist party and the Bulgarian Agrarian National Union, was forced to resign just two months after 10 November 1989, under broad pressure from both elites and the masses. Since the opposition forces and the Agrarian Union refused to form a coalition government with the Communist party, a new, "pure" communist government was formed with Andrej Lukanov as prime minister. The excommunist government initiated economic reform in early 1990 at a time of deep economic crisis. The primary objectives were to stabilize the budget deficit and the currency, curb expansion of the black market, and tackle the problem of a severe shortage of goods.

To secure favorable conditions for the implementation of the reform package, the two Bulgarian Socialist Party (BSP) governments entered into regular negotiations and consultations with CITUB. The government of the former communists also needed public support and political legitimacy on the eve of the June 1990 elections, and CITUB needed public legitimacy in

[9] Information materials from the Bulgarian Chamber of Commerce and Industry.
[10] Information materials from the Union of Private Economic Enterprising.

the new conditions of rapid union pluralization. In February 1990, CITUB and the Atanassov government began bilateral negotiations.[11] They agreed to regular consultations on problems of vital importance to working people, such as rising unemployment and rapidly falling living standards.[12] Later agreements were reached to include NUEM and other actors (chiefly Podkrepa).

Unlike the official unions, Podkrepa CL opposed negotiations with socialist governments, and it embraced strikes and other open protest actions as well as active political participation at the elite level. Podkrepa was one of the thirteen independent opposition groups, which merged on 7 December 1989, to form the opposition umbrella organization Union of Democratic Forces (UDF). Podkrepa was successful in organizing widespread social protest, including labor union actions (there were some 500 strike actions in the months immediately following the November events), which quickly undermined the government's legitimacy and forced the communists to grant political concessions. A mass prodemocracy demonstration on 10 December 1989 directly challenged the Communist party's leading role. The Bulgarian government and the UDF opened round-table negotiations on the political future of the country in January 1990, which ended in April 1990. Outcomes included elimination of the Communist party's legal monopoly on power and arrangements for free parliamentary elections in June 1990. Podkrepa CL's next big strike initiative was the miners' strikes in January and March 1990, and Podkrepa held separate negotiations with the government on behalf of striking miners on 6 March 1990, the day on which the first tripartite negotiations between the government, CITUB, and NUEM began.

The most important tripartite activities among the Atanassov government, CITUB, and NUEM included the signing of national agreements on urgent social and economic problems: the General Agreement among the government of Bulgaria, CITUB, and NUEM, signed on 15 March 1990; the General Guidelines on the Conclusion of Collective Labor Contracts and Agreements during 1990; and the Agreement on Indexation of Incomes, concluded in August 1990. The creation on 5 April 1990 of a National Commission for Coordination of Interests (NCCI) marked the institutionalization of social dialogue in Bulgaria.

[11] "Pyrvite pregovori mezhdu Bulgarskite profesionalni syjuzi i chlenove na pravitelstvoto" (First Negotiations between the Bulgarian Trade Unions and Members of the Government), *Trud*, 29 December 1989; "Bylgarskite profsyjuzi predlagat: Generalno sporazumenie s pravitelstvoto" (Bulgarian Trade Unions Propose General Agreement with the Government), *Trud*, 5 January 1990.

[12] "Osnova za konstruktiven dialog. Nachalo na konsultatsiite mezhdu pravitelstvoto i sindikatite po zhisneno vazhni za trudovite hora problemi" (The Basis for a Constructive Dialogue. Start of Consultations between the Government and the Trade Unions on Problems of Vital Importance for the Working People), *Trud*, 1 March 1990.

The General Agreement targeted both political and economic objectives.[13] On the one hand, the agreement was a rational effort to combat the economic crisis and to control social protest before the start of economic reforms. The main provisions of the agreement envisaged social protection in the areas of employment, wages, living standards, social development (holidays and social funds), health and safety, rest and recreation, and democracy in firms and enterprises. On the other hand, the agreement ensured political legitimacy for the socialist government, CITUB, and NUEM, which were all offspring of the old system and were under vigorous attack from the unified anticommunist opposition. Podkrepa CL was invited to sign the agreement, but it refused to engage in official negotiations with a socialist government. However, realizing the importance of negotiations as a mechanism for the defense of the interests of its members, Podkrepa CL joined the recently created social dialogue forum at the end of April 1990.

The General Agreement provided for the institutionalization of social dialogue through a *National Commission for Coordination of Interests* (see Table 1). Founding members of the commission became the signatories of the General Agreement: the government, CITUB, and NUEM.[14] The commission was open to other parties, without any legitimization or recognition requirements, as long as they signed the General Agreement. Equal numbers of representatives – three – from each member participated in the sessions of the commission. The government was represented at the level of deputy prime minister, while the social partners sent deputy leaders. Participation by interested political and other organizations as observers was also regulated. Decisions became final only when consensus was reached.

The *Agreement on Indexation of Incomes*, concluded in August 1990,[15] modified the General Agreement's provisions on wages and launched a system by which incomes were indexed to compensate for price hikes. It marked a step forward in the institutionalization of social dialogue by forming standing working groups at the commission on living standards,

[13] Generalno sporazumenie mezhdu Konfederatzijata na nezavisimite sindikati v Bulgaria, Pravitelstvoto na NR Bulgaria i Natzionalnija Syjuz na stopanskite rykovoditeli v Bulgaria. (General Agreement among CITUB, the Government of the PR Bulgaria, and the Union of Economic Managers in Bulgaria), Sofia, 15 March 1990.

[14] "Prieti sa Obshti pravila. Zaraboti Natsionalnata komnisija za syglasuvane na interesite" (General Guidelines Were Adopted. The National Commission for Coordination of Interests Started Its Work), *Trud*, 5 April 1990.

[15] Sporazumenie mezhdu pravitelstvoto na NR Bulgaria, Konfederatzijata na nezavisimite sindikati v Bulgaria, Konfederatzijata na truda Podkrepa i Natsionalnija syjuz na stopanskite rykovoditeli za reshavaneto na njakoi ostri sotzialni problemi, porodeni ot zadylbochavashtata se ikonomicheska krisa" (Agreement among the Government of Bulgaria, CITUB, Podkrepa CL, and NUEM for the Resolution of Some Urgent Social Problems, Caused by the Deepening Economic Crisis), *Trud*, 15 August 1990.

unemployment, wages, privatization, economic legislation, labor law and social security, rest and recreation, conditions of work, and health and safety. The National Commission aimed to arrive at mutually acceptable decisions concerning economic reform and its social consequences; solutions to major problems revolving around labor relations, social security, and living standards; and the resolution of nationally important labor conflicts, including those in areas where strike actions were legally forbidden.

The commission produced important results despite the government's reluctance to fulfill its obligations. From April 1990 until the fall of the second Lukanov government in November 1990, a total of fourteen meetings concerning the signing and implementation of the provisions of the General Agreement were held by the commission.[16] One of the commission's most important successes was the *General Guidelines on the Conclusion of Collective Labor Contracts and Agreements during 1990*. Signed on 5 April 1990, the Guidelines concerned the development of social dialogue at lower levels and laid the basis for a new collective bargaining approach to replace the system of centrally fixed wages.[17] The commission also agreed on procedures for layoffs in enterprises and negotiations on plant closures, and in May 1990 it suspended all layoffs until after the June 1990 elections.

Another round of negotiations within the National Commission concerned wage regulation according to the Agreement on Indexation of Incomes. During the era of state socialism, wages were regulated centrally according to a Soviet-style tariff system. Centralized wage regulation was modified in 1989–90 by the so-called new system of basic wages, which granted some freedom to enterprises in distributing the wage fund. Indexation of wages in enterprises and organizations was introduced in September 1990, and an agreement was reached for the negotiation of indexation within each enterprise and organization. In October 1990, an automatic indexation mechanism was introduced.[18] The agreement also included a 300-day moratorium on strikes, proposed by Prime Minister Lukanov and accepted by the unions. However, the Lukanov government implemented the agreement only after the unions proclaimed a national strike alert in October 1990.

[16] Archive data: Minutes of the work of the Tripartite Commission; interviews with its secretary. See also "Izpylnenie na Generalnoto sporazumenie mezhdu Konfederatsijata na nezavisimite sindikati v Bulgaria, pravitelstvoto i Natsionalnija syjus na stopanskite rykovoditeli" (Fulfilment of the General Agreement between the CITUB, the Government and the National Union of Economic Managers), *Trud*, 20 July 1990, no. 142.

[17] "Obshti pravila za skljuchvaneto na kolektivni trudovi dogovori i sporazumenija pres 1990 godina" (General Guidelines on the Conclusion of Collective Labor Contracts and Agreements during 1990), *Trud*, 9 April 1990.

[18] Council of Ministers Decree no. 103 of 4 October 1990 for the Creation of Conditions Facilitating the Practical Implementaiton of Indexation of Incomes.

From the start, the mechanism for compensating wage earners for inflation was influenced by the restrictions imposed by the IMF on wages, as part of its conditions for granting loans for macroeconomic stabilization. Within these restrictions, the social partners negotiated a 30 percent decline in living standards. Wages for various categories became more equal, dropping to their lower ends. The rise in inflation and the production decline undercut the continued viability of the indexation mechanism.

Meanwhile, the polarization of Bulgarian politics lent such a strong political coloration to the country's transition that economic reforms were considerably delayed. The economy was additionally damaged by the collapse of the CMEA markets and ruptured trade relations with the former Soviet Union (Beleva et al. 1995). In addition, unlike most of the former socialist countries, Bulgaria began economic reforms without foreign financial assistance. In the June 1990 elections the democratic opposition UDF did not gain the majority in the Grand National Assembly, and political tensions increased. The socialist government continued to pursue social partnership, in order to secure social peace as the unpopular economic reforms were finally effected. Both Podkrepa and CITUB rejected the reform plan, however, especially its call for rapid privatization. The political and economic crisis in the country deepened.

By the end of 1990, the number of labor conflicts reached 1,300, with 1.4 million participants.[19] The strikes were regulated by a new *Law for the Settlement of Collective Labor Disputes* initiated and prepared by CITUB and passed by Parliament on 6 March 1990.[20] Although the law prohibited strikes with political demands, in November 1990, Podkrepa CL called for a national strike action to force the resignation of the Lukanov government. CITUB later joined the strike, and the government collapsed in December 1990. Thus, the unions used the tripartite forum in combination with active strike actions to speed up both political and economic reforms.

The resignation of the Lukanov government sparked conflicts within CITUB of an ideological-political nature, between the reformist leadership of the confederation and the prosocialist leaders of branch unions affiliated with CITUB. This led to a horizontal split of the confederation and the emergence of the People's Trade Union "Edinstvo" at the end of 1990. In 1991, Edinstvo claimed a membership of 184,000. The union emerged as a left alternative in trade unionism and a supporter of the socialist government, although it rejected official links with the BSP.

[19] Materials of the Third Congress of CITUB, Sofia, 8–10 October 1993; materials of CITUB's "Individual and Collective Labor Disputes" Department.

[20] Zakon za urezhdane na kolektivnite trudovi sporove (Law on the Settlement of Collective Labor Disputes). See also Nikolay Angelov and Ivan Neikov, "Pravila ili haos: Zakonyt za kolektivnite trudovi sporove ima za kakvo da byde kritikuvan, no ne i otrichan" (Rules or Chaos: The Law on the Settlement of Collective Labor Disputes Can Be Criticized but Not Negated), *Trud*, 27 August 1990.

3.2. Economic Reform and Tripartism

After a year of stagnation and mass shortages in 1990, economic reforms, more specifically, macroeconomic stabilization measures, began in February 1991. They were passed by the BSP-dominated Parliament and led by the Popov coalition government (BSP, UDF, and Agrarians), formed in December 1990 as a government of compromise. The Agreement for Peaceful Transition Towards a Market Economy, concluded by fifteen political parties and organizations (including CITUB) on 3 January 1991, became the basis of the government program. The main task of the government was to initiate the first stage of economic reforms: macroeconomic stabilization. The reform did not differ basically from those in other countries in Eastern Europe and was, in its way, as radical and as comprehensive as the Polish "big-bang" package of the previous year. It included a package of measures such as liberalization of prices and interest rates, restrictive wage and incomes policy, tight control on credit, and provisions to keep the decline of living standards within tolerable limits. These liberalization measures were accompanied by an IMF-backed stabilization program.

Social Peace and Institutionalization of Tripartism

For the success of its unpopular stabilization program,[21] the government needed not only political consensus within Parliament but also broad mass support, including the cooperation of trade unions. Social dialogue, which had been cut short in October 1990 by the nationwide strike that toppled the socialist government, was restored in January 1991. Following the recommendations of the IMF, the government signed two social peace agreements and reached a temporary six-month consensus with the social partners.

The *Agreement on Preservation of Social Peace*, signed on 8 January 1991, had purely economic objectives and was directly linked to economic reforms.[22] It was signed by the government, Podkrepa, the CITUB, and several employers' organizations from the state, cooperative, and private sectors: the NUEM, the Vazrazhdane Union of Private Producers, the Union for Private Economic Enterprising, the Union of Producer Cooperatives,

[21] As a result of the liberalization program, prices increased at least 100 percent in February and a further 50 percent in March, so that by the end of March prices were three times as high as in January. GDP fell 26 percent during the first two years of liberalization. The decline in industrial output was even sharper: 37 percent. Employment fell as rapidly as output. At zero in 1989, the unemployment rate reached 1.7 percent by the end of 1990, then escalated to 15.2 percent by December 1992 (Beleva et al. 1995: 195). On the effects of the liberalization program, see also in Wyzan 1996, 1998.

[22] Sporazumenie za zapazvane na sotsialnija mir (Agreement for the Preservation of Social Peace), *Korespondentsko obuchenie* (Sofia: CITUB), no. 1 (January 1991).

the Central Cooperative Union, and the Bulgarian Industrial Association. Unions promised to abstain from national industrial action and to discourage their structures – union federations – from industrial action at lower levels. In exchange, the government agreed to introduce some social protections for the population. The agreement included an increase in the basic interest rate; a liberalization of prices over several stages; a fixed ratio between minimum wages and the social minimum, with a mechanism for fixing the social minimum and the minimum wage; the beginning of wage bargaining at the enterprise level; a revised mechanism for indexation; provisions for other social security and training benefits; and changes in labor and social legislation. Employers' organizations were given some preferential treatment in obtaining state loans and credits. The agreement was legally endorsed by government decree in January 1991.

To coordinate the activities of the partners in securing social peace in the course of macroeconomic stabilization, the *National Standing Tripartite Commission for Coordination of Interests* was established on 15 January 1991. Founding members of the commission became the signatories to the Social Peace Agreement. The commission was also open to other interested organizations and institutions, and initially the National Student Confederation participated in its sessions. The commission's goal was to establish dialogue and negotiation as the basis of social partnership in the resolution of major labor conflicts.[23] Seven subcommissions were set up, covering Financial and Credit Policy and Banking; Employment, Layoffs and Training of the Labor Force; Social Minimum Wages and Compensations of Incomes; Industrial Conflicts; Privatization, Expert Evaluation and Autonomization of State and Municipal Property; Social Insurance and Social Care; and Labor and Social Legislation. Discussions in the subcommissions (the expert level) were a precondition for official negotiations in the commission (at the leadership level).

Consensus was a requirement for decisions within the commission. In cases of disagreement, the government, as well as the other social partners, could act independently. Following a special government decree in April 1991, in an attempt to transform the consultative forum into a joint decision-making body, all decisions of the commission became mandatory for the lower levels of state administration. The mandate of the commission also authorized the creation of branch and regional commissions for coordination of interests. The process was facilitated and expedited in April 1991 by a special government ordinance for the creation of such commissions.[24]

[23] Statut na Postojannata tristranna komisija za syglasuvane na interesite (Statute of the Standing Tripartite Commission for Coordination of Interests), *Korespondentsko obuchenie* (Sofia: CITUB), no. 5 (March 1991).

[24] Council of Ministers Decree no. 102 of 23 April 1991 for the Creation of Sectoral and Regional Subcommissions for Coordination of Interests.

The reception given the neoliberal reforms when they were initiated in February 1991[25] showed that Bulgaria enjoyed a broad sociopolitical consensus on the need for radical change. Despite a drastic fall in living standards of 40 to 45 percent, there were no major industrial conflicts or civil unrest. The number of labor conflicts and strikes dropped from 1,300 in 1990 to 850 in 1991.[26] For the nine-month period of its existence (until October 1991), the Tripartite Commission functioned actively and regularly, meeting forty-six times, which was more than once per week on average.[27]

The commission and its subcommissions discussed all important issues in the field of labor, social insurance, and standards of living, such as the introduction of wage bargaining at national, industry-wide, and enterprise levels and the adjustment of wages and other incomes with price liberalization. They focused specifically on liberalization of prices and adjustment of incomes, procedures for layoffs in enterprises, guidelines for collective bargaining during 1991, the introduction of wage bargaining and a procedure for legitimization of the partners in collective bargaining, the process of collective bargaining in the public sphere, privatization issues and development of small business, employment issues, and amendments to the Labor Code. The reduction of personnel in state enterprises was counterbalanced by a procedure to prevent chaotic and unjustified layoffs. The Guidelines on Collective Bargaining during 1991 fostered the development of collective bargaining at the enterprise level and forced enterprise managers to bargain with unions.

In June 1991, as political conflict over the new constitution intensified (it was condemned by radical members of the UDF), another tripartite agreement was concluded, the *Agreement on the Further Course of Economic Reform and Preservation of Social Peace*.[28] This second social peace agreement contained a program for the continuation of economic reform that went beyond labor relations. It envisaged stabilization of employee incomes, social security, restructuring of the economy, and privatization. At the same time, the agreement emphasized the need for attention to labor market issues and social support for those suffering the greatest decline in economic welfare.

With price liberalization and the fall in real wages, compensation became a major concern of the social partners. The tripartite commission prescribed

[25] Council of Ministers Decree no. 8 of 29 January 1991 for the Liberalization of Prices and Social Protection of the Population.

[26] There is no official statistical data on strikes in Bulgaria; the numbers used in this study are based on estimates of CITUB's Organizational Department and "Individual and Collective Labor Disputes" Department.

[27] Archive data: minutes of sessions held by the National Standing Tripartite Commission for Coordination of Interests.

[28] "Sporazumenieto e podpisano. Sindikatite i bog da pazjat reformata!" (The Agreement Is Signed. The Trade Unions and God Should Guard the Reform!), *Trud*, 14 June 1991.

maximum permitted ceilings on wage growth in each enterprise, and wage payments in excess of the ceiling were subject to an excess wage tax. The recession necessitated, however, the introduction of a new wage policy for the second stage of economic reform. In July 1991, with the incomes policy and the excess wage tax in place, a new system of decentralized wage bargaining was introduced in the state sector by decree no. 129.[29] The new policy abandoned compensation and indexation, and introduced branch-, regional-, and enterprise-level wage bargaining in parallel with existing national bargaining. Two tasks delegated to national wage bargaining were fixing the minimum wage and suggesting a formula for setting wages based on education and skill levels. The state concentrated its efforts on the regulation of wage funds in order to control inflationary pressures, rather than on the management of individual wages, and the excess wage tax remained the only operative restraint on wages. (Private firms were not subject to the excess wage tax.) This tax, however, was substantially reformed to soften the effect of the abandonment of compensation and indexation. The government raised the threshold below which wage tax growth was untaxed and liberalized the excess wage tax (Troxel 1993).

The Tripartite Commission and the two social peace agreements effectively bound the unions to preserve social and industrial peace in the country, so that the economic reforms could be implemented. But while unions were enjoined to abstain from strike action, at least at the national level, they could express their dissatisfaction by other means, such as breaking off participation in the commission. Thus, in February 1991 CITUB officially withdrew its participation for several days, and in July 1991 Podkrepa CL also left for about a month.

Social Dialogue at Stake: A Clash of Commitments

The temporary, six-month consensus allowed a variant of shock therapy in Bulgaria, which brought inflation down to 5 percent monthly, from 60 percent in December 1989. However, the monetarist program and the coalition government were short-lived. In the summer of 1991, the structural measures that had been agreed upon were undermined by political pressures (inside and outside Parliament) for new elections, and a new deadlock in economic reform set in. Active preparation for the October 1991 elections led to a discontinuation of social dialogue at the end of August 1991.

The shift in power from the former communists to the opposition that began with the Popov coalition government was consolidated in the second free elections for Parliament in October 1991. The 1991 parliamentary

[29] Council of Ministers Decree no. 129 of 5 July 1991 on the Introduction of Wage Bargaining.

elections brought a modest victory for the UDF-Movement.[30] The UDF formed a minority government – the Dimitrov government – with strong parliamentary backing from the Movement for Rights and Freedoms (MRF), and continued to carry out the economic reforms. Its platform was more distinctly neoliberal than those of the previous governments had been. Determined to continue shock therapy on a large scale, it sharpened the restrictive financial and incomes policy. The strategy was to keep wages down and to create macroeconomic conditions that would both stimulate the spontaneous development of private enterprises and allow the rapid privatization of the state sector. The UDF government met with success in real estate, small-scale privatization, and, especially, large-scale restitution of properties nationalized in the late 1940s, but overall privatization proceeded more slowly than in other postcommunist countries (Dimitrov 1996).

The Bulgarian democratic forces, like those in Poland, had firm neoliberal commitments and favored a U.S.-U.K. pluralistic and adversarial model of relations between government and labor. Although Podkrepa was one of the founding members of the umbrella organization UDF, it was not as bound to it as the Solidarity union was to the Solidarity movement. Thus, while in Poland the Solidarity-led government, despite its firm neoliberal orientation, was involved in an informal social dialogue with the Solidarity union, in Bulgaria the UDF government's strong antiunion policies threatened to push trade unions to the periphery of the political process, especially after the government declared that trade unions were the main obstacle to the creation of a free market economy and that the tripartite structure was an unnecessary second center of power in the country. The government decided to replace the national tripartite commission with consultations at the level of the Ministry of Labor instead of at the level of the council of ministers.

Podkrepa became increasingly hostile to the Ministers of Industry and Finance, who dominated economic policy within this firm antiunion framework. Podkrepa annulled its status as an observer in the UDF, effectively withdrawing its signature from the Agreement on Social Peace, and requested the resignation of the Ministers of Finance and Industry, Ivan Kostov and Ivan Pushkarov. Moreover, in official declarations, both Podkrepa and CITUB protested the government's abandonment of tripar-

[30] The elections were preceded by a split in the UDF, which became clear in the struggle over the adoption of a new constitution (Troxel 1993). Three new groupings were formed: UDF-Liberals (rump members of the Green Party and the Federation of Clubs for Democracy), UDF-Center (the rump of Ecoglasnost and the Bulgarian Social Democratic Party), and UDF-Movement (remnants of the old UDF, followers of thirty-nine parliamentary deputies, who walked out of the Grand National Assembly in June 1991 to protest compromises in the new constitution).

tism and initiated bipartite actions with the major employers' organizations in the country.

Podkrepa's opposition to the UDF government resulted in increased tensions and the pluralization of union structures. New, pro-UDF trade union organizations appeared. The National Trade Union (NTU) was founded in January 1992 with 30,000 members in the transport (seafarers and dockworkers), metal, chemical, and energy sectors. The NTU supported the UDF and participated in pro-UDF demonstrations in Sofia in June 1993. The Geology, Metallurgy and Chemical Union also emerged, under the influence of the UDF. Thus, in 1992, in conflicts that were crucial to the development of the reform process, these unions took positions of unquestioning support for the UDF government and against CITUB and Podkrepa. The Association of Democratic Trade Unions was also a spin-off from Podkrepa. It was formed in December 1992 with a membership of 30,000, mainly persons and organizations that had either left Podkrepa or were excluded from it. The association also affiliated politically with the UDF, and the UDF leadership has attempted to use the association electorally in the role played by Podkrepa in the 1990 and 1991 elections. A group from the miners' federation also split from Podkrepa in February 1994 and formed the National Trade Union Federation "Miner" (Petkov and Gradev 1995: 45–46).

The government attack on social dialogue and tripartism affected CITUB to an even greater degree. To diminish the power of CITUB, on 19 December 1991, UDF radicals adopted a law mandating the confiscation of the remaining property of totalitarian organizations; CITUB was included in its list as the successor of the Bulgarian Trade Unions.[31] These antiunion policies and the disastrous fall in wages and rise in unemployment provoked CITUB to organize, in January 1992, a national "warning" strike favoring the renewal of the activities of the National Tripartite Commission and opposing any confiscation of union property.

Under pressure from the IMF, the UDF government reconsidered its social partnership policy. By early summer 1992, the government had reshuffled the Ministries of Finance and Industry and appointed a new Deputy Prime Minister, Nikola Vassilev, who was charged with maintaining contact with the trade unions. Meanwhile, however, the government discussed a draft proposal for introducing works councils in enterprises,

[31] The question of trade union property became a political issue, as in Hungary. The property of CITUB was confiscated by the state in December 1991. This issue played a significant role in the development of interunion relations and tripartism. Starting from total confrontation between CITUB and Podkrepa, on the one hand, and with the government, on the other, the issue was resolved in 1993 through the redistribution of assets between the state, CITUB, and Podkrepa by a formula of 10:55:35. Because of protests from the other unions, CITUB decided to give up its share in favor of the creation of a fund for additional social security benefits.

which brought a new dose of hostility into relations among the social partners. Podkrepa CL and CITUB, joined by the employers' organizations, refused to engage in any negotiations with the government until social partnership was again institutionalized. Podkrepa CL backed up its demands with a national miners' strike in March 1992. It brought a new government crisis, and on 20 May 1992, a new UDF cabinet was formed under the same Prime Minister, Filip Dimitrov.

On 29 May 1992, Guidelines for the Activities of the National Social Partnership System were signed by the government, Podkrepa CL, CITUB, the Bulgarian Industrial Association, and the Union for Private Economic Enterprising.[32] The *National Council for Social Partnership* was created as its "supreme organ." The council was to discuss and adopt agreements concerning social insurance, living standards, the definition of the poverty level, the rate of unemployment, the resolution of labor and social conflicts, and national aspects of the conditions of labor.[33] The parties were the government; unions, represented by Podkrepa CL and CITUB; and employers' organizations, represented by the Bulgarian Industrial Association, the Vazrazhdane Union of Private Producers, the Association of Free Entrepreneurs "Alternative 2000," and the Union for Private Economic Enterprising. The council was open to other interested organizations, but they had to meet criteria established by the founding members. Like the previous forums, the council had standing commissions and working groups, denominated by function: Labor Force (labor, employment, training, and retraining); Incomes and Prices; Collective Labor Disputes; Social Insurance and Social Aid; Privatization and Restructuring of the Economy; Financial, Tax and Credit Parameters of Social Partnership; and Specific Problems of Employees in the Budgetary/Public Organizations. The Regulations for the Functioning of the Council regulated the formation of branch and regional councils.

The council functioned, however, for only about three months and met only five times. At the same time, bilateral meetings between the social partners increased considerably. Most of these meetings were between the two union confederations; they were held mainly to discuss property confiscated from the former Bulgarian Trade Unions and its redistribution among union organizations, but also to organize joint actions in opposition to the government's antiunion policy. Thus, two philosophies clashed as the

[32] "Sindikati i rabotodateli pak dadoha shans na pravitelstvoto. Prieti sa pravilata za rabota na Natsionalnata sistema za sotsialno partnerstvo" (Trade Unions and Employers Gave a Chance to the Government, Once Again. The Guidelines for the Work of the National System for Tripartite Partnership Were Adopted), *Podkrepa*, 30 May 1992; "Profesoryt i Trenchev se poglednaha syuchastnicheski, vitsepremieryt Nikola Vasilev se okazva myzhko momche," *Trud*, 30 May 1992.

[33] "Pravila za rabota na Natsionalnata sistema za sotsialno partnerstvo" (Regulations for the Work of the National System of Social Partnership), *Sindikalna praktika*, no. 6 (1992), 7–11.

neoliberal government rejected tripartism in principle, while trade unions and employers recognized the role of social partnership.

The clash of commitments led to permanent destabilization in the industrial and political arenas. From January 1992 through November 1992, there were more than forty big strikes at the branch level and a considerable increase in the number of local labor conflicts, which totaled 1,070 in that period, with 1.1 million participants. Social dialogue was ignored, and conflict and pressure prevailed as the means of coordinating individual and group interests. This case showed the crucial role of political commitments, especially those of the state, in maintaining and shaping social partnerships.

Legal Endorsement of Social Dialogue

During the fourteen months of the UDF-led government, neoliberal policies failed to produce any significant economic recovery. Throughout 1992, unemployment rose, real wages stagnated at low levels, and national output fell. The government struggled on, following a reshuffling in May 1992, but in December, weakened by internal disagreements and a parliamentary split, it was unable to win a confidence vote initiated by the MRF, and was forced to resign.

A new "government of experts" came to power at the end of 1992: the Berov government, elected with the support of the Turkish Minority Party (MRF). The government was a compromise among all of the parliamentary parties and coalitions other than the UDF and had support from rival political forces. Its major aim was to avoid early parliamentary elections, although in his Program Declaration, the Prime Minister declared much more ambitious intentions, such as the correction of the restrictive incomes policy and the start of large-scale mass privatization (Petkov 1994).

Pressed by the unions, in need of some way to counteract political crisis, and convinced that structural reform could not be realized without broad extraparliamentary support, the government enacted a new Labor Code, to take effect on 1 January 1993, that established the legal grounds for social partnership.[34] Starting that month, social dialogue acquired formal legal status in Bulgaria. The Labor Code required that the state regulate the terms and conditions of social insurance and employment "after consultations and in partnership with the representative organizations of employees and employers."[35] The order and organization of such consultations were to be determined by the Council of Ministers, again after consultations with representative union and employers' organizations.

[34] *Tripartizmyt v Bulgaria: Normativna uredba, institutzii, sotsialni partnjori* (Tripartism in Bulgaria: Legal Framework, Institutions, Social Partners) (Sofia: CITUB and BIA, 1993); Mruchkov 1993; Mruchkov et al. 1993.

[35] Bulgarian Labor Code 1993.

The Labor Code regulated the conditions for recognition of employers' and unions' organizations as representative. Union recognition was first regulated in agreements between the social partners, then in the 1991 normative documents on the introduction of wage bargaining, while the new Labor Code, based on agreement reached within the tripartite forum, reiterated the principle of recognition. Complex criteria for representation at all levels were introduced, including official registration of nationwide organizations and a certain number of branch and regional structures.[36] For a union organization, the criteria for recognition were at least fifty union organizations with at least five members at the workplace level in each branch, and regional organs in at least 80 percent of the district cities, with at least fifty union workplace organizations, each having five or more members, in each district. For an employers' organization, recognition required coverage of at least two branches with at least fifty employers in each of them; and regional organs in at least 50 percent of the district cities, each regional structure comprising at least ten employers. Only nationally representative union and employers' organizations could participate in social dialogue and collective bargaining at lower levels.

In January 1993, the government recognized several union and employers' organizations as representative at the national level. Of the unions, Podkrepa CL and CITUB were recognized, but the Edinstvo NTU failed to meet the legal requirements for recognition and was denied access to the national tripartite body. On the employers' side, the Union for Private Economic Enterprising, the Bulgarian Chamber of Commerce, the Bulgarian Industrial Association, and the Vazrazhdane Union of Private Entrepreneurs were recognized.[37]

In line with the requirements of the new Labor Code, and after negotiations with the social partners, the new institutions of tripartite cooperation were created at all levels.[38] The Berov government reinstated the *National Council for Tripartite Cooperation* in March 1993.[39] It comprised representatives of the government and of the organizations of employees and employers recognized by the Council of Ministers as representative. The government was represented at the level of deputy prime minister, and

[36] Council of Ministers Decree no. 7 of 22 January 1993 on Regulation of the Principles, Terms and Order of Recognition of Workers' and Employers' Organizations as Representative at the National Level of Tripartite Partnership.

[37] See more in Kamenov et al. 1996; "Sotzialno partnjorstvo: Sistemata na sotzialnoto sytrudnichestvo i rabotodatelskite syjuzi" (Social Partnership: The System of Social Cooperation and the Employer Associations), *Korespondentsko obuchenie*, vol. 6 (April 1993).

[38] "Kodeksyt na truda otvarja pytja na istinskoto kolektivno trudovo dogovarjane" (The Labor Code Opens the Floor for True Collective Bargaining), *Sindikalna praktika*, no. 1 (1993), 26–53.

[39] Council of Ministers Decree no. 51 of 15 March 1993 on the Adoption of Rules for the Work of the National System for Tripartite Partnership.

the unions and employers' organizations sent deputy leaders. Sessions of the Council were organized by a Secretariat and were held on a regular basis. Standing expert commissions on the Labor Force were created, covering Employment, Unemployment, Qualification and Requalification; Incomes, Prices and Living Standards; Collective Labor Disputes; Social Insurance and Social Aid; International Labor Legislation and Work with the ILO; Conditions of Work; Privatization and Restructuring of the Economy; Financial, Credit and Tax Relations; and Specific Problems of Employees in Budget Organizations.[40]

During 1993, the economic situation deteriorated in most sectors, especially in the budget-financed sectors (state enterprises and services). Naturally, the Tripartite Council focused much of its attention on wages. The social partners had to agree on the minimum wage,[41] as well as on other protected payments – monthly supplemental children's payments and unemployment benefits – that were calculated as a percentage of the minimum wage. The social partners also negotiated wage increases and protections against inflation in material production in both the public sphere and state enterprises. The goals, principles, criteria, and mechanisms of incomes policy have also been a major area of discussion within the tripartite forum. Consensus about the defense of real incomes against galloping inflation has been reached only with difficulty.

Strategies and policies in the area of employment and unemployment were also regularly discussed, and important laws and normative documents issued by the government have been prepared in the council. The council has also concerned itself with the creation and effective functioning of labor market structures; the development of national and regional employment programs and measures against unemployment, including mechanisms for setting unemployment benefits; the system of training and retraining of unemployed workers; the defense of the national labor market; and the formation, governance, and budget of the Professional Training and Unemployment Fund. The council also discussed amendments to legislation on collective labor disputes, the mechanisms of social insurance, pensions, social aid, and the methods for privatization of the state sector (Bankov 1994).

Most aspects of the economic reforms also were discussed in the council. These included price controls on selected basic goods produced by state monopolies, legislation concerning the financing of small- and medium-sized enterprise development, and privatization and industrial restructuring, among others.

[40] Working Rules of the National System of Tripartite Partnership (in Bulgarian).

[41] The agreement was reflected in the Council of Ministers Decree no. 65 of 26 March 1993 for the Calculation of the National Minimum Wage and for the Compensation of Some Incomes of the Population; and in Council of Ministers Decree no. 71 of 6 April 1993 for the Indexation of Wages in the Budget-Supported Organizations and Activities.

With its formal legalization, social partnership enjoyed a second surge in development. The number of local labor conflicts in the country decreased as social dialogue boomed. In 1993, conflicts were down to 750, in 1994 to 620, and in 1995 to 538.[42] If before 1993 social dialogue disintegrated with each election campaign and government reshuffling, the adoption of the new Labor Code reduced *politically* initiated breaks in tripartism to a minimum.

IMF Constraints and Fragility of Compromise, 1994–1996

The stability of Bulgarian tripartism did not solely depend on a solid normative-legislative basis and the good will of the social partners, however. The constraints imposed by the IMF and World Bank's lending conditionalities, especially on wage increases, challenged significantly the compromise at the heart of social dialogue. This was sharply manifested in the spring of 1994, when the economic situation in the country deteriorated. Cumulative inflation over the period from 1990 through 1994 was 4,000 percent; the real incomes of the population, as a result of wages, pensions, and social payments that did not keep pace with inflation, were 55 percent lower in 1994 than they had been in 1990. At the end of 1994, the decrease in average real wages and pensions was more than 30 percent; according to official government estimates, more than 80 percent of the population received incomes below the social minimum.[43]

In April 1994, however, the Berov government – severely constrained by the continuing economic crisis and the mandates of the IMF and the World Bank – refused to reconsider wage adjustments after financial destabilization necessitated price increases of 20 to 25 percent. In addition, in light of the dominance of state property, unions insisted on the direct involvement of the state in branch collective bargaining, while employers, backed up by the state, preferred that the state withdraw from the negotiation and conclusion of bipartite union-management agreements. This disagreement led to open conflict among the social partners and to discontinuation of social dialogue. The conflict culminated in a national strike action initiated by CITUB on 4 May 1994.

The Indzhova interim government, in office until the December 1994 parliamentary elections, supported social dialogue and concluded a temporary agreement with the social partners. The agreement aimed to reduce the trend toward the impoverishment of the Bulgarian population, to increase labor productivity, to create new jobs, and to facilitate the privatization

42 Data from CITUB.

43 *Sotzialno-ikonomichesko razvitie na Republika Bulgaria prez perioda '90–94 godina* (Social and Economic Development of the Republic of Bulgaria in the Period 1990–94) (Sofia: National Statistical Institute, 1995).

process. A new minimum wage, 18 percent above the old rate, was agreed to as the basis for computing social and other payments and wages in the public sphere. It was agreed that the government would start to liberalize the tax on excess wages in material production. Unions agreed to abstain from strikes and other social protests for one month before the December 1994 elections. Employers agreed to cooperate toward optimizing social services' funds and organization.

With living standards dramatically down, the country was once again divided on the eve of elections, this time, like Poland in the same year, along economic, not political, lines. The elections brought victory to the BSP, which promised a less radical variant of economic reforms and a gradualist approach to the extrication from state socialism. However, the left-wing Videnov government, formed in January 1995, inevitably pursued policies that were politically to the right, albeit less restrictive than the policies they replaced. The socialist government needed social consensus on very unpopular policies, such as increases in the prices of electricity, telephone services, water, and postal services, on which the international monetary institutions insisted. Such restrictive economic policies led to a substantial increase in the scope of social partnership at all levels.

In its Program Declaration, the Videnov government declared a policy of active cooperation with trade unions and all the social partners within the National Tripartite Council and its intention to develop and improve the social partnership system at all levels: industry-wide, branch, and regional. The government even made an attempt to expand the scope of consultations through cooperation with other legitimate but nonrepresentative organizations of employees and employers, as well as other nongovernmental organizations with social-protective functions, by creating a National Social Council to deal with problems of unemployment and pensions. The government hoped to include the Union of the Unemployed, the Union of the Disabled, the Union of Pensioners, and other bodies in the council, but the project failed when both Podkrepa and the CITUB accused the government of attempting to replace and devalue the existing national tripartite structure.

As part of its effort to expand social dialogue, the Videnov government recognized, over the acute protests of Podkrepa and CITUB, another trade union – the Alliance of Free Trade Union Organizations in Bulgaria (OSSOB) – as representative at the national level. The core member of OSSOB was the National Free Trade Union "Business," founded in December 1989 with more than 20,000 members. This union united employees in tourism, restaurants, and trade, in both the state and cooperative sectors; but the goals, membership, and organizational structure of this new organization made it difficult to identify it as either purely a trade union or purely a business union. In 1995, OSSOB claimed membership of around 200,000 and united workers from thirty-one branches. The union has avoided political involvement, although it has often been accused of sympathizing with the Socialist party and being a "progovernment" trade union.

During the tenure of the Videnov government, social dialogue within the National Council for Tripartite Cooperation was shaped by union demands that further cuts in the real purchasing power of the population be stopped and that the tight restrictions on wage increases and other social payments be ended. In 1995, negotiations in the forum focused primarily on protecting incomes from inflation. Debates about wages in the budget sphere and other budget payments were intense, and disagreements threatened to put an end to the social partnership. The dialogue reached an impasse, and the government sent its draft 1995 budget to parliament without consensus among the social partners. The unions, CITUB in particular, sent a memorandum to the National Assembly defending their position. The conflict affected more than 550,000 teachers, doctors, cultural and scientific workers, and highly qualified state administration employees. Despite this failure, the social partners did negotiate a substantial liberalization of restrictions on wage increases. Decree no. 67, of 24 March 1995, although still restrictive, significantly liberalized compensation by regulating wages in companies with more than 50 percent state and/or municipal ownership (including joint stock companies with foreign capital).[44]

Pensions were another major union concern in 1995. The unions insisted on a 60 percent increase in the maximum pension and improvements in the structure and distribution of pensions. For the first time, a differential compensation was introduced for those whose pensions had been calculated long before and under very different conditions, and whose standards of living were most affected by the inflation of the past few years.

3.3. Currency Board, EU Accession, and Reinforcement of Tripartism

Social dialogue within the National Council for Tripartite Cooperation was discontinued in the fall of 1996, because of the deteriorating economic situation caused by mismanagement of the Videnov cabinet. The crisis had led to real wages dropping to $10 per month as a result of the devaluation of the Bulgarian currency. Industrial conflicts, protests, and strike actions were increasing, culminating in mass street protests in December–January

[44] Thus in cases of increases up to 2 percent, no penalty was applied. In cases of more than 5 percent increase, the tax penalty had to be differentiated according to the concrete amount of the average gross wage during the respective quarter of 1995: If the wage did not exceed two minimum wages, the tax had to be 50 percent; up to three minimum wages, 150 percent; up to four minimum wages, 300 percent; and above four minimum wages, 500 percent. Or in the last case a wage increase of 5 percent led to 500 percent excess wage tax.

1997, led by both CITUB and Podkrepa. In January 1997, the Videnov government was forced to resign.

An interim government with Stefan Sofijanski was formed in February 1997. In March, the interim cabinet signed an agreement for the preservation of social peace with the Bulgarian Industrial Association, Podkrepa, and CITUB. The trade unions took serious responsibility for preserving social peace, and wages were deregulated.

In July 1997, the Kostov cabinet was formed, after the UDF won an impressive 52 percent of the vote in the April 1997 early parliamentary elections. To combat the situation of hyperinflation, the Currency Board pegged the Bulgarian currency, the lev, to the German mark. Such an arrangement is designed to instill credibility in economic policy, and it has been highly successful in Bulgaria in bringing down inflation and interest rates. Consumer price inflation had dropped to only 1 percent in December 1998, from 578 percent a year earlier, and stood at 1.7 percent in the twelve months prior to July 1999. Under the currency board arrangement, wages have recovered to precrisis levels. The average monthly wage in the public sector, which had fallen to $25 in February 1997, recovered by May 1999 to $124, close to the postcommunist peak of $128 in September 1993 (Done 1998; Wyzan 1999).[45]

Charter for Social Cooperation and Memorandum for Priority Joint Action

Social dialogue was restored. The new government initiated the signing of a Charter for Social Cooperation and Memorandum for Priority Joint Action with the social partners. Interdependently, the Charter and the Memorandum served as the basis for the Currency Board's start-up. The trade unions (CITUB and Podkrepa) supported the currency board, and affirmed their commitment to its mechanism as the only way to manage the country's resources in the current economic situation. The extensive loss of financial and economic sovereignty that resulted from the currency board arrangement, although still restrictive, has led to a commitment by all social partners to more directly coordinate their activities with the international financial institutions.

The Charter for Social Cooperation and the Memorandum for Priority Joint Action identified so-called authentic social partners from among the seven trade unions and the four employer associations that had participated in social dialogue since 1995–96. Although all eleven organizations continued to participate in the work of the tripartite council, the government

[45] See also in *Ikonomikata na Bulgaria pres 1998 godina, Godishen doklad* (The Bulgarian Economy in 1998, An Annual Report) (Sofia: Agency for Economic Analyses and Prognoses, 1998).

invited only those social partners that had previously signed the social peace agreement with the interim government of Sofijanski – the CITUB, Podkrepa, and the Bulgarian Industrial Association – to sign the charter and the memorandum.

The *Charter for Social Cooperation*, signed on 2 October 1997 by the Prime Minister and the presidents of CITUB, Podkrepa, and the BIA, had the aim of generating broad social support for continued economic and social reform, democratization, and efforts to improve the social dialogue in the spirit of the European standards, principles, and rules.[46] The social partners agreed to maintain five basic principles of social co-operation: (1) in the interest of social peace, collaboration in creating and adopting the normative regulations of social and economic relations, for the fulfillment of the government program "Bulgaria 2001"; (2) explicit recognition that reforming the system of social dialogue in the sphere of economic, social, and industrial relations, and creating new forms of institutionalized social cooperation, were in the partners' mutual interests; (3) acceptance of responsibility for fulfilling obligations stemming from consensus-based selection of participants in the new collective bargaining–based model of social dialogue; (4) coordination of efforts and actions to integrate Bulgaria into the European and global structures, with a balance between the economic and social dimensions of reforms backed by international financial institutions and the ILO; and (5) transparency of the process of social dialogue and of the intentions and positions of the social partners, to help maintain public support for reforms.[47]

The *Memorandum for Priority Joint Action*, signed in October 1997 by the Prime Minister and the presidents of Podkrepa, CITUB, and the BIA, underscored the necessity of maintaining social and civil peace as a condition for the success of the reforms and the development of market relations, and was a concrete step in the fulfillment of the Charter for Social Cooperation. The memorandum outlined sixteen priorities for the social partners. These ranged from purely social and industrial-relations issues to broader macroeconomic responsibilities. Priorities included elaboration of a draft law on a tripartite Economic and Social Council for the management of the national insurance institutions and social rehabilitation, along with a whole package of social laws, a new labor code, and a draft law for social funds; concordance of the Bulgarian social and labor legislation with international standards, especially with the EU *acquis*, the European Union's common law; adoption of a national structural program

[46] Harta za sotzialno sytrudnichestvo (Charter for Social Cooperation) (Sofia: Ministry of Labor and Social Policy, 2 October 1997), 1.

[47] Harta za sotzialno sytrudnichestvo (Charter for Social Cooperation) (Sofia: Ministry of Labor and Social Policy, 2 October 1997).

for employment and a new employment policy through stimulation of investment activity; and adoption of coordinated sectoral programs for financial stabilization and restructuring.

According to union reports, the government reacted variously to the memorandum, responding to some of its points with impassivity and to others with positive, constructive action.[48] The areas in which the government, despite its participation in the broad tripartite discussions, did not follow through on its agreements with the social partners were the tax reform and the living standard parameters. Also not implemented was a mechanism for free wage negotiations in state enterprises in the real sector. Achievements were accomplished in three broad areas of social partnership: cooperation in the normative sphere for the adoption of the basic social laws, creation of institutions of social cooperation such as an Economic and Social Council, and technical coordination of tripartite cooperation.

Further, the social partners closely cooperated in negotiations with the IMF missions on issues concerning the social sphere. They participated in meetings to determine the government's strategy in its relations with the IMF; they were kept constantly informed about the outcome of the IMF-government negotiations; and several of their important proposals were borne in mind by the government as it formulated its position in negotiations with the IMF.

Civic and Institutional Expansion of Social Dialogue

Until 1997, the sole approved arena for discussion of all questions related to the social and employment sphere in Bulgaria was the National Council for Tripartite Cooperation (NCTC), with its regional and branch structures. Initially, the NCTC was the only institutionalized form of an active civil society (Meininger and Radoeva 1996; Dimitrov 1998).[49] As Bulgarian civil society developed, however, it placed increasing pressure on the council to discuss a broad range of issues concerning the consolidation of civil society. Many civil organizations wanted to become members of the tripartite council, so that their voices could be heard.[50] Before long, the council had acquired new members who were not representative according to the 1993 labor code; moreover, the council began to assume responsibilities much broader than those officially assigned to it, some of which even contradicted some constitutional stipulations.

[48] "100 dni Memorandum za prioritetni obshti dejstvija (Analiz)" (100 Days Memorandum for Priority Joint Action (An Assessment)) (Sofia: Konfederatzija na nezavisimite sindikati v Bulgaria, January 1998).

[49] By 1998, over 7,500 organizations of the third sector were registered in Bulgaria (Dimitrov 1998: 54).

[50] Interview with Ivan Neikov, Minister of Labor and Social Policy, Sofia, July 1999.

As a result, the Kostov government initiated two major revampings of Bulgarian tripartism: first, a systematic evaluation to confirm the qualifications of organizations for social partner status (the so-called authentication or verification of social partners), an important part of which was the enumeration of members, those of unions, in particular; and second, expansion of the scope of tripartism through the creation of a well-elaborated web of tripartite institutions and, consequently, inclusion of additional social actors, mostly from the "third sector," in the work of the newly created tripartite forums. Eight additional institutions of tripartism and five specialized social funds, governed with the broad participation of the social partners, were created on the basis of the social legislation adopted during 1997 and 1998 (see Table 2).

From 1995 until the end of 1998, the trade union side in national tripartism was increased from two unions (CITUB and Podkrepa) to seven, with the five additions officially recognized by the Videnov government and later by the Kostov government. In 1996, OSSOB – officially recognized by the Videnov government in 1995 – split into OSSOB and the General Centrale of the Branch Trade Unions in Bulgaria. The cabinet, in the few days before its 6 February 1997 resignation, recognized three more unions: the Edinstvo National Trade Union, the General Centrale of the Branch Trade Unions in Bulgaria, and the Promjana National Trade Union.[51] The Promjana Alliance for National, Trade Union and Civic Action was created in October 1996 by the UDF, as a broad civic formation to topple the Videnov government as a reaction to the financial crisis. Promjana included not only trade unions but also political parties, the Women's Union, the Physicians' Union, and the Union of Royal Military. By 1999, the alliance had already split into two, one of them being the Promiana National Trade Union. The interim cabinet of Sofijanski recognized one more trade union, the Association of Democratic Trade Unions, on 20 May 1997.

In March 1998, to prevent interunion quarrels from weakening social dialogue, the Kostov cabinet initiated verification or enumeration of trade union membership across the country. The three criteria for union "representativeness" were membership of at least 50,000, members in more than half of the branches of the economy, and regional structures in at least 80 percent of the regions.[52] According to the results, officially announced

[51] Decree no. 181, for the Recognition of the Edinstvo Independent Trade Union as a Representative Organization; Decree no. 182, for the Recognition of the National Trade Union as a Representative Organization; Decree no.183, for the Recognition of OSSOB; all 6 February 1997, *Dyrzhaven vestnik* (State Gazette), no. 13, 1997.

[52] Procedure for the Identification of Criteria for Representativeness of the Organizations of Workers, Adopted with Decree no. 41 of the Council of Ministers, 17 February 1998.

in December 1998,[53] only CITUB and Podkrepa fulfilled the requirements for national representation. CITUB and Podkrepa had memberships of 607,883 and 154,894, respectively, compared with fewer than 8,000 for the next-largest trade union, NTU Promjana; 4,000 for OSSOB; and 2,100 for the Association of Democratic Trade Unions. In terms of the second criterion, CITUB had members in twenty-two branches and Podkrepa in nineteen, whereas NTU Promjana registered members in only two branches, and OSSOB and the General Centrale of Branch Trade Unions had members in only one branch each. In terms of the third criterion, CITUB had regional organizations in all twenty-eight regions, Podkrepa in twenty-three, and the remaining trade unions had none in any regions.

The enumeration and evaluation of union members in Bulgaria showed that the trade unions excluded from tripartism had a total membership of less than 15,000, and that they were highly politicized and answered to the will of various political entities.

Through a series of laws adopted in 1997–98, the Kostov government created additional tripartite organs to complement the NCTC in all major areas of the social sphere, in accordance with the priorities set in the government program Bulgaria 2001 for the period 1997–2001. The program emphasized the social market economy as the economic guarantee for the development of industry and for the rights and freedoms of individuals.[54] The government policy in the social sphere included several major high-priority goals, among which were a panoply of reforms – in social security, incomes policy and social assistance, and in health and safety at work, for example – and the creation of labor markets. The government program emphasized the tripartite character of the management and control of a variety of social funds.

Consistent with the social-dialogue orientation of the new government, a total of thirteen civic-tripartite structures arose in Bulgaria after 1997, all normatively regulated in the new social and labor legislation adopted in 1997–98: eight tripartite forums and five tripartite boards for the management of social funds.[55] Many of the tripartite organs departed from their classical tripartite character and became multipartite, including nongovernmental organizations and various professional organizations. Moreover, the tripartite organs developed not only as organs of consultation but

[53] Concluding Statement of the Commission on Par. 6(1) of the Procedure for the Identification of Criteria for Representativeness of the Organizations of Workers . . . , 14 December 1998.

[54] Bulgaria 2001. Programa na pravitelstvoto na Republika Bulgaria 1997–2001 (Program of the Government of the Republic of Bulgaria for the Period 1997–2001 "Bulgaria 2001"), p. 39.

[55] "Social Dialogue Reality in Bulgaria," *From Guidelines to Action*, Bulgarian Ministry of Labor and Social Policy Bulletin, vol. 2 (November 1998).

as organs through which social groups became directly involved in the decision-making process in the respective sphere.

The *National Council for Tripartite Cooperation*, established by virtue of the Labor Code, remained a purely tripartite structure, comprising the government, the representative organizations of employers, and the representative organizations of workers. According to the working rules adopted by the social partners, cochairmen of the NCTC became the three deputy prime ministers. The first session of the council was held on 1 June 1997, and since then the council has held twenty-four meetings over a period of twenty-five months, through the end of July 1999.[56] In 1997, the Council held ten meetings; in 1998, eleven; and through mid-1999, three. Compared with previous years, 1999 saw a definite decrease in the intensity of sessions. This resulted from the channeling of most of the discussions into other, newly created structures of social dialogue. Discussions in the council focused on the Charter for Social Cooperation and the Memorandum for Priority Joint Action, as well as on several matters of national importance, such as wage and income policies, especially the minimum wage and the basic "minimal income"; draft laws in the labor and social spheres – health insurance, social security, and social assistance; the reform of state administration; taxation issues; the state budget for 1997 and 1998; and privatization of state enterprises.

CITUB, Podkrepa CL, and the BIA also concluded bipartite national agreements, such as the National Agreement on Collective Bargaining, signed on 7 April 1998. This agreement regulated collective bargaining agreements at lower levels between the two unions and the Bulgarian Industrial Association. The social partners also regulated the creation of a Voluntary Labor Arbitration body comprising representatives of the two unions and the BIA.

As in Poland, a separate tripartite structure concentrating on issues of employment and unemployment emerged in Bulgaria, but at a later stage of the reforms. Transition eventually requires a forum that deals exclusively with employment and unemployment issues, rather than with the whole breadth of economic policy. The tripartite *Supervisory Board of the Vocational Training and Unemployment Fund* was created in December 1994. At regional levels, similar tripartite consultative committees were established as part of the National Program on Temporary Employment. The Supervisory Board comprises representatives of the government and the representative organizations of employers and unions and is chaired by one of its members for a period of six months. Board decisions require only a simple majority. At least three times a year, the central management of the

[56] Archive data: minutes of the sessions of the National Council for Tripartite Cooperation (secretariat of the NCTC); interviews with the secretary of the council.

National Employment Office organizes sessions of the board. The board was created with the aim of securing control over the expenditure of funds from the Vocational Training and Unemployment Fund. Although the fund is supervised by the Minister of Labor and Social Affairs, its six-month and annual balance reports are adopted by the tripartite Supervisory Board. Additional responsibilities of the board include issuance of opinions and recommendations on the annual budget of the fund, and on draft programs financed by the fund.

The *National Council on Unemployment Protection and Employment Promotion* was created as a permanent organ of tripartite cooperation to regulate unemployment insurance policy, employment promotion, and vocational training of persons of working age. Participating in it, in equal numbers, are representatives of the government, of representative organizations of employers, and of representative organizations of workers.

The *National Council on Vocational Training* is a consultative organ attached to the Ministry of Labor and Social Policy in the area of vocational training. It comprises representatives of the Ministry of Labor and Social Policy, the Ministry of Education, and the representative organizations of employers and employees. The council approves the state policy in the area of vocational training. It makes proposals to the government for the approval of regulations on vocational training and the issuance of professional certificates. Another of its duties is to approve, under the auspices of the Minister of Labor and the Minister of Education, a list of all professions and specialties in the country for which specific vocational training, work experience, or both are required.

The *Supervisory Board of the National Employment Office* is another tripartite structure. The National Employment Office was created to manage the Vocational Training and Unemployment Fund and to implement state policy on employment promotion, organization of professional training and retraining, and unemployment protection. Under the new law, the National Employment Office is managed by a Management Board and a Supervisory Board. The Supervisory Board is formed on a tripartite basis, with equal numbers of representatives of the government and the nationally representative organizations of employers and employees. The chairman of the board is elected for a period of one year, on a rotating basis, from each of the three parties. The board holds meetings at least once a month and requires a two-thirds' quorum to conduct business. Decisions require the vote of at least two thirds of the present members. The Supervisory Board approves the basic guidelines and oversees the activities of the National Employment Office. It also exercises control over the management of the National Vocational Training and Unemployment Fund, by approving its annual budget. The Supervisory Board also approves draft normative regulations regarding unemployment insurance, vocational training, and employment promotion before their official discussion in the appropriate government organs. The board further nominates the head of the National Employment Office to the Council of Ministers.

The *National Council on Working Conditions* became part of the tripartite structures at national, regional, and branch levels for coordination of state policy for the promotion of health and safety at work. The council is a standing tripartite body of social dialogue for the elaboration and maintenance of national policy on health and safety at work. It includes representatives of the government, representative organizations of employers and workers, the National Social Security Institute, and the Council for Mutual Insurance of Members of Producer Cooperatives. Its chairman is the Minister of Labor and Social Policy, and it has two vice-chairmen: one from the representative organizations of employers and another from the representative organizations of employees. The council discusses working conditions and proposes measures for their improvement, including the creation of sectoral and branch organs for tripartite cooperation on working conditions. It coordinates the activities of the state control organs in this field.

The *Managing Board of the Working Conditions Fund* exercises control over the management of the Working Conditions Fund. The fund was created to finance activities for the improvement of health and safety on the job. The board comprises a chairman, a vice-chairman, and five members. While the Minister of Labor and Social Policy appoints the chairman and three of the members, the National Council on Working Conditions elects the vice-chairman and two of the members of the Managing Board from among its members. The Managing Board develops and coordinates the annual budget of the fund with the National Council on Working Conditions, and it approves the procedures for financing various projects and programs through the fund.

The *Council for Social Assistance* was created as a public consultative organ of the Ministry of Labor and Social Policy. It comprises representatives of the government (the Ministry of Labor and Social Policy, Ministry of Finance, Ministry of Health Care, Ministry of Education and Science, and Ministry of Regional Development), the National Alliance of Municipalities in Bulgaria, representative organizations of employers and workers, and charitable/humanitarian nongovernmental organizations active in the sphere of social assistance. The council analyzes annual reports on the development of social assistance in the country issued by the National Office for Social Assistance. It also oversees the activity of the Social Assistance Fund, in collaboration with the Managing Council of the Social Assistance Fund.

The *Managing Board of the Social Assistance Fund* exercises control over the fund. It comprises a chairman, a vice-chairman, and three members. The chairman and vice-chairman are appointed by the Minister of Labor, while the members are put forward by the Council on Social Assistance. The Managing Board develops and coordinates the annual budget of the fund with the Council on Social Assistance, and it proposes the annual budget of the fund to the Minister of Labor, after coordinating it with the Minister of Finance. The Managing Board also produces annual financial statements and reports on the activities of the fund.

The *Supervisory Board of the National Social Security Institute* was created to supervise the institute, which in turn manages and oversees the Social Security Fund. The fund is used for the payment of compensation, aid, annual child support, the indexation of pensions, and the operating budget of the National Social Security Institute and other organizations. The Supervisory Board comprises an equal number of representatives from the government and nationally representative organizations of employers and trade unions. The board approves the general guidelines for the activities of the institute as well as the annual budget of the Social Security Fund. It approves draft laws and normative documents in the area of social security before their official approval by the respective state organs. The board convenes meetings at the request of at least one third of its members. Decisions require a simple majority.

The *National Council on Rehabilitation and Social Integration* was created as a consultative organ to the Council of Ministers in the area of rehabilitation and social integration. It includes representatives of the Cabinet of Ministers, representative organizations of disabled persons, and representative organizations of employers. The organization of the council's activities is determined by the Council of Ministers.

The *Managing Board of the Rehabilitation and Social Integration Fund* exercises control over the fund. The fund finances projects and programs for prevention, rehabilitation, and social integration and for social aids to disabled people. The board includes fifteen people: a chair, a vice-chair, and thirteen members, including one representative each from the Ministries of Labor and Social Policy, Finance, Health Care, Education, Science and Technology, Regional Development, and Transport; one representative of employers; and three representatives of the nationally representative organizations of disabled people. The board develops prognoses and programs for the activities of the fund, decides its budget, organizes a competitive forum for financing rehabilitation programs and projects, and prepares an annual report on the fund's activities.

The Act on Health Insurance, adopted in June 1998,[57] stipulated the creation of a tripartite *Meeting of Representatives* as a governing body of the *National Health Insurance Bank*. The Meeting of Representatives comprises eighteen representatives of the state, the trade unions, and the

[57] *State Gazette*, vol. 70 of 19 June 1998, last amended vol. 153 of 23 December 1998, in force from 1 January 1998.

employer associations. It adopts and amends the guidelines for the activities of the National Health Insurance Bank; elects and dismisses the members of the Managing and Supervisory boards of the bank; and adopts guidelines for the activities of these organs, as well as for the amount of remuneration for their members. The meeting also adopts guidelines on the activities of regional health insurance banks, and drafts laws on the annual budget of the bank. The Managing Board of the bank comprises members elected from among the members of the Meeting of Representatives, in addition to other persons.

In addition to these tripartite structures regulated by the 1997–98 labor and social legislation, a *Parliamentary Consultative Council for Legislative Initiatives* was created in October 1997, under the initiative of the chairman of the Standing Parliamentary Commission on Labor and Social Policy. The Consultative Council aimed to improve the quality of the social dialogue in Bulgaria and to guarantee transparency of public debates on the most important areas of social legislation: social reforms and harmonization of Bulgarian social and labor legislation with European common law.

The council became an organ for spurring involvement of, and exchange of opinions among, all legitimate groups in society. It comprises representatives of the Standing Parliamentary Commission on Labor and Social Policy; chairs of all standing parliamentary commissions; representatives of all parliamentary groups; and representatives of the government, the presidency, all employer organizations, all trade unions, and all NGOs that have a say in the specific aspects of legislation that are under discussion in the council. The Consultative Council is chaired by the chairman of the Standing Parliamentary Commission on Labor and Social Policy.

The agenda of each council meeting is largely determined by its chairman. However, in such a broad social dialogue forum, proposals for agenda items sometimes come from the social groups, and issues stretch to draft laws with a wider economic range. For example, at the suggestion of some unions, the council discussed the draft law on privatization. Between its founding meeting in October 1997 and mid-1999, the Consultative Council met five times, and discussed several important draft laws, including those on privatization, social assistance, the protection of children, the supplemental voluntary pension insurance fund, and family aid and benefits for children. On average, seventy to eighty people participate in each of the sessions of the council.[58] Many of the proposals made at the council are later

[58] The June 1999 meeting of the council, for example, discussed a draft law on family aid and children's benefits, and was attended by twenty-nine different institutions and organizations: trade unions (CITUB, Podkrepa, Promjana NTU, OSSOB, Edinstvo Peoples Union, and the Association of Democratic Trade Unions), employer and business associations (the Bulgarian Chamber of Commerce and Industry, the Bulgarian Industrial Association, and

considered by the Standing Parliamentary Commission and are included in the final draft laws before their discussion in Parliament. As a result of these discussions, the draft laws proposed by the commission are accepted in Parliament with less dissent and fewer debates.[59]

An overall good indication of the importance of social dialogue in Bulgaria since 1997 is the fact that all draft laws that have been discussed in the tripartite councils and then introduced in Parliament have been adopted with almost no changes and almost unanimously. Another indicator is the social partners' own assessments of social dialogue, which are generally positive.[60] The social partners still argue, however, that their opinion is not heard enough. They cite, in particular, cases in which they have been invited to participate in the preparation of latter-stage draft laws, without having been given a chance to help work out the *philosophy* underlying the law. According to the two main social partners, unions and employers, the institutional pluralization and decentralization of social dialogue has to some extent diminished its importance at the top level, within the NCTC, where strategic documents of national importance are discussed, such as draft laws, price increases, the budget, and taxation. Moreover, given the presence of thirteen civic-tripartite structures, inevitably there are problems in function and coordination, as well as shortages of experts to represent each of the social partners at the many meetings and forums.

The IMF, the World Bank, and Tripartism

With the introduction of the Currency Board, international institutions and organizations such as the IMF gained a prominent role in the Bulgarian tripartite system, by becoming more openly involved in shaping the framework of its deliberations. The IMF's three-year standby agreement with the Bulgarian government (reached in 1997) put some clear restrictions and constraints on tripartite bargaining. For example, the IMF set clear ceilings on wage increases and linked them with productivity (Minassian 1999). Also noteworthy is the fact that the major requirements of the standby agreement with the IMF were drafted in accordance

the Union of Private Producers), government representatives and parliament members; representatives of UNICEF and various nongovernmental organizations (the Dobbut Foundation, the Social Protection Foundation, the Open Society Fund, the Center for Independent Life, Parents of Children with Epilepsy, Parents of Hearing Impaired Children, Women's Alliance for Development, the Bulgarian Association of University Women, Mothers and Women Against Violence, and the Foundation for Child and Family Development), and media representatives.

59 Interview with Svetlana Djankova, vice-president of the Parliamentary Group of the UDF, chairman of the Permanent Parliamentary Commission on Labor and Social Policy, and chairman of the Parliamentary Consultative Council for Legislative Initiatives, Sofia, 30 July 1999.

60 Opinion of the Bulgarian Industrial Association on the Fulfillment of Part VIII.1 "Social Policy" of Program "Bulgaria 2001."

with the EU requirements and criteria for accession and reflected discussions among the social partners about the degree to which the agreement should conform with the European social model.[61] Even when faced with a strike threat from major unions, the government could not avoid these restrictions.

Further, the tripartite forum had to take into consideration the macroeconomic framework laid out by the Currency Board. The unions accepted their role in preserving social peace within these macroeconomic constraints, but with the condition that they would be consulted in the areas that directly concerned their members: structural reform, employment, prices and incomes, and social protection.[62] The unions insisted on the expansion and deepening of social dialogue, which was accomplished with the 1997–98 social laws, as discussed above.

The IMF has never elaborated any official position on social dialogue in Bulgaria, beyond its requirement that the government and social partners maintain social peace as a condition for granting loans to implement the stabilization programs. At the latest congress of the International Confederation of Free Trade Unions (ICFTU), the president of the IMF, Michel Camdessus, stated that the IMF wished to see a greater openness toward the trade unions. Subsequently, almost every mission of the IMF to Bulgaria initiated meetings with the trade unions at its insistence. The first social peace agreement in the country, reached in 1991, was also the result of such meetings.

The evolving discussions between unions and the IMF reflect a general shift in public perception of cooperation with the IMF, from a "necessary evil" to an "indispensable prerequisite for progress" (Minassian 1999). Discussions focus on the positions of trade unions on a variety of issues related to economic reform. The greatest debates between the IMF and the trade unions were connected with the macroeconomic parameters of reform: While the IMF wanted wage restrictions and regulations, the unions favored the abolition of wage regulations. The IMF has remained firm on its wage policies, however, and even the big 1996–97 economic crisis in Bulgaria could not change its policies, despite persistent trade union opposition. There were other differing views, as, for example, on the incomes policy and the classification of labor for early retirement. According to CITUB assessments, the effect of their consultations with

[61] Memorandum na KNSB za minimalno neobhodimite merki za podkrepa na trigodishnoto Sporazumenie na Bulgaria s Mezhdunarodnija valuten fond i Svetovnata banka (CITUB Memorandum for the Minimal Requirements in Support of the Three-Year Agreement between Bulgaria and the International Monetary Fund and the World Bank) (Sofia: CITUB, 1997).

[62] International Round Table, "The Currency Board and the Strategy of the Authentic Trade Unions," Sofia, 14–17 May 1997 (Sofia: CITUB and Podkrepa CL, 1997).

the IMF missions has been that the worker-managerial form of privatization has been preserved, although the IMF had initially insisted on its abolition.

The World Bank has also played a role in Bulgarian tripartism, though not so powerful as the IMF. After September 1990, when Bulgaria became a member of the bank, its assistance has facilitated the transition to a market economy and expanded private sector activity through structural reforms in the enterprise and banking sectors. Bank assistance was also aimed at supporting macroeconomic stabilization, including lower inflation and a sustainable balance-of-payments position. In parallel, bank assistance has been aimed at reducing poverty and improving living standards in the country. The bank has supported complementary efforts by the government to help the poor directly, such as its establishment of effective and sustainable social sector policies and institutions, including a social safety net. With its first two loans, the bank offered policy advice and institution-building support. A Structural Adjustment loan of $250 million approved in August 1991 was the centerpiece of the bank's initial activities, supported by a Technical Assistance Loan of $17 million approved in June 1991. Altogether, by the end of 1998, the bank made loans to Bulgaria in fifteen separate operations, totaling over $1 billion. These operations were focused on energy development, telecommunications, water and sanitation services, development of commercial and industrial consumers, debt and debt service reduction, railway rehabilitation, improvement of the efficiency of health care service, and financial and enterprise sector adjustments.[63]

As with the IMF missions, each World Bank mission to the country has increasingly included social partners and various NGOs in discussions and working groups related to the bank's lending policies. The draft law on a World Bank–sponsored Social Investment Fund was part of the tasks included in the social partners' 1997 Memorandum for Priority Joint Action. In December 1998, the government created a special working group for the preparation of the draft law, which included representatives from the World Bank office in Sofia and the social partners.

Tripartism and Accession to the European Union

If the PHARE Social Dialogue Project initiated in Bulgaria in 1993 played a positive role for the organizational development of the social partners and the consolidation of tripartism,[64] the EU's Agenda 2000, the accession partnership agreement with Bulgaria concluded in 1998, and the EU decision to open accession negotiations with Bulgaria in February 2000 have

[63] The World Bank, Europe and Central Asia Region materials.

[64] Interim Report on the Social Dialogue in Bulgaria (ISA Consult/NJM and PHARE Management Team at the Bulgarian Minstry of Labor and Social Welfare, 2 October 1994).

determined Bulgaria's future direction and the priorities of the Kostov government. Since 1997, the process of European integration has developed domestically at the level of institutional infrastructure and judicial norms: All draft laws require special certificates that show the degree of their harmonization with European standards and directives.[65]

Directly linked with the European integration process was the creation of a fourteenth social dialogue forum: the *Council for the Ratification of the Social Charter (Revised)*. One of the few firm accession requirements of the EU in regard to the social *acquis* has been the ratification by each applicant country of the Social Charter (Revised) of the Council of Europe. On 21 September 1998, Bulgarian Minister of Labor and Social Policy Ivan Neikov signed the European Social Charter, and national preparation began for its ratification. The Ratification Council was established with the aim of giving voice to the government regarding the ratification of the Social Charter by mid-2000 and of implementing the obligations following the ratification. The council must work to win acceptance not only of specific articles that need to be ratified according to the requirements for ratification, but also of an additional number of articles or numbered paragraphs, to make a total of not less than sixteen articles or sixty-three numbered paragraphs.[66]

The Bulgarian government has to keep the Ratification Council informed concerning its relations with the Council of Europe and its committees, and members of the council in turn must keep the Bulgarian government up to date concerning their activities with various European organizations with consultative status at the Council of Europe. In the course of its work on the ratification of the European Social Charter and the fulfillment of all obligations subsequent to ratification, the council must follow the social policy of the Council of Europe. It thus plays the role of intermediary for all adopted European measures, for the European facets of Bulgarian social cohesion, and for full harmonization of Bulgarian social legislation with the basic standardizing and coordinating documents of the Council of Europe. One of the strategic goals of the council is to increase the transparency in its activities and to promote mutual trust between state institutions and civil society.

Each organization participating in the council's work nominates one representative to the council. The council includes representatives of state institutions, organizations of employers, organizations of workers,

[65] *Bulgaria and the European Union: Towards an Institutional Infrastructure* (Sofia: Center for the Study of Democracy, 1998); "Bulgaria zapochva da izpylnjava ikonomicheskite kriterii ot Kopenhagen" ("Bulgaria Is Beginning to Fulfil the Copenhagen Economic Criteria"), *Pari*, 26 July 1999.

[66] *Revised European Social Charter* (Council of Europe, November 1998), pp. 40–41.

professional organizations, nongovernmental organizations, local authorities, and research institutions and organizations, for a total of some forty different institutions and organizations. This is the widest institutional structure among any of Bulgaria's tripartite organizations to date. Members of the council can form factions or working groups, according to various group interests. As many as six working groups, with each group comprising at least three members, can coexist at any given time. Each member must participate in the work of at least one working group. Opinions on finished draft documents are voted on at a plenary session of the council and are adopted by a three-fourths' majority.[67]

The council is chaired by the Minister of Labor and Social Policy. Its Standing Secretariat is formed by employees of the Ministry of Labor and Social Policy. The secretariat is charged with administering the activities of the council and preparing drafts of all documents to be adopted by the council. It maintains contacts and correspondence with the Council of Europe, the Ministry of Foreign Affairs, the Information Center of the Council of Ministers, and all organizations and institutions represented in the Council for the Ratification of the Social Charter.

The council had four sessions by mid-1999. The third session, in February 1999, was a joint meeting with representatives of the council of Europe. The work of the council focused on the selection of articles for ratification in three major groups of social rights: protection of employment, protection outside the workplace, and "social protection" (for example, unemployment benefits and health insurance) for the population.

The formation of the *EU-Bulgaria Joint Consultative Committee* (JCC) was another major tripartite development initiated by the process of European integration. The decision to form the Consultative Committee was made by the EU-Bulgaria Association Council on 15 September 1998, and the committee's inaugural meeting was held in Bulgaria in January 1999. It is multipartite, comprising six representatives from the economic and social interests of the EU (Economic and Social Committee (ESC)) and six from Bulgarian economic and social interests.[68]

The Bulgarian part of the committee was constituted at the end of October 1998, with the presence of the Foreign and Labor ministers. It comprises three groups: employers (only the BIA); trade unions (only CITUB and Podkrepa); and various interests (the Federation of Consumers in Bulgaria, the Bulgarian Women's Union, and a farmers' Federation of the Cooperatives in Bulgaria). The ESC part of the Consultative

[67] Pravila za dejnosta i organizatsijata na Syveta za ratifikatsija na Evropejskata sotsialna harta (Regulations for the Work and Organization of the Council for the Ratification of the European Social Charter) (Sofia: Ministry of Labor and Social Policy, 1998).

[68] Press Release, EU-Bulgaria Joint Consultative Committee, 17 January 1999.

Committee also comprises three groups: employers (the Assembly of French Chambers of Commerce and Industry; the General Italian Confederation of Commerce, Tourism and Services; and the Confederation of Finnish Industry and Employers); employees (the Netherlands Trade Union Confederation and the French Democratic Confederation of Labor); and various interests (the Greek Economic Chamber and the Central Union of Agricultural Producers and Forest Owners, Finland). The Bulgarian secretariat to the JCC is administered by the BIA, and the chairman of the BIA was elected chairman of the Bulgarian part of the committee. The ESC's Division of External Relations organizes the secretariat of the ESC part of the committee.

The purposes of the committee are to prepare the ground for enlargement of the EU by promoting dialogue and to support the professional organizations of the partner country in their efforts to create a functioning society in which their consultation by the government is an integral part of the decision-making process. This is particularly important with the start of accession negotiations between the Bulgarian government and the EU. Another task of the committee is to assist and consult the EU-Bulgaria Association Council on the promotion of dialogue and cooperation between the economic and social interest groups in the EU and those in Bulgaria. The dialogue covers all economic and social aspects of EU-Bulgaria relations in light of the Association/Europe Agreement and the Accession Partnership Agreement between the EU and Bulgaria.

The committee is scheduled to hold meetings twice a year. Its constitutive meeting was on 17 January 1999. The members of the committee exchanged views on the current economic situation in Bulgaria, the social dialogue in the country, and the progress of agricultural reform. In the fall of 1999, the members of the committee met in Brussels to discuss the challenges of the preaccession process. The committee will present concrete proposals on economic and social issues to the European Commission and the Bulgarian government. At the first meeting of the Bulgarian part of the committee the members decided to present to the government a draft law for the creation of a National Economic and Social Council.

The screening of social legislation as part of the overall screening process initiated by the EU in 1998 was an area in which the Bulgarian social partners became actively involved, through the elaboration of a Joint Action Plan with the Ministry of Labor and Social Policy.[69] Moreover, with the opening up of accession negotiations in early 2000, the government decided to include the social partners from the NCTC in the EU accession negotiations, specifically in the discussions on the free movement of people, social

[69] Statement of Ivan Neikov, Minister of Labor and Social Policy of the Republic of Bulgaria at the Informal Meeting of EU and Applicant Countries' Ministers of Labor and Social Affairs (Brussels, Belgium, 9 March 1999).

policy, and employment. The social partners will also take part in the management of the resources of the EU preaccession funds.[70]

With time, virtually all influential groups in Bulgaria have come to accept the need for harmonization of Bulgarian legislation with the EU social *acquis*, because they expect improvements in living standards to follow harmonization. Legislative harmonization is considered easier in the social sphere than in the economic sphere because the EU requirements in the former are minimal, and because Bulgarian social legislation in some areas, such as social dialogue, already exceeds EU norms. The EU requirement is for the establishment of an *Economic and Social Council* as a purely consultative organ, whose recommendations need not necessarily be followed by the government; still, all draft laws have to be submitted beforehand to the Economic and Social Council for review. This council directly corresponds to the European standards for economic and social councils. Its creation was envisaged under the PHARE program, and a draft law for the Economic and Social Council is still under discussion. This council is expected to expand to overlap civil society and develop as a multilateral interinstitutional structure, with representatives of trade unions, employers, women's organizations, consumers' organizations, and organizations of cooperatives, and a chair jointly appointed by the Council of Ministers, the chairman of the Parliament, and the President.[71] In light of the extensive tripartite system that has developed so far in the country, the Economic and Social Council will not mean an end to the NCTC, but is expected to complement that institution with its outreach to society at large.

[70] *Pari Daily News*, 11 January 2000.

[71] Draft law on the creation of Economic and Social Council (Sofia: Ministry of Labor and Social Policy, 1999). See also in Daskalova 1999: 4–5.

4

National Social Dialogue in Poland

4.1. Negotiated Extrication from State Socialism

Unlike the other postcommunist countries, Poland had a history of prolonged and painful resistance to the communist regime. While other countries experienced only occasional eruptions of mass discontent and attempts to radically reform the system, Poland was regularly shaken by such events. In 1956, 1968, 1970, 1976, and, especially, 1980–81, the rationales for Polish communism were challenged by the masses and, increasingly, also by reformist elites. The roots of Poland's pioneering exit from state socialism should be sought in the legacy of these numerous initiatives of a united civil society (Kolankiewicz and Lewis 1988; Poznanski 1996; Ekiert 1998). Poland's extremely strong, unitary, and politically militant civil society was able to weaken the whole Soviet bloc in the 1980s and provide other countries in the region with a path-breaking example of how to effect the peaceful collapse of a communist regime.

The events of 1980–81 broadened the cracks within the Soviet empire. Especially after Gorbachev initiated a process of liberalization in the form of glasnost and perestroika in 1985, the Soviet empire could no longer be propped up by military means, and Solidarity could fully realize the opportunities stemming from the corporatist concessions of 1981. Initially, however, in accordance with the requirements of the 1982 Trade Union Act, the official All-Poland Trade Union Alliance (OPZZ) emerged between 1982 and 1984, while Solidarity remained underground. The Communist authorities set up the alliance as a controlled substitute for Solidarity. The union was allowed to develop from the bottom up for a period of two years, and the national alliance was registered in 1984. The OPZZ was structured as a loose federation of "independent, self-governing" trade unions organized in more than 100 occupational branches, but it was, in reality, a centrally controlled attempt to divert workers' protest into harmless channels. At its high-water mark in 1986, OPZZ enrolled some 6.5 million members.

The strike wave in the spring and summer of 1988 brought about a radical shift in the balance of power between regime and opposition in Poland (Staniszkis 1991). The 1989 Round Table assumed, as did the Gdansk negotiations, that compromise was possible and continued the Gdansk negotiations' emphasis on political demands (Osiatynski 1996). The primary and indispensable demand of "Solidarity-Opposition" was its own legal reinstatement. An agreement signed on 5 April 1989 ratified several explosive political concessions the government felt compelled to make. The agreement provided for Solidarity's legal reinstatement, guaranteed trade union pluralism at the workplace, and promised genuine parliamentary pluralism. The provision of the October 1982 law on trade unions that had prohibited the existence of more than one trade union in a given factory was annulled. The free formation of national trade unions, in line with ILO conventions, was allowed, and "equality of all trade unions, especially equal powers for trade unions, representing the majority of work establishments" was also negotiated (Kemp-Welch 1991).

The price the opposition paid for these concessions was also high. "Contractual" parliamentary elections guaranteed a communist majority.[1] The creation of the post of President (with power over the armed forces and control over foreign policy), to be held by General Wojciech Jaruzelski, also ensured continued communist domination of the government. The creation of the Senate marked a complex political compromise closely interwoven with the deal over the presidency.

However, the June 1989 elections brought a total victory for Solidarity. The Solidarity union was legally reregistered on 17 April 1989, and its candidates won all of the Sejm seats they could contest and ninety-nine of the 100 seats in the resurrected Senate. A later agreement between the democratic opposition and reformists within the Communist party prepared the way for Poland's peaceful, early exit from state socialism: The presidency went to the party (Jaruzelski was elected President by the assembled Houses on 19 July 1989) and the government to Solidarity, following the rejection of Jaruzelski's proposal for a "grand coalition" government of all parties, including Solidarity (Ost 1990). In August 1989 the Soviet bloc's first noncommunist government, headed by Poland's Tadeusz Mazowiecki, had taken power.

Poland's "negotiated" (Karl and Schmitter 1991), "pacted" (Linz and Stepan 1996: 253–92) extrication from state socialism in 1989, a political-corporatist compromise between broad opposition forces united around an independent trade union and reformist party elites, is widely and rightly praised for its historic contribution to the end of state socialism. And Polish society of the pre- and postbreakthrough period may be the most studied

[1] The round table allocated 65 percent of seats in the Sejm to the party or its coalition partners; free elections would be allowed only for the remaining 35 percent.

European people of the modern era. Yet while many have emphasized the trend toward diversity in civil society since 1989 (Synak 1993; Poznanski 1996; Millard 1999), others have underscored its uniqueness as an "ethical" civil society (Ogrodzinski 1991), representing "truth" and ethical values rather than well-articulated interests. Poland's polity represented a particularly strong instance of a civil society–state dichotomy, one that had strong historical, cultural, and religious roots. Within such a dichotomy, each camp attaches an extremely high value to "unity," while "the ideas of compromise or internal conflict are spoken of pejoratively" (Linz and Stepan 1996: 271). The "unity" value leads to "immediacy, spontaneity, and antiformal modes of operation" as widely accepted ethical standards for personal and collective behavior. Linz and Stepan have eloquently argued that Poland's ethics-based civil society was "one of the most powerful and innovative features of the Polish opposition and, ultimately, of the Polish path to democratic transition" (Linz and Stepan 1996: 271).

In the post-1989 era, Poland's legacy of an ethics-based civil society retarded efforts to create the political institutions necessary for democratic consolidation. To consolidate, a democracy needs to legitimize and accept conflict within its democratic framework, and it requires organizations that articulate and represent the conflicting interests of society. It is true that everywhere in the region, thanks to the slow and difficult processes of interest formation/differentiation (especially in regard to material interests, because of the legacies of highly egalitarian societies), organizational restructuring, and self-definition, problems related to representation were drawn-out and profound. As argued by Linz and Stepan, however, the long duration and distinctive ethos of the pre-1989 opposition activities in Poland made it unique in the region with regard to the general postcommunist problem of interest representation and the legitimation of political society. The political system in the aftermath of 1989, Millard observed, was dominated by the Solidarity movement, not by parties (Millard 1994). The monolithic and ethics-based civil society that came to power in Poland in 1989 fostered the elevation of the situational ethics of oppositional behavior into a general principle.

As Linz and Stepan concluded, the oppositional ethos that incubated at high temperature in Poland for many years prior to 1990, as well as the legacy of the 1989 political compromise with General Jaruzelski, substantially retarded the necessary shift from the ethics-based civil society of opposition to a political society of democratic consolidation. A stark consequence of the ethical principle was Solidarity's "nonparty bloc" in Parliament, which, Staniszkis has argued, in cooperation with the government, succeeded in implementing a virtual blockade against the articulation and representation of interests (Staniszkis 1991).

The "ethos and values" of Solidarity, however, also prevented Poland from embracing a neoliberal pluralistic mode of interest articulation.

Poland's ethics-based civil society engaged in "ethical," informal corporatist bargaining with the state over the introduction of neoliberal economic reforms. Based on the politics of "immediacy," "spontaneity," and "anti-formalism," Poland's "ethical" corporatism was initially equal to securing social peace against potential civil and industrial discontent. With impressive poise, it outlived the first pain of shock-therapy adjustment. Its triumph, however, was short-lived. A few years of pain and plummeting living standards efficiently catalyzed the crystallization of diverse material interests in Polish society, which were readily apparent by 1993. Challenged by the great industrial unrest of 1992–93, the mechanism of ethics-based compromise that had guided the transition was displaced by an interest-based institutionalized arrangement. By early 1994, as the next two sections reveal, clear-cut interest-based institutionalized arrangements linked state and working society in Poland, as they had in the other former communist countries by the turn of the 1990s.

4.2. The Truce of Neoliberal Reform

The main goal of the Mazowiecki "government of national responsibility" was to start economic reforms. The Balcerowicz plan was an IMF-backed neoliberal program aimed at fighting hyperinflation by discontinuing state protection of the economy, withdrawing state subsidies, opening national markets for importers, and giving real value to the national currency. The plan included privatization of business enterprises by sale or lease; reform of the banking system; wage restraints designed to stifle inflation; an end to price controls, subsidies, rationing, and centralized planning; drastically reduced import barriers; and establishment of a convertible currency.

Broad social consensus was needed to guarantee "social peace" when the government implemented such drastic measures, which were guaranteed to have dramatic short-term consequences for the majority of wage-earners. In any event, in the immediate aftermath of 1989, the monolithic and powerful civil society was of one mind on the major contours of needed post-communist reform: democratization of politics and society, introduction of the market, and movement toward private ownership transformation. Because of the monolithic and underdeveloped organizational nature of the social partners, Poland did not need to develop specialized tripartite "social peace" arrangements to guarantee social peace in the course of neoliberal reform and to play the major instrumental role of a political fuse in the transformation. It was possible to mobilize the high political and moral consensus developed prior to the election of 1989 to gain almost universal approval of Finance Minister Balcerowicz's "shock therapy" plan, which was to be implemented beginning in January 1990.

As a result, the government was able to introduce a unique and radical freeing-up of prices in January 1990, and simultaneously institute strict controls over nominal wages. Prices of consumer goods increased almost sevenfold between 1989 and 1990, and twofold between 1990 and 1991, bringing inflation down to a rate of 5 to 10 percent per month, and thus ending the pre-1990 hyperinflationary spiral (Brada 1991).[2] Shock therapy also, however, resulted in sharp increases in unemployment, decreases in real wages and private wealth held in the form of cash, and reduced living standards for salaried employees and older people living on pensions. Between 1989 and 1990 alone, the cost of living for workers and employees increased by 50 percent more than wages and salaries (Wade et al. 1994).

The willingness of Poland's society to sacrifice individual and group economic interests in the name of a broader political interest counterbalanced these enormous economic difficulties and allowed good progress in the difficult transition to a market economy. Real GDP fell sharply in 1990 and 1991, but in 1992 Poland became the first country in the region to resume economic growth, with a 2.6 percent increase. Growth increased to 3.8 percent in 1993 and 5.5 percent in 1994, the highest rate in Europe outside Albania. All of the growth since 1991 has come from the private sector, which has accounted for at least 55 percent of GDP. Industrial production increased 12 percent in 1994 and was well above the 1990 level. Inflation, which had approached 1,200 percent annually in early 1990, was down to about 30 percent in 1994, as the government held the budget deficit to 1.5 percent of GDP. The trade deficit was sharply reduced in 1994, due mainly to increased exports to Western Europe.[3]

Purely corporatist-like adjustments did emerge, however, in Poland with the start of neoliberal reform. The most significant one was the legal endorsement of a specialized tripartite institution – the national system of tripartite employment councils – to combat the most acute problem of economic reform, namely, unemployment. Reflecting the ethical bonds of Poland's civil society, informal tripartite developments found expression in Poland's Parliament and in informal bargaining among the government, labor unions (mostly Solidarity), and emerging employers (mostly the Confederation of Polish Employers (KPP)).

The Main Employment Council

The urgent need to combat the greatest social problem of the transformation, unemployment, led to the establishment of a specialized tripartite structure on employment at national and regional levels. Successive govern-

[2] The rise of prices has been much more gradual in Hungary, for example, where prices increased by less than 30 percent between 1989 and 1990 and by about 35 percent between 1990 and 1991. In the former Czechoslovakia, price increases have been even more moderate, and increased by only 10 percent between 1989 and 1990 and by less than 60 percent between 1990 and 1991 (Brada 1991: 11).

[3] Country map of Poland, 1995.

ments have attempted to combine implementation of a free market economy with an active social and employment policy. In 1989, 1991, and 1994, the Sejm included the principle of full employment in legislation.[4]

The employment legislation provided employment services and vocational counseling to the unemployed, as well as active means such as job training and retraining programs. It authorized employment offices to undertake initiatives to create new jobs. All of the unemployment legislation has been linked strongly with privatization policies. Government employment offices were authorized to grant financial assistance to employers who create new jobs for the unemployed and to organizers of public works and temporary work projects. The unemployed were also eligible for a one-time loan to carry out their own business activities, 50 percent of which is forgiven if they stay in business for more than two years. Standard unemployment benefits amounted to 36 percent of a recipient's previous average salary or wage and were payable for up to twelve months. The costs of these programs were covered by the National Labor Fund, which was supported by employer contributions and government subsidies (Sewerynski 1995).

The government's policy on economic growth included a commitment to guaranteeing the participation of employers and employees in the management of employment offices. Toward this end, employment councils were created comprising representatives of trade unions, employers, state administration, and local government. Direct participation in state governance was secured through participation in the supervisory boards of some social funds, such as the Labor Fund and the Guaranteed Workers' Benefits Fund.

The employment structure brought together a wide variety of interest groups and, especially at the regional level, included wide segments of society in a civic web, in efforts to resolve regional unemployment and restructuring problems. It has a dual administrative/tripartite character. Labor offices at the national level (the Main Employment Council), the provincial level (provinces, or *voivod*ships, a total of forty-nine),[5] and the regional level (*rejon* and *gmina*, a total of 267) are part of the state bureaucracy, while tripartite employment councils at these levels complement the administrative structure and help counterbalance the instabilities of emerging labor markets.[6]

[4] Act on Employment from 29 December 1989 (*Dziennik Ustaw*, 31 December 1989, no. 75, Text 446); Act of 16 October 1991, concerning Employment and Unemployent (*Dziennik Ustaw*, 20 November 1991, no. 106, pp. 1417–28, Text no. 457); Act on Employment and Combatting Unemployment from 14 December 1994 (*Dziennik Ustaw*, 6 January 1995, no. 1); Piotrowski 1994: 15–18.

[5] The book does not reflect developments within the new territorial-administrative structure in Poland since 1999.

[6] Order of the Minister of Labor and Social Policy, dated 21 March 1995, in the matter of the organization, specific basis and scope of activity of the National Labor Office, as well as the *voivod*ship and regional labor offices (*Dziennik Ustaw*, 11 April 1995 r., no. 38, pp. 1351–54, Text 187).

The *Main Employment Council* was set up in 1990. It comprises twenty-four members, six each from trade unions, employers' organizations, the state bureaucracy, and self-government (local government). The employers' representatives come from the Confederation of Polish Employers, the Lower Silesia Employers' Organization, the Association of Stone Coal Mining Employers (ZPGWK), and the National Local Self-Government Diet. Solidarity, OPZZ, Solidarity '80, the Federation of Railway Workers' Unions, Rural Solidarity, and the National Union of Farmers and Farmers' Organizations represent the trade unions (Morawski and Hausner 1994).

The council advises the Minister of Labor and Social Policy on issues of employment and devotes the bulk of its deliberations to initiatives to achieve full and rational employment. The council also advises the government on projects of the Labor Fund[7] and on draft legislation regarding employment issues. The council is required to give opinions on all draft normative acts regulating employment issues. It is also obliged to report on its activities, and the activities of the regional employment councils, to the Minister of Labor and Social Policy. On some occasions, most often when it is supporting the position of the Ministry of Labor on a particular employment-related issue, the council can send its opinions directly to the Marshal of the Sejm or to the Prime Minister. The council can also propose the appointment of the chairman of the Central Employment Office.

Being only a consultative body, the Main Employment Council does not require a consensus of all participants in order to function; its major purpose is to give opinions, which may differ for the different members of the council. Members of the council are not necessarily experts, and can be people from different social groups.

The council held ten meetings in 1995, eight in 1996, eleven in 1997, and twelve in 1998.[8] At each session, the council exchanged current information about the situation of the labor market in the country. Its members discussed draft decisions of the Ministry of Labor and Social Policy on a variety of issues, and proposed amendments to them. They also discussed projected activities of the State Employment Office.

Two examples of the many issues the council considered concerning the impact of economic conditions on labor markets were uncontrollable imports (with particular regard to their effects on the labor market in the leather and shoe industry) and the restructuring of the coal and textile industries. A significant part of the council's deliberations covered activities aimed at full and rational employment, and it gave opinions on many draft

[7] The Labor Fund is administered by the Minister of Labor and Social Policy. It pays, among others, for unemployment benefits, the costs of training and retraining unemployed workers, social insurance contributions, loans for the creation of new jobs, and vocational training programs for apprentices.

[8] Archive data: minutes of the sessions of the Main Employment Council; interview with H. Odachowska, Secretary of the Council, Warsaw, May 1995, March 1999.

laws concerning employment and unemployment (eighteen in 1995 alone). More particularly, these draft laws addressed issues of rural unemployment, the enhancement of workers' training, flexible work scheduling as a device to alleviate unemployment, unemployment among women, programs for the promotion of youth employment, and unemployment problems in the former agricultural cooperatives. Additional deliberations focused on amendments in health legislation and social and professional rehabilitation for the disabled. With respect to public administration reform, in 1998 the council discussed draft amendments to a law on employment and unemployment that was prepared within the framework of such reform. The council provided the Prime Minister and the Chairman of Parliament with a critical assessment of the project on new labor administration. Also, by 1998 the council had already discussed employment policy from the perspective of EU integration.

The Main Employment Council and its regional structures also report opinions on the distribution of resources from the Labor Fund (the council provided forty-five opinions in 1995 alone) and the Guaranteed Wages Fund. The Labor Fund is administered by the Minister of Labor and Social Policy. It funds unemployment benefits, training and retraining for unemployed workers, social insurance, loans for the creation of new jobs, vocational training programs for apprentices, and other projects. By law, the regional labor offices can provide establishments with loans from the Labor Fund for the creation of additional jobs for the unemployed, and it can provide the unemployed with lump sums to fund business start-ups. The Main Employment Council makes special efforts to allocate Labor Fund resources through nongovernmental institutions and organizations.

Furthermore, the council gives annual opinions on the activities of the Central Employment Office. It also periodically assesses the contracting of tasks through various NGOs by regional labor offices, a program that was introduced in 1997.

A "Corporatist" Parliament

Up to 1993, the Polish variant of postcommunist transformation was heavily colored by a distinctive mixture of union and political party, and in particular by close contacts between the Solidarity trade union and the Solidarity governments. Direct engagement with political parties and direct participation in Parliament substituted for the political legitimation of the Polish social partners. This peculiarity – despite the 1991 legislation on trade unions and employers – retarded the organizational and functional separation of the Polish social partners and the crystallization and articulation of economic interests within Polish society.

After 1989, the Solidarity trade union had to decide whether to take part in decision-making or concern itself solely with the defense of workers' rights. Having previously identified communist rule as the enemy,

Solidarity's first response was to support neoliberal reform. Starting in late 1989, the union was directly represented in Parliament and had the chance to influence neoliberal reforms at the highest level. Solidarity put up a separate list of candidates in the 1991 elections and focused its campaign on populist criticism of the Balcerowicz reforms, featuring calls for state intervention, employee buy-outs of state enterprises, and higher taxes on private entrepreneurs. Winning 5.1 percent of the vote, or twenty-seven seats in the Sejm (out of 460) and twelve seats in the Senate (out of 100), the union had enough representation to form a lobby within Parliament.

Solidarity's official support of the Solidarity-rooted governments and direct participation in Parliament led to a profound identity crisis and sharp debates and conflicts over the extent to which the union should involve itself in politics (Morawski 1994; Matuchniak-Krasuska 1996: 156–69). Activists at central and regional levels, who mixed politics with their work in the union movement, supported government's efforts to minimize the risk of costly strikes. Trade union activists at the enterprise level favored concentration on defending workers' rights through greater emphasis on employee participation in management and employee buy-outs of companies (Kulpinska 1994). The eventual vertical split in Poland's labor movement was an inevitable by-product of Solidarity's success in seizing control of government at a time of decreasing living standards and increasing mass discontent.

The direct involvement and representation of unions in the Polish Sejm and Senate continued with the 1993 parliamentary elections. The Solidarity union received only 4.9 percent of the vote, below the 5 percent threshold for seats in the Sejm, but it won ten seats in the Senate. Following Solidarity's return to legal status, the OPZZ attempted to win support from dissatisfied industrial workers by demanding an immediate improvement in the standard of living. In the elections, the OPZZ, the National Teachers' Union, and several other groups won sixty-two seats in the Sejm and five in the Senate under the banner of the Democratic Left Alliance (SLD). The SLD comprised seven political parties and eleven trade unions (OPZZ, six large member federations of OPZZ, and four independent autonomous unions).

Overall, direct union representation in Parliament further complicated the process of organizational restructuring and consolidation of the Polish social partners. Some union parliamentarians, especially Solidarity's, reportedly have come into conflict with the union leadership, because they identified themselves as "delegates of the whole nation" rather than delegates exclusively of the union members.[9] Still, the unions were able to focus parliamentary discussion on some particular issues of great importance to

[9] Interview data (interview with Ewa Tomaszewska, member of the Solidarity National Commission and MP).

their members. Solidarity had two major parliamentary-political initiatives: a separate project of mass privatization, and proposed amendments to the Polish constitution.

While a variety of unions with different ideological orientations were directly represented in the Polish Parliament, and could in general use this important channel for the defense of the particular interests of their members, the emerging employers were hardly represented at all in Parliament. After 1989, several groups of employers, entrepreneurs, and businessmen appeared in Poland, all with roots in the Solidarity movement. Among them were the KPP, the National Economic Chamber, and the Business Center Club. The Business Center Club is an association of private sector firms. The National Economic Chamber represents economic self-management, and it focuses predominantly on marketing for all companies, supporting joint ventures, influencing draft laws in the economic sphere, and creating conditions favorable to the development of enterprises.

The KPP emerged in the early 1980s, paralleling the formation of Solidarity. At that time, private entrepreneurs seeking to introduce a market economy in Poland founded the Economic Society (Towarzystwo Gospodarcze). The society was denied registration by the communist authorities and acted underground. When the creation of regional economic societies became legal in the beginning of 1989, organizations quickly appeared in many regions and soon merged to form an organization called Economic Action (Akcja Gospodarcza). In November 1989 the KPP was formed from the merger of various employers' organizations from both the private and the state sectors: the Economic Society, the Association of Polish Employers, the All-Polish Association of Managers, and the Central Union of Craftsmanship.

In September 1991, the KPP held its First Congress in accordance with the new law on employers' organizations. The 1991 law on employers' organizations guaranteed their independence from state and local authorities and their right to express opinions on fundamental principles and draft laws, as well as on issues concerning their statutory activities. With only five member organizations in 1989, by 1994 the KPP claimed 49, most of them branch organizations. As of April 1995, KPP had a membership of twenty regional, twenty branch, and nine mixed (branch and regional) organizations. The employers associated in KPP employ over 30 percent of Polish labor, or about 3 million employees.[10]

The KPP had three representatives in the Senate and one in the Sejm before the 1993 elections, and it had no representatives in the Parliament formed after the elections. Based on the general weakness and the underrepresentation of employers in Parliament, some right-wing parties regarded

[10] Information materials from the Confederation of Polish Employers.

the presence of unions in Parliament as a danger to democratic consolidation in Poland.[11]

The 1997 parliamentary elections gave forty-two Parliament seats to the OPZZ and sixty to the Solidarity union. Other unions were also represented in Parliament, in the SLD caucus.

Informal Negotiations

In 1991, the government passed three laws to regulate its relationship with interest groups: the Act on Trade Unions, the Act on Employers' Organizations, and the Act on the Resolution of Collective Labor Disputes.[12] The 1991 labor legislation favored bargaining that was national-level, nonmonopolistic (for all trade unions and employer organizations), and informal and consultative. It stipulated that all draft laws and acts of government, before being submitted to Parliament for debate and adoption, must be submitted to trade unions and employer organizations for comment. This led to regular, informal meetings of officials from the Ministry of Labor, trade unions, and, occasionally, employer organizations such as the Confederation of Polish Employers.

In the beginning of the 1990s there were several big trade unions in Poland: Solidarity, OPZZ, Solidarity of Individual Farmers, and the Trade Union of Agricultural Workers. There were also numerous smaller unions, mostly spin-offs from the Solidarity union, which had begun to fragment after its victory in 1989. Spin-offs included the Christian Trade Union Solidarity (16,200 members) and its militant rival Solidarity '80 (156,000 members), which claimed to be the true descendant of the original Solidarity, and from which the "August 80" group broke. The Kontra union, set up by the Confederation for Independent Poland, had some regional significance. By 1993 there were some 1,500 registered trade unions in Poland, of which 200 claimed to be national in scope (Millard 1999: 111).

The Ministry of Labor held consultations mostly with the two major unions, Solidarity (with some 2 million members at that time) and OPZZ (with some 4.5 million members), while the Ministry of Agriculture held talks with the two major agrarian unions: Solidarity of Individual Farmers and the Trade Union of Agricultural Workers (a union dating from communist times). Through both planning and practice, these informal practices were gradually becoming institutionalized. By 1990 the Ministry for Liaison with Trade Unions was merged with the Ministry of Labor, where a special department for contacts with trade unions was established, mainly

[11] Interview data.

[12] Law on Trade Unions from 23 May 1991; Law on Employers' Organizations from 23 May 1991; Law on the Settlement of Collective Labor Disputes from 23 May 1991 – *Dziennik Ustaw* Nr. 55, 1991. See also Sewerynski 1995: 33–37.

to discuss the minimum wage. In meetings, the government was represented by the Statistical Office, the Ministry of Finance, the Ministry of Planning, and the Ministry of Labor.

Real differentiation of interests, however, was as yet inchoate. In these informal negotiations, the Solidarity trade union functioned as a "protective screen" for the reform policies of the new government. Although it symbolically withdrew that "protective screen" in the spring of 1991, it remained loyal to the aims of government policy (Deppe and Tatur 1994). Also consistent with informal conduct was Solidarity's reluctance to engage in negotiations jointly with OPZZ; union-government talks were mainly between Solidarity and the Solidarity government, excluding all political forces "hostile to reform." Strikes were viewed as part of a political campaign to derail reform.

The 1991 labor legislation did not favor the development of tripartism at the level of industrial branches. It was built on the belief that the state should be excluded from bargaining below the national level and that there would be a fully developed market economy with private employers as labor's negotiating partners. Initially, the government tried to observe the terms of the legislation and refused to participate in negotiations with trade unions and strike committees. But given that the state and the other social partners were the dominant employers in Polish industry, social and political pressure soon forced their direct involvement in worker disputes and the resolution of numerous conflicts at lower levels. In most cases, these protests led to negotiations with the direct participation of government representatives.

Despite Solidarity's efforts to lobby directly in Parliament and in informal talks with the government for social mechanisms to counterbalance neoliberal reforms, the considerable losses in real income quickly undermined the sociopolitical consensus for radical change and provoked serious unrest. The government's restrictive wage policy – part of the stabilization program recommended by the IMF – became the major focus of open discontent. Under central planning a low-wage policy prevailed, but the onset of the transformation process in Poland led to even lower wages under a wage regulation system that was more centralized than under the centrally planned economy. Under the restrictive wage policy introduced in 1990, wage increases have been directly and centrally regulated, while at the same time prices have been liberalized. Initial regulation covered the total wage fund of the enterprise; by 1991 it focused on the average wage growth in enterprises. Whereas under central planning wage growth was determined by administrative regulation, the new wage regulation applied a system of tax penalties (Kabaj 1998).

The "apple of discord" thus became the *popiwek*, a punitive tax of up to 100 percent on all wage increases above wage norms, linked to a government "inflation coefficient," set for certain state firms (not including those producing for export). While it was obvious that in order to achieve the objectives of the stabilization program, its architects had to rely largely on wage control, the issue in question was how far wage growth should lag behind the inflation rate. Polish authorities did not agree with the IMF's proposal to completely freeze wages, and a compromise was reached. But even in this compromise the wage adjustment coefficient was very restrictive. In January 1990 it was 0.3 (meaning that the wage fund could increase, at most, to compensate for 30 percent of the cost of living increase). Under the *popiwek* system, enterprises that exceeded the allowed wage fund by up to 3 percent paid 200 percent in taxes on the additional wages paid out, and for each additional 1 percent the tax was 500 percent (Adam 1999: 25).

The tax had a negative effect on production and productivity, and its enforcement effectively discouraged enterprise-level and even sectoral-level collective bargaining on wages. The tax amounted to centralized control on wages and inevitably shifted social dialogue to the central political arena. Declining standards of living forced trade union activists at the enterprise level to insist on the abolition of *popiwek* and to call on Solidarity to take a more aggressive approach that included the use of strikes as a political weapon. Total strikes had declined from 900 in 1989 to only 250 in 1990, and in 1991 that figure increased only marginally to 305, but in 1992, as a wave of grass-roots social discontent swept Poland, the number increased twenty-fold, exceeding the 6,000 mark. The strike wave peaked in 1993 with 7,443 strikes.[13] Most strike demands concerned wages and the *popiwek* (Kloc 1992).

Under pressure from an increasingly discontented rank and file, Solidarity adopted a tough bargaining line in negotiations on the excess wage tax. However, the union did so on the grounds that the tax had become socially and politically untenable and could provoke the public to reject both the government and its entire economic program (Vinton 1991). Throughout 1993, despite such protests and appeals, the government continued to impose the *popiwek*, in an effort to link wages to increases in productivity, reduce inflationary pressures in the state industrial sector, and, overall, speed up privatization.

The fragile compromisal nature of social dialogue, manifested in other postcommunist societies mainly in the relations *among* governments, unions, and emerging employers, found political expression in Poland *within* the organizational structure of Solidarity, and generated acute tensions between different levels of the union's organization. Rising social discontent and unrest challenged both the government and union elites. The strike wave in the summer of 1992 marked an important step in the erosion of informal tripartite negotiations at the top of the Polish polity.

[13] *Rocznik Statystyczny 1995* (Warsaw: Glowny Urzad Statystyczny, 1995), 130. See also Buchner-Jeziorska 1994; Kulpinska and Warzywoda-Krusynska 1995.

4.3. Institutionalization of Tripartism

Overall, the recession proved to be much deeper and longer-lasting than either politicians or the population expected. The enthusiasm of 1989 and 1990, sparked by regained independence, gave way to disillusionment as the standard of living declined and unemployment increased. The breaking up of the social consensus on fast-track transition was reflected in the emergence of economically rooted distinctions within the polymorphous Solidarity movement (parties and President), and the trade unions more or less detached from it (Deppe and Tatur 1994). Strikes and other forms of mass protest could no longer be neutralized by informal social dialogue at the elite level between the government and Solidarity, nor by Solidarity's direct representation in Parliament.

Torn between militant cadres and a mass membership critical of government policies on the one hand, and its leadership, which supported those policies, on the other, Solidarity concluded a formal agreement with the government in June 1992, in an attempt to decrease the scope of worker protests. For the trade unions, after two years' domination by adherents of the liberal doctrine, the agreement was a breakthrough. It favored negotiations before any active protest, and it regulated the negotiation process and defined the social partners at each level. In all-nation disputes, the parties were to be national or central organs of the state administration (Council of Ministers, ministries, or central government administration) and the National Commission of Solidarity. In cases of all-industry disputes, the parties were to be ministries or representatives of the central government administration and the branch secretariats of Solidarity. In local disputes (county, province, region), the *voivod* and the regional governing organ of the union would negotiate. To prevent overcentralization of conflict resolution, the agreement required preliminary approval from the upper state and union bodies before a problem could be transferred to the upper level for resolution.

Solidarity's leaders further distanced themselves from government policies by becoming more militant in their strategy and tactics, organizing, for example, a major strike among school and hospital workers and even threatening a general strike. At the same time, the government attempted to distance itself from Solidarity by proposing to include both employers' organizations and other trade unions along with Solidarity in comprehensive negotiations concerning the privatization of state enterprises. The removal of practical barriers to government-union talks, the conclusion of the Enterprise Pact, and the formal institutionalization of social dialogue through the creation of the National Tripartite Commission on Socio-Economic Issues were all important steps toward institutionalization of Poland's societal compromise on reform and consolidation of democracy.

The Enterprise Pact

As strikes reached a peak in the summer of 1992, it became clear that purely economic instruments (such as the excess payroll tax for state enterprises), combined with informal social dialogue at the top, no longer sufficed to bring the stabilization program to a successful end. A more formal and inclusive mechanism was needed to limit mass discontent and guarantee continuation of economic reforms. The Suchocka government and, in particular, the Minister of Labor, Jacek Kuron, proposed negotiations to develop a social pact: the Enterprise Pact. The pact would regulate the distribution of the social costs of transformation and the rules governing the new economic system. The government's main intention was to grant effective guarantees of minimum security in return for the continuation of reforms and the acceleration of the privatization process.

Initially, all parties were wary of the pact. The government was divided; employers' organizations and the political circles linked to them looked on the proposal with disfavor and insisted on the parallel conclusion of a pact on private enterprises; and union leaders were cautious, distrustful, and unsure of their authority. The union elites, who had been late in joining the strikes, feared that by consenting to the government's proposals, they might be seen as distancing themselves from the protests. Most workers surveyed by public opinion polls, meanwhile, felt that "nobody" represented their interests in the government or the workplace, and that Solidarity – like the old trade unions – was the long arm of government policy (Deppe and Tatur 1994).

In September 1992 the government invited fifteen unions[14] and three employers' formations[15] to participate in the negotiations. The negotiations were greatly facilitated by the Social Dialogue Project, which the EU's PHARE, with the participation of experts from the ILO, ran from 1991 to 1993 (Sobotka 1995). Workshops attended by representatives of all the organizations that later signed the pact were an important preliminary to the actual negotiation of the Enterprise Pact. A unique compromise prevented the blocking of negotiations by Solidarity's reluctance to have other trade unions, especially the OPZZ, join it in negotiations with the

[14] These were NSZZ Solidarity; the All-Poland Trade Union Alliance, OPZZ; NSZZ Solidarity '80; the Rev. J. Popieluszko Christian Trade Union, Solidarity; the Federation of Miners' Unions; the Polish Miners Union; the Union of Miners' Inspectorates "Kadra"; the National Union of Transport Workers; the Municipal Transport Workers' Union; the Federation of Railway Workers' Unions; the Engineers and Technical Workers' Union; the Confederation of Energy Workers' Unions; the "Kontra" Trade Union; the Machine Industry Trade Union; the Polish Engine-Drivers' Union.

[15] These were the Confederation of Polish Employers, the Cooperative Supervisory Board, and the National Chamber of Commerce. Representatives of the Business Center Club and the National Local Self-Government Diet joined the talks in the capacity of observers.

government. The government and the employers' organization, KPP, held separate negotiations with the different unions. Negotiations were organized in three working groups dealing with finance, privatization, and social policy. The negotiations with Solidarity ended in October 1992 and those with the other trade unions in November 1992.

On 22 February 1993, three versions of the Pact on State Enterprises in Transformation were signed simultaneously, one with Solidarity, the second with OPZZ, and the third with seven branch unions: the Federation of Railway Workers' Unions, the Confederation of Energy Workers' Unions, the Union of Miners' Inspectorates "Kadra," the Engineers and Technical Workers' Union, the Polish Engine-Drivers' Union, the Municipal Transport Workers' Union, and the Machine Industry Trade Union. In each case the pact was signed by the Confederation of Polish Employers and by the Minister of Labor and Social Policy, Jacek Kuron, representing the government. The three versions of the pact were basically the same, although OPZZ did not agree to sections dealing with amendments to the Labor Code in the area of collective labor agreements and collective agreements at the plant level.[16]

The Enterprise Pact was a compromise between neoliberals striving for an acceleration of privatization and trade unions favoring a more gradualist approach. In return for trade union acceptance of the privatization of state-owned enterprises, workers were granted important concessions. They would help determine their enterprise's privatization strategy, they would receive 10 percent of their enterprise's stock, and union representatives would sit on the boards of newly privatized companies.

The Enterprise Pact was divided into three parts, corresponding to issues dealing with privatization, the financing of state enterprises, and social problems. The section on privatization included agreements authorizing the employee representatives of a given enterprise to present a plan for its privatization to its founding organization; entitling employees to 10 percent of the total number of the company's shares free, and another 10 percent at preferential prices; and guaranteeing workers participation in the management of the company. Employees were further granted the right to have representatives on the supervisory board and the board of directors. The part of the pact concerning the financing of state enterprises included agreements that the tax on net profits (*dywidenda*), calculated in relation to the initial (founding) value of the enterprise, would be eliminated and that the excess wage tax, *popiwek*, would not be paid out of net profits. The part of the pact concerned with social issues dealt with the principles governing collective labor agreements and collective agreements at the plant level (OPZZ refused to sign this section of the pact); stated guidelines for the

16 *Pact on State-Owned Enterprise in the Process of Ownership Transformation* (Warsaw: Ministry of Labor and Social Policy, 1993).

establishment of a Guaranteed Workers' Benefits Fund, which would protect workers' claims in the event of bankruptcy and other unusual contingencies; and called for the establishment of social insurance funds at all workplaces, including private ones, within five years.[17]

Bipartite and tripartite mechanisms of control over the implementation and functioning of the agreements contained in the pact included a tripartite board for supervision and control over the Guaranteed Workers' Benefits Fund and a tripartite commission charged with the task of monitoring economic processes and macroeconomic policies.[18] The Tripartite Commission for Control over the Implementation of the Enterprise Pact was set up in April 1993. It became the prototype of the National Commission on Socio-Economic Issues, which was created in February 1994.

The launch of the EU's PHARE Social Dialogue Project in 1992–93 was a decisive step toward bringing together the social partners at the negotiation table. Financed by the EC Commission, the Social Dialogue Project covered two major topics for trade union and employer education: tripartism and labor relations, and a system for resolving collective labor disputes. The instructional program for each of these topics involved a two-week study tour by the Polish social partners (representatives of the trade unions, employers, and the state) to selected Western European countries: Belgium, Ireland, and Italy on the first topic, and Germany, the United Kingdom, and Belgium on the second topic. Each of the two Social Dialogue topics was later discussed by a wider group of people including union and economic activists, as well as scientists. As Elzbieta Sobotka, the then Project Coordinator, noted, at the seminar devoted to tripartism, which was organized a few days after the signing of the Enterprise Pact, representatives of fifteen trade unions sat together for the first time at the negotiation table, an achievement that had not been possible during the pact negotiations (Sobotka 1994: 16).

The Tripartite Commission on Socioeconomic Issues

The government anticipated that the 1991 Trade Union Act and the collective bargaining aspects of the Enterprise Pact would discourage labor disputes, but the austerity of economic reforms and the absence of a stable process for resolving disputes increased tensions on the shop-floor in 1993, and many strikes occurred before the legislation could be passed. January 1993 saw a major strike in the Silesian coal basin, and public service workers organized a simultaneous work stoppage. Tensions in the public sector led to another strike in April 1993. Paradoxically, in May 1993,

[17] Ibid. [18] Ibid.

under pressure from the pact's signatories (Solidarity and OPZZ), the Parliament passed a no-confidence vote in the same government that had devised the pact. The dissolution of the Polish Parliament in 1993, almost immediately after the successful negotiation of the Enterprise Pact, was clear evidence of both the fragile balance of Poland's corporatist compromise and the beginning of its organizational normalization.

The public revolt against laissez-faire capitalism led to a significant leftward shift in the September 1993 parliamentary elections, with advocacy of more gradual reforms.[19] Much of the electorate expected the left-wing parties to increase welfare programs, slow down privatization, increase subsidies for farmers and prices of agricultural products, raise taxes on the wealthy, extend state control of the economy, pursue preferential credits for Polish investors, and slow both foreign investment and the flight of Polish capital. However, while the SLD was committed to a slower, less painful transition, it had no plans to abandon the economic reforms of the Solidarity-backed governments of the past four years, and the left coalition faced the same socioeconomic challenges as the last Solidarity government, led by Suchocka.

With the dissolution of Parliament, however, work on legislation to implement the pact was slowed down. This included amendments to seven laws, all designed to guarantee workers greater rights, as agreed upon in the Enterprise Pact. The SLD-PSL coalition government of Waldemar Pawlak was very slow to proceed toward any form of privatization, including mass privatization. Not until the advent of the Oleksy government, which was formed in February 1995, was the Act on Privatization and Commercialization of State-Owned Enterprises adopted by Parliament (June 1995) to supersede the 1990 Act on Privatization of State-Owned Enterprises.

Overall, the Polish model of ownership transformation included a decisive role of the workers in the enterprises to be privatized.[20] On the positive side, this had the effect of minimizing or avoiding conflicts as to whether the enterprise should or should not be privatized. On the negative side, however, it provoked distributive conflicts with the new buyers, especially foreign investors, over the social packages for workers and man-

[19] Of the postcommunist parties, the Democratic Left Alliance (SLD) received more than 20 percent of the general vote, and the Polish Peasant's Party more than 15 percent. A newly emerged left-wing party, the Labor Union (UP), took an additional 7.3 percent of the vote and contributed to the overwhelming predominance of the left. Right-wing parties such as the National and Christian Union (ZChN), the Center Civic Alliance (PC), and the Liberal Democratic Congress (KLD) were unable to break the 5 percent election threshold. In the 100-seat Senate, the dominance of the two leading parties was even more pronounced, with the Democratic Left Alliance taking thirty-seven seats and the Polish Peasant's Party thirty-six.

[20] See in Bogdanowicz-Bindert and Czekaj 1999: 75.

agement. This tendency continued to keep Poland's civil society generally contentious and robust, despite the institutionalization of social dialogue in early 1994 to monitor the implementation of the Enterprise Pact.

The functions of the Tripartite Commission on Socio-Economic Issues envisaged in the Enterprise Pact were laid out in a government decree of 15 February 1994, amended on 18 June 1996 and 17 December 1996, and the guidelines for the work of the commission adopted in February 1994.[21] Legislative recognition of the Tripartite Commission was partly achieved through a December 1994 law establishing a system for negotiated average wage increases within enterprises, which replaced the *popiwek*. The law more specifically stipulated that the criteria for increases in remuneration were to be elaborated by the Tripartite Commission. The December 1994 law on wage-setting in the public sphere also recognized the Tripartite Commission. However, the will for consensus became more important than any legal regulations granting authority to tripartite bodies.

The regulations on the work of the tripartite commission did not stipulate criteria for representativeness. Furthermore, while the Labor Code defined criteria for representativeness in collective bargaining, it did not define any criteria for representativeness in the tripartite bodies, especially the tripartite commission. In the absence of other guidelines, a "historical" criterion was applied: The signatories of the Enterprise Pact automatically became members of the commission. Each of the big players – the government, KPP, Solidarity, and OPZZ – has four representatives on the commission and one vote, while each of the seven branch unions has one representative, and the seven representatives together share one vote. The government is represented by the Minister of Finance, the Minister for Labor and Social Policy, the Minister for Trade and Industry, and the Minister-Director of the Central Planning Office. In addition, a representative of the chairman of the Main Statistical Office participates as an observer. Before 1996, the chair of the Tripartite Commission was a deputy minister, and since 1996 he or she has been the Minister of Labor and Social Policy.

The commission was established to monitor economic processes and basic macroeconomic relations, to assess the instruments and mechanisms applied, and to formulate opinions and proposals about the priorities of social and economic policy, looking, in particular, at wages and employment policy in the public sector, social benefits policy, the instruments of wage policy, the relation between consumption and investment, and the pattern of consumption. The main task of the commission is to establish the annual growth index for the average industrial wage, taking

[21] Resolution no. 7/94 of the Council of Ministers of 15 February 1994 on appointment of a Tripartite Commission for Socio-Economic Issues and Working Regulations of the Tripartite Commission for Socio-Economic Issues (Warsaw: Ministry of Labor and Social Policy, March 1994).

into consideration the prognosis for growth in the GNP as well as the projected rate of inflation.

The commission set up six working groups dealing with pay and social security, employment and the prevention of unemployment, the reform of social insurance and insurance benefits, health care, housing, and culture and education. In terms of organization, the working groups are subordinated to the appropriate ministries: Labor and Social Policy, Health and Social Care, Regional Economic Development and Housing, and Education. The problem groups were increased to eight in 1995, and dropped to seven beginning in 1996.

The most noteworthy function of the Tripartite Commission is to set target maxima for wage increases in public and private sector enterprises employing over fifty persons. The Law of 16 December 1994 on the establishment of a new national collective bargaining system for determining wage increases abolished the *popiwek*. The new system, effective in January 1995, represented, as M. Kabaj noted, "a turning point" in the relations between government, employers, and unions (Kabaj 1998: 241). By 20 July of each year, the government provides the commission with projected macroeconomic indicators for the following year on real GDP growth and the inflation rate, and proposes a maximum annual increase in average monthly wages. By 31 August of each year, the commission is required to determine the maximum annual increase in average monthly wages and approximate indicators for each quarter relative to the same period of the previous year. If no target maxima are determined by the commission, they are set by the government. The target maxima set by the Tripartite Commission or the government, together with the financial situation of each enterprise, are taken into account in enterprise bargaining over wage increases (Kabaj 1998: 241).

By the end of 1998, the commission had held fifty-five sessions, of which fifteen were in 1994, eighteen in 1995, twelve in 1996, ten in 1997, and eight in 1998.[22] The commission was able to reach consensus on some of the most important labor, social, and incomes issues.[23]

The commission extensively discussed issues of wages and incomes, and reached consensus on the coefficient for annual wage increases within enterprises during the third and fourth quarters of 1994. It achieved

[22] Archive data: minutes of the sessions of the Tripartite Commission on Socio-Economic Issues.

[23] Interviews with Zbigniew Zegarski, Secretary of the Tripartite Commission, Warsaw, May 1995, August 1996, March 1999; interviews with Elzbieta Sobotka, Deputy Minister of Labor and Social Policy, Warsaw, May 1995 and March 1999; interview with Maciej Manicki, vice-chairman of OPZZ, MP, and head of the OPZZ delegation to the Tripartite Commission, Warsaw, May 1995; interview with Longin Komolowski, head of NSZZ Solidarity Delegation to the Tripartite Commission, Warsaw, May 1995; interviews with Henryk Wilk, vice-chairman of the Confederation of Polish Employers and Head of the KPP Delegation to the Tripartite Commission.

consensus on the maximum annual coefficient for average monthly wage increases within enterprises, and coefficients for the average monthly wage increases in all quarters, for the years 1995 through 1998. For 1995 the commission set the wage increase index at 23.5 percent, which was about equal to the projected price increases and cost of living. In August of that year, the index was increased to 27 percent due to higher than expected inflation. The wage growth recommended for 1996 was 21.8 percent. The commission also set the average wage increases of workers in the public sphere. The commission's agreement of 3 January 1995 regulated wage levels in the public sector and effectively ended prolonged strikes. The commission periodically assessed the implementation of the law on the negotiated average wage increases within enterprises.

The commission rendered opinions on the draft budget laws concerning the distribution of government financial resources. It also produced opinions on amendments to laws regarding, among other things, employment and unemployment, pension insurance, social security, and the health care reform. Members of the commission participated in the work of the Provisional Parliamentary Commission on Social Security Reform. The commission also provided an opinion concerning the use of 1.6 million zlotys from the government reserve for the training of worker representatives in the state treasury supervisory boards. In addition, the commission discussed regional differences in electric energy consumption.

It is noteworthy that strikes, after peaking at 7,443 in 1993, fell to 429 in 1994, forty-two in 1995, and twenty-one in 1996.[24] The dramatic decline in strike activity may have owed as much to fears of layoffs, however, as to the work of the commission.

With time, the Tripartite Commission's relationship with Parliament appears to be changing from competitive to complementary. When the commission was established in 1994, Parliament showed at least a slight "allergy" to it, as some Solidarity MPs recall. The Enterprise Pact had been of crucial importance to the course of Poland's economic reform, and some Parliament members felt they had not been part of it; they feared that someone besides themselves was behind the decision.[25] Later, however, competition between Parliament and the Tripartite Commission diminished and even changed to constructive complementary action. All decisions of the Tripartite Commission were reflected in the draft laws prepared in a final form by the government before their submission for parliamentary discussions and adoption.

In contrast to unions, employers have no representatives in Parliament, and it is generally more difficult for them to defend their interests. If the social

[24] *Rocznyk Statystyczny 1996* (Warsaw: GUS, 1996), 133; *Rocznyk statystyczny 1997* (Warsaw: GUS, 1997), 139.

[25] Interview with Ewa Tomaszewska, Parliament member and member of Solidarity's National Commission.

partners, for example, cannot reach consensus in the Tripartite Commission on a draft law, and the draft then enters Parliament for discussions, it is much harder for employers to lobby than it is for unions to do so, since the latter can engage in another "round" of negotiation and the former cannot.[26]

While OPZZ and Solidarity have no official links at the national level, in parliamentary commissions they are beginning to show solidarity on trade union issues.[27] More recently, the Sejm has created a special parliamentary commission to study the Enterprise Pact. It suggested some changes in legislation in accordance with the arrangements of the Enterprise Pact, and six laws were adopted on the basis of its recommendations, including legislation to protect employee wages in cases of employers' insolvencies, and a new law on privatization, which granted 15 percent of the company's shares to employees free of charge – 50 percent more than the share negotiated in the Enterprise Pact.

Under the AWS-UW Rule: Social Dialogue on a Slow Track

With the September 1997 elections, social dialogue in Poland deteriorated. The elections resulted in a return to government of the post-Solidarity parties, grouped under the Solidarity Electoral Action (AWS) umbrella, after the coalition of the excommunist SLD and the PSL lost despite presiding over four years of economic growth.[28] In comparison with the former SLD/PSL government, the coalition AWS-Freedom Union (UW) right-wing government of Jerzy Buzek has been guided much more by the ideology of neoliberalism, and has been less committed to enforcing social dialogue in Poland, basically reserving it only for normatively regulated cases, conditions, and situations. Balcerowicz, the leader of Freedom Union, was a key figure in pushing tripartite compromise to the edge of breakup.

In 1997–98, the work of the Tripartite Commission closely reflected the government's administrative-territorial reform and its reforms in pension insurance, health care, and education.[29] The commission created special working groups on these issues, members of which would later work together with the parliamentary commissions and participate in parliamentary discussions, some as Parliament members, some as official representatives of the Tripartite Commission who were invited as observers during the discussions of the social laws. Large swaths of policy-making and many local conflicts remained outside the scope of the commission's activities, however.

[26] Interview with Maciej Manicki, vice-president of OPZZ, member of the Tripartite Commission on Socio-Economic Issues, and Parliament member, Warsaw, May 1995.

[27] Information about the Work of the SLD Parliamentary Club.

[28] The AWS won 33.8 percent of the vote, the SLD 27.1 percent, the center-reformist Freedom Union (UW) 13.4 percent, and the PSL 7.3 percent.

[29] See, e.g., in Bieniasz and Uscinska 1999.

The weakening of social dialogue has been of great concern to the trade unions. The OPZZ initiated discussions with the Solidarity leadership in the summer of 1999 on the principles and the future of social dialogue in Poland. While the Tripartite Commission continued to function relatively regularly, by the deterioration ("worsening") of social dialogue the social partners meant the greater difficulties they encountered in reaching social consensus with the government on issues of vital importance to their members.[30] In August 1997 the commission reached an impasse over public sector pay rises for the coming year, and the same impasse occurred in 1998.

On the other hand, even if agreements were reached in the Tripartite Commission, the minority ruling partner, the neoliberal Freedom Union, could block some of them, one of its prerogatives as part of the ruling coalition. Since the AWS has no parliamentary majority, compromise with the Freedom Union is important. It is difficult, however, to find political compromise within the ruling coalition, as the Freedom Union defends the interests of people with high incomes.

Besides being hurt by increasingly diversifying commitments over social dialogue among the Polish social partners, trade unions were progressively and steadily losing members. Union membership decline was fostered by the acceleration of privatization and the trade union law abolishing the formation of trade unions in companies with fewer than ten employees (currently, many newly founded companies have three to five employees). In 1997 Solidarity claimed a membership of 2.2 million, strong numbers despite the problems remarked above. In 1999, Solidarity's membership dropped to 1 million, administered by thirty-seven regional offices and sixteen branch secretariats, with more than thirty professional sections. In 1997 OPZZ claimed 4.5 million members, and in 1999 its membership dropped to 2.5 million. OPZZ has 105 federations, and has regional organizational structures in sixteen *voivod*ships and 250 *powiaty*, and 15,000 local enterprise organizations. According to ILO data, trade union membership in Poland shrank by 42.5 percent between 1985 and 1995, and by 1995 only one third of the Polish labor force belonged to trade unions.[31]

An issue with increasing importance is representation on the commission (Pliszkiewicz and Seweryski 1995). The commission is, in principle, open to new participants, and their inclusion is jointly regulated by the constituting members. The regulations for the work of the commission provide that the Prime Minister may, upon petition by the commission, grant membership to new groups representing other trade unions and employers' organizations. Since March 1994, a total of thirty-six organizations, mostly

[30] *RFE/RL Newsline*, 2 August 1999.

[31] International Labour Organization, *World Labour Report 1997–98* (Geneva: International Labour Office, 1997), cited in Millard 1999: 111.

unions, have applied for membership in the commission.[32] Among them are the Confederation of Trade Unions of Polish Miners, the Federation of Trade Unions of Health Workers, the Trade Union of Civil Servants at the Ministry of National Defense, and Solidarity '80. The constituting members, however, did not reach consensus in favor of admitting additional members.

These and other developments have prompted public discussion in Poland as to whether the historical criterion for representation should be preserved in the future. Important segments of society have no representation in the commission, such as Solidarity '80, the farmers' unions, and some large autonomous unions such as the Union in Health Care (67,000 members). At the same time, some of the OPZZ's branch unions, such as the Confederation of Energy Workers' Unions and the Machine Industry Union, have separate memberships in the commission because they were separate signatories to the Enterprise Pact. On the employers' side, a new formation emerged in March 1999, the Confederation of Polish Private Employers (KPPP), closely linked with the Freedom Union. Its creation confronted the social partners with the question of whether or not to include it in the work of the commission. Another representation problem is how and on what side to include "self-government" (local government operations) in the tripartite structures, since such organizations are both employers and government institutions.

These developments, however, do not point toward monopoly of representation in Poland. Irrespective of the position taken by the Tripartite Commission in terms of new members, the government, in accordance with

[32] These include NSZZ Solidarity '80; Confederation of Trade Unions of Miners in Poland; All-Poland Professional Union of Physicians; Federation of Trade Unions of Healthcare Workers; August-80 Trade Uion; National Trade Union for Heating System Workers; National Trade Unions of Workers in the Army; Trade Union of Workers in Agriculture "Self-Defense"; Confederation of Trade Unions of Agricultural Employers; Trade Union of Agricultural Workers in Poland; National Union of Agricultural Workers, Units and Organizations; Trade Union of Civil Workers of Ministry of Internal Affairs; Trade Union of Workers in Enterprises for Mechanical Coal Processing in Poland; Federation of Unions of Polish Teachers in Higher Education and Science; Trade Union of Functioners and Workers in the System of Prisons; Trade Union of Polish Officers and Mariners; Trade Union of Miners in Poland; Trade Union of Workers in Polish National Parks; Convention of Entrepreneurs, Traders and Producers in Agriculture (NGO); Trade Union of Workers in the Judicial System; Parliament of Students of the Republic of Poland; All-Poland Alliance of Constant Movement; Union of Polish Cities; Main Council of Nurses and Obstetricians; Federation of Craftsmen; Independent Trade Union of Workers in the Regional Court in Lodz; Independent Trade Union of Workers in Police; All-Poland Trade Union of Professional Obstetricians; All-Poland Federation of Trade Unions of Workers in Administrative Councils; All-Poland Trade Union of Nurses and Obstetricians; Polish Trade Union of Pensioners and Disabled People; Federation of Trade Unions of Financial Workers; Union of Polish Forest Workers; Independent Trade Union of Judicial Workers in Poland; Federation of Trade Unions in Public Radio and Television; Trade Union of Bus Drivers.

the existing labor legislation, has to consult *all* statutory trade unions and employers' organizations in preparing any draft law.

At a seminar in February 1999 celebrating the fifth anniversary of the Tripartite Commission's founding, none of the social partners criticized the commission as unnecessary, and all of them acknowledged the importance of maintaining social dialogue in Poland. The commission came into being as the result of strong pressures from below from the social partners, with the start of the privatization process and the negotiation of a social pact on the privatization of state enterprises. A voluntary and highly inclusive form of corporatism emerged that represented a step away from the articulation of civil society's ethical values and a move toward the articulation of more or less clearly distinguished interests. While agreements were reached in the commission, however, they "were frequently subject to protest and mutual accusations of bad faith," especially the commission's agreed wage guidelines for public sector workers in 1994–96 (Millard 1999: 113). These developments have inspired continuous debates over the regulation of tripartism in the Polish constitution.[33]

Civic and Institutional Expansion of Social Dialogue

In addition to direct representation in Parliament and the institutionalization of the Tripartite Commission on Socio-Economic Issues, to cope with the various challenges of transition Poland developed a variety of other more specialized, mostly single-issue tripartite structures (see Table 3). Some of them were created earlier than the Tripartite Commission. According to data from the KPP, there are some thirteen tripartite and multipartite organs for social dialogue in Poland, including the Tripartite Commission and the Main Employment Council.[34] Some of them include various organizations from Poland's rapidly expanding civil society. By 1995, some 20,000 nongovernmental organizations were operating in the country, including political, professional, cultural, ecological, and single-issue groups and associations, women's groups, think tanks, and student organizations (Michta 1997: 99; Ekiert and Kubik 1999). The inclusion of civil society in various tripartite structures, especially in the social sphere, was not the major form of its public participation, however. As Ekiert and Kubik assert, due to continuing politicization of the organizations of civil society, and at the same time fragmentation and isolation from political parties, Poland's ethics-based civil society has relied more heavily on grass-roots activism and protest to make its voice heard (Ekiert and Kubik 1997: 17).

[33] A draft law on the Tripartite Commission for Socio-Economic Issues has been under public discussion since 1994 (Guidelines for the Draft-Law on the Tripartite Commission for Socio-Economic Issues).

[34] "Organs in Whose Work KPP Representatives Take Part" (Warszawa: Konfederacja Pracodawcow Polskich, information material, 1999).

A variety of tripartite commissions for labor protection spread at the local level, but the primary agency at the national level was the *Council for Labor Protection*. The council was established by the Law on State Labor Inspection (1981) as a supervisory body to oversee health and safety at work and labor inspection activity. It is composed of Parliament members, representatives of the government, trade unions, employers, and various organizations from the third sector, experts, and academics. The council's functions include elaboration of opinions concerning labor protection and evaluation of the activity of the Agency for Labor Inspection. The council also expresses positions on problems in the area of health and safety at work, and gives opinions on candidates for the posts of General Labor Inspector, deputy, and local labor inspector.

Another tripartite organ is the *Council for Social Assistance*, established by the Law on Social Assistance (1990) and a 1991 regulation of the Minister of Labor and Social Policy. It is an advisory body to the Minister of Labor and Social Policy in the area of social welfare. The council comprises representatives of the Ministry of Labor, trade unions (OPZZ and Solidarity), employers (KPP), representatives of local social assistance centers at the level of *voivod*ships, NGOs, religious organizations, and academics. Meetings are held at least twice a year. The council provides opinions on draft legislation in the area of social assistance, expertise on social assistance issues, and opinions on social assistance policy.

According to the Act of 29 December 1993 concerning the protection of workers' claims in the event of insolvency of their employers,[35] workers' claims that are not satisfied are to be paid by the Guaranteed Workers' Benefits Fund, administered by the Central Labor Office. The fund's supervisory board – the *Council of the Guaranteed Workers' Benefits Fund* – is a bipartite body whose members are drawn from representative employers' organizations (two thirds) and representative trade union organizations (one third). Members are appointed by the Minister of Labor and Social Policy. The council approves the financial plan of the fund and annual reports on its implementation. It also determines the conditions for loan reimbursement and performs overall evaluations of the functioning of the fund.

The *Supervisory Board of the Social Security Institute* was established by the Law on the Social Security System (1998) and a 1998 regulation of the Council of Ministers. It comprises fifteen members, of whom five are nominated by the Minister of Labor and Social Policy, five by employers' organizations, and five by trade unions and organizations of pensioners.

[35] Act of 29 December 1993, concerning the protection of workers' claims in the event of the insolvency of their employer (*Dziennik Ustaw*, 4 January 1994, no. 1, pp. 1–4, text no. 1).

The *Commission on Collective Bargaining Issues* was established by the law amending the Labor Code (1994)[36] and a 1995 regulation of the Minister of Labor and Social Policy. It comprises representatives of the social partners, the Ministry of Finance, and the Ministry of Labor and Social Policy. The commission's responsibilities include promoting collective bargaining in the country, assisting the parties in collective bargaining, and providing information about law and jurisprudence. It meets only once or twice a year.

Another tripartite forum is the *Tripartite Commission for Cooperation with the International Labor Organization*, established through a 1990 decision of the Prime Minister. It is comprised of twenty representatives of the government: ten from trade unions (Solidarity and OPZZ, but also Solidarity '80), and ten from employers' organizations. The commission meets twice a year to discuss issues concerning national and international aspects of cooperation with the ILO. It elaborates opinions on the ILO's draft conventions and recommendations and initiates ratification of ILO documents in Poland. The commission also helps the development of relations between Poland and the ILO, and promotes the principles of the ILO's constitution in Poland.

Other tripartite bodies include the *Supervisory Board of the State Fund for Rehabilitation of Disabled People*, the *Commission on Minimum Payments* (created in 1991 as a government–trade union commission; in 1994 it included the KPP as well), and the *Commission for Labor Law Reform* (a multipartite forum for amendments to the 1994 labor legislation, established in 1989).

4.4. Integration and Tripartism

International donors and institutions have played an important role in Poland's transition, though the financial aid they have offered has proved to be limited and not well structured (Wedel 1998). Poland was one of the first two countries to receive assistance from the international community, under the PHARE assistance program. Aid programs were set up in virtually all sectors concerned with the reforms leading to a free market economy. Overall, EU funds offered to Poland annually amount to some EUR 200 million, which is 0.2 percent of Poland's GDP, or 0.5 percent of the state budget.[37] The country's assimilation of Western institutions was strengthened when, on 11 July 1996, it was granted membership in the Organization for Economic Cooperation and Development (OECD).

While partners to the IMF and the World Bank are exclusively governments, not private businesses or trade unions, and these international

[36] Act to amend the Labor Code and other acts in respect of collective bargaining, dated 29 September 1994 (*Dziennik Ustaw*, 26 October 1994, no. 113, text no. 547, pp. 2017–25).

[37] "A Summary of EU Aid Programmes," PAP (Polish Press Agency), 14 May 1999.

lending organizations are not linked directly with civil society, both organizations have consulted the social partners in Poland on the major parameters of granting loans and conditions for preserving social peace in the country. In the World Bank's social adjustment loan projects, the bank regularly consulted trade unions and employers, concerning two matters in particular: measures to enhance the transparency of social reform, and "macro" conditions for the bank's loans, namely, a relatively good economic and political situation in the country, with little social unrest.

Although Poland – with a relatively stable recovery from its economic crisis by 1994 – stopped using IMF assistance loans in 1996, the World Bank retains a prominent presence in the country. More important, the bank's recent policy is to establish partnerships with unions and employers of its lending countries. The aim is to reflect their concerns in the bank's recommendations to governments in the economic memoranda it regularly prepares for each client country. These bank-union-employer talks in Poland have tended to focus not on unemployment – the unions acknowledge the need for layoffs – but, rather, on wages (the unions insist on higher minimum wages, for example, and on securing the so-called family wage, or a wage equal to supporting a family), working conditions, and worker rights.

In May 1997 the bank approved a new Country Assistance Strategy for Poland. The program was developed in close consultation with the government of Poland, the social partners, and also a broad range of Poland's civil society, such as Polish foundations, economic development institutions, and research institutions. The new strategy recognized that, the country having gained good access to international markets, its need for the bank's financial assistance was small. Poland's expected accession to the EU will further reduce the bank's policy leverage. Therefore, the strategy formulated the bank's new role as an independent advisor in policy formulation and as a partner in building and strengthening market-oriented institutions, in three major ways: by helping formulate and implement policies needed for sustained growth; by providing independent evaluation, as well as investment support in selected areas such as the environment and labor market policies; and by helping to ensure the social sustainability of reform and reduce poverty. The new strategy covered the period through the turn of the century and provided for continued lending and technical assistance and policy advice from the bank. The program's main objective is to help Poland maintain strong economic growth and meet the requirements for accession to the EU (Landau 1997).

The role of the IMF and the World Bank as heavy lenders in the early years of transition was gradually eclipsed by the impact of EU integration.

No major restructuring of Polish tripartism occurred as a result of the process of accession to the EU. As part of the accession obligations of the Polish government, the European Social Charter had to be ratified, and preparations for that action were channeled through tripartite institutions.

A separate multipartite commission based on the tripartite principle – the *Commission for the Ratification of the European Social Charter* – was established in 1992 to coordinate social partners' activities for the ratification of the charter. Participating in this body were wide segments of society, including but not limited to government ministries and agencies, trade unions and employers, nongovernmental and professional organizations, and academics.

Poland did not ratify the European Social Charter until June 1997, however. The many debates within the commission divided the social partners and various social groups on the issue of how many charter articles (above the required minimum) should be ratified. While the unions insisted on the ratification of many more than the required number of articles, with the hope of thereby effecting a general improvement in employment conditions and health and safety at work, Polish employers were against many of the EU standards contained in the Social Charter, most of which exceeded existing Polish standards. Employers lost in their bid to gain the right to lock out during industrial disputes (a right not granted them by Polish labor law, in contrast to the recognized right of workers to strike): Poland did not ratify clause 4 of Article 6 of the European Social Charter, which extends the right of collective action to employers and employees alike (Bell and Mickiewicz 1999: 132).

Processes of European integration led to expanded consultation between the Polish social partners and various European structures. As part of the PHARE Social Dialogue Project, the Tripartite Commission regularly interacted with similar institutions (social economic councils) in Belgium, Netherlands, Spain, and Italy, as well as the Economic and Social Committee of the EU. Most recently, in 1998, the whole commission visited Brussels to discuss accession issues. The members of the Tripartite Commission were informed about the progress of work related to EU accession.

The fifth meeting of the joint EU-Poland Association Council, held on 10 November 1998, agreed to form a *Joint Consultative Committee* that would involve economic and social partners from Poland and the EU in accession preparations. As part of the accession effort, the session of the EU-Poland Association Committee had previously (on 6 March 1998) concluded plans to create the Consultative Committee, which was established in October 1998. The committee comprises members of the EU's Economic and Social Committee and members of the Polish Tripartite Commission, as well as representatives of other interest groups.

The Joint Consultative Committee is intended to constitute a forum for dialogue between the social partners of both sides, Poland and the EU. Through its work, the Polish social partners are expected to become familiar with the process of consultation taking place within the EU's Economic and Social Committee and with the dialogue between the social partners in the EU in general. The social partners in the EU are in turn expected to familiarize themselves with the social dimension of the economic and social reforms taking place in Poland. The Consultative Committee also has the major function of consulting the EU-Poland Association Council on matters of social interest. On 21–22 May 1999, the EU-Poland Joint Consultative Committee held a session discussing CEE countries' preparations for EU accession.

The Tripartite Commission does not discuss particular issues of accession to the EU in its regular meetings. The social partners have been consulted, however, on the social *acquis* during the screening exercise on Polish legislative readiness for accession. Screening of the social *acquis* was relatively trouble-free for Poland. The questions were mostly technical ones concerning how to adjust Polish labor legislation to EU common law. Collective bargaining and social dialogue are not sticking points; EU standards in these areas are minimal, and tripartite structures already exist in Poland.

The social partners have made large strides toward harmonizing social and labor legislation with EU common law by establishing the Commission on Labor Law Reform. Much of Poland's social and labor legislation is already in harmony with the European standards, in all six areas specified by the community's labor standards: (1) the right to work and employment and the right to a fair wage; (2) creation of a legal framework for the free movement of workers; (3) equal treatment of men and women in employment law; (4) enterprise restructuring and modernization of the employment relationship; (5) protection of health and safety at the workplace; and (6) dialogue, consultation, and sharing of information among the social partners (Matey 1995).

Unfortunately, dialogue with different groups within Polish civil society in the period of accession to the EU is not a straightforward matter. Anomie, confusion, and apathy characterize many of Poland's civic organizations, reflecting the fact that people have concentrated more on trying to keep up their deteriorating standard of living and ensuring their children's future than on participating in public and civic life. Because new social strata and groups are incompletely formed, their interests have not yet fully crystallized and are poorly represented. As a result, there are now many weak organizations, representing small interest groups, which cannot establish a common platform and reach consensus. The accession process, however, will help crystallize interests, as political groups search for new allies among these developing groups (Kolarska-Bobinska 1999).

Considering the weak regulation of tripartism by Polish labor law and the distinctly neoliberal attempt of the Buzek government (especially in the person of the prominent neoliberal Balcerowicz) to marginalize tripartism in Poland since 1997, it is perhaps mostly the EU accession requirement to maintain social dialogue and consultation among the social partners that keeps tripartism still functioning, though at lower speed. The EU's PHARE Social Dialogue Project, completed in Poland in 1992–93, played a decisive part in the breakup of the politics of opposition and the shift toward negotiated compromise in concluding the Enterprise Pact in February 1993. The process of harmonizing Polish law, including labor law, with the EU standards, and especially the requirement to maintain social dialogue among the social partners, is another recent development that reinforces tripartism and, to some extent, counteracts the Buzek government's attempts to marginalize it.

5

The Politics of Sectoral Tripartism

5.1. Sectoral Tripartism in Bulgaria

Sectoral tripartism in Bulgaria emerged as an integral part of national social dialogue, and stretched to the company level as well. In January 1991, to reduce the overwhelming, dense direct involvement of the state and the national social partners in the resolution of local problems, the social partners negotiated with the Agreement for Preservation of Social Peace the development of social dialogue at lower sectoral and regional levels, to complement the activities of the National Standing Tripartite Commission for Coordination of Interests (created in January 1991). Based on the Agreement for Preservation of Social Peace and the statute of this commission, a special government decree required all sectoral ministries and local government structures to initiate the creation of sectoral and regional *sub*-commissions for coordination of interests.[1] The new Labor Code of 1993 mandated the creation of tripartite bodies for social dialogue in all industries and branches of the national economy, and the development of collective bargaining at the enterprise level and at sectoral and industry levels. Tripartite sectoral agreements then began to be signed in each sectoral ministry, and by the end of 1994, sectoral tripartite forums were functioning at each ministry. At some bigger ministries, such as the Ministry of Industry, more than one tripartite body was created, each dealing with issues of its subsector.

The next sections consider the emergence and development of social dialogue at the Bulgarian Ministry of Industry and the Committee of Posts and Telecommunications, focusing, respectively, on the electronics industry and the telecommunications industry. Those two industries faced different levels of economic crisis and social tension, as well as different speeds of

[1] Council of Ministers Decree no. 102 of 23 April 1991 for the creation of sectoral and regional subcommissions for coordination of interests.

economic restructuring. While electronics was severely hit by the collapse of its Council for Mutual Economic Assistance (CMEA) markets, the telecommunications industry was among the few sectors of the national economy able to recover and stabilize relatively quickly. Thus, employment in the electronics and electrotechnical industry decreased sharply – from 197,800 in 1990 to 89,400 in 1993 to 54,400 in 1997 – while employment in communications remained stable – 45,000 in 1990, 44,000 in 1991 and 1992, 45,000 in 1993, and 47,000 by 1997.[2] The reasons for these differences are to be found mainly in the international economy. While 90 percent of the electronics markets were linked with the CMEA system, the Bulgarian communications industry did not face international competition and its domestic markets remained stable after 1989. Because of the general delay in privatization in Bulgaria, even by 1998 privatization remained low in both sectors. State ownership stood at 94 percent in 1993,[3] still defining the structure of industrial production. In 1996, employment in the private sector of the electronics and electrotechnical industry was 15 percent of total employment, and in 1997 it increased to no more than 36 percent. In communications, employment in the private sector remained extremely low: 4.1 percent in 1996 and 1997.[4]

Despite the different levels of economic crisis and social tensions, both sectors developed social dialogue structures, backed by national-level normative prescriptions of the social partners. Yet the depth and focus of these forums differ substantially.

Social Dialogue at the Ministry of Industry

Social dialogue emerged at the Ministry of Industry in 1991, in accordance with the January 1991 Agreement for the Preservation of Social Peace. The Minister of Industry and Trade signed an agreement with the central leadership of Podkrepa and CITUB to regulate social partnership.[5] The ministry became the social partner to some forty union federations. In exchange for some job security, retraining, and social benefits, these unions agreed not to organize strike actions before negotiations were held in tripartite forums at the ministry. The organizational structure of conflict resolution at the Ministry of Industry included four levels: (1) at the enterprise level, bipartite

[2] *Statisticheski spravochnik, 1998* (Sofia: National Statistical Institute, 1998), 40.

[3] *Sotzialno-ikonomichesko razvitie na Republika Bulgaria prez perioda '90–94 godina (Social and Economic Development of the Republic of Bulgaria in the Period 1990–94)* (Sofia: National Statistical Institute, 1995), 87.

[4] *Statisticheski spravochnik, 1998* (Sofia: National Statistical Institute, 1998), 40.

[5] Sporazumenie za syglasuvane na interesite v sistemata na industrijata, tyrgovijata i uslugite (Agreement for the Coordination of Interests in the System of Industry, Trade and Services) (Sofia: Ministry of Industry, Trade and Services, April 1991). See also Pravila za osyshtestvjavane na sotsialnoto partnerstvo na nivo Ministerstvo na promishlenostta (Regulations for the Realization of Social Partnership at the Ministry of Industry).

union-management commissions served to coordinate interests; (2) bipartite union-employer commissions at the Ministry of Industry provided a forum for discussion of labor and social conflicts that could not be resolved at the enterprise level; (3) when consensus could not be reached, the problem was transferred to one of the six tripartite sectoral commissions that involved the participation of representatives of the ministry; and (4) if the social partners at the ministry could not reach consensus, the national tripartite forum would be sent a protocol for differences in opinions.

From the time of its establishment in 1991, tripartism at the Ministry of Industry functioned relatively smoothly, with only one major break in activity occurring in 1994–95. The conflict began with a dispute over the involvement of the state in the signing of the sectoral collective agreements for 1994 in the Sectoral Commission on Machine-Building. Initially, the prevalence of state property had brought the state in as a third partner in the negotiations. The unions favored continued direct state involvement. The employers, however, insisted that they and the unions be the only signatories to the industry-wide collective contract. The conflict also involved specifics of the sectoral contract, such as the procedure for mass layoffs and the minimum wage level for the sector. Since the unions and employers could not reach an agreement, the employers withdrew their signatures from the 1993 collective contract.

The interlinking of the levels of bargaining was immediately manifested in this conflict and some other national disputes related to the process of economic reform. In April 1994, the unions discontinued their participation in the National Council for Tripartite Cooperation, and national social dialogue ceased until the election of a new provisional government in early October 1994. Nevertheless, some sectoral tripartite councils did continue to function after April 1994, to resolve major industrial conflicts either in the sectors as a whole or in major enterprises of the sectors. The law prohibiting unions from striking unless they first took their complaint to the appropriate upper state organ (ministry) for negotiations[6] contributed to the preservation of sectoral social dialogue.

At the Ministry of Industry, social dialogue was restored in June 1995 by the Videnov socialist government. An Agreement for Tripartite Cooperation was then signed between the Minister of Industry and the numerous social partners involved in negotiations with the ministry: twelve sectoral chambers of the Bulgarian Industrial Association; thirteen CITUB federations and sectoral unions; six Podkrepa unions; and six unions of the newly recognized trade union confederation OSSOB.[7] This agreement reduced the

[6] Law on the Resolution of Collective Labor Conflicts, adopted 6 March 1991.

[7] Sporazumenie za osyushtestvjavane na tristranno sytrudnichestvo v Ministerstvo na promishlenostta (Agreement for the Realization of Social Cooperation at the Ministry of Industry), *KNSB Dokumenti*, July (1991), 14–15.

state's role in the sectoral social dialogue occurring at the Ministry of Industry, and the state became only a mediator and guarantor of the collective agreements signed by unions and employers.

In substantive terms, the agreement established a trend away from discussions of purely local issues and the resolution of enterprise labor conflicts. Tripartite cooperation was to be focused on the conclusion of sectoral collective agreements and on issues such as employment levels, training, wages, incomes, social insurance, and collective disputes. Tripartite negotiations also covered work conditions – labor legislation on work time, holidays, leisure time, rest hours, and recreation – as well as the social aspects of privatization and restructuring.

Social partnership at the Ministry of Industry occurs at two levels: all-industry, spanning industries; and subindustrial or sectoral, involving one sector or a group of sectors with similar activities or problems (see Table 2). At the all-industry level, social partnership occurs through a Departmental Council. The Departmental Council is chaired by the Minister of Industry and includes representatives of the ministry, the chairs of the sectoral councils for tripartite cooperation, the chief of the "Leasing of Management and Social Policy" department, the chairs of the federations of the three nationally recognized trade unions, and the chairs of the sectoral associations that include the nationally recognized employers' organizations. The council meets once a month and takes decisions by consensus. Its jurisdiction covers general problems in the ministry, such as the coordination of draft labor legislation, wages, social insurance, employment, training, corruption, privatization, ecology and safety of work, and collective bargaining at the enterprise level. The Departmental Council also deals with the resolution of specific problems that have not been resolved in sectoral councils. It is also responsible for communicating with the social partnership organs in other ministries and with the social partnership structures at the national level.

At the subindustry/sectoral level, social partnership occurs through sectoral councils covering the following eight sectors: Machine-Building; Electronics and Electrotechnics; Chemistry and Mineral Oil Processing; Metallurgy; the Timber, Forestry and Furniture Industry; Light Industry; Mineral Resources; and Special Production. According to the 1995 agreement, the major task of each sectoral council is to conclude collective contracts regulating the employment relationship in all companies in the respective sector. The main focus of the sectoral tripartite commissions has, thus, gradually shifted from the resolution of restructuring-driven local labor conflicts and the prevention of strike actions to the preparation of annual sectoral collective agreements. The agreements reached by these councils regulate wages, labor efficiency, inflation, employment, working time, holidays, training, and health and safety.

Tripartite cooperation was again interrupted in 1997 because of difficulties in concluding the sectoral contracts that year. The Podkrepa and

CITUB unions had insisted on the automatic renewal of the old collective contracts for 1996, in order to prevent the new, smaller union organizations from signing them and thereby gaining not only the right to participate in social dialogue at the Ministry of Industry, but also national legitimation. An initiative of the national social partners called for national recognition for participation in social dialogue, and one official criterion for such recognition was the conclusion of sectoral collective contracts. In 1994–96, the new union formations had not participated in the conclusion of any sectoral collective contracts. Podkrepa and CITUB wanted to maintain that status quo in 1997, and consequently refused to sign new sectoral contracts for that year.

In March 1998 an agreement was reached, however, among the unions, the employers, and Minister of Industry Bozhkov for restoring tripartite cooperation at the Ministry of Industry.[8] On the employers' side, the agreement was signed by twenty-five sectoral chambers of the Bulgarian Industrial Association, the Union of Private Economic Enterprising, the Bulgarian Chamber of Commerce and Industry, and the Vazrazhdane Union of Private Producers. On the union side, the agreement was signed by fourteen CITUB unions, nine OSSOB unions, four Edinstvo unions, the Association of Democratic Trade Unions, and the General Centrale of Branch Trade Unions in Bulgaria. The Podkrepa Unions, nine in number, refused to sign the agreement as a result of the union battles for national recognition and the enumeration of union members that was initiated by the government at that time. But the Podkrepa sectoral unions did not refuse to participate in the work of the tripartite forums that were established on its basis.

The agreement regulated the creation of nine sectoral councils for tripartite cooperation to deal with issues of employment, training and retraining, wages and incomes, social security, work conditions, rest and recreation, amendments in labor legislation, social aspects of privatization, liquidation and restructuring, and the conclusion of collective contracts. The activities of the sectoral councils[9] are illustrated by the council on "Electronics and Electrotechnics."

The Case of Electronics

The Bulgarian electronics industry developed in the 1950s as a priority industry under state socialism. Bulgaria specialized within the CMEA in the area of computers and automated management systems, including those used in the military-industrial complex. Over 90 percent of electronics

[8] Sporazumenie za osyshtestvjavane na tristranno sytrudnichestvo v Ministerstvoto na promishlenostta (Agreement for the Realization of Social Cooperation at the Ministry of Industry) (Sofia: Ministry of Industry, March 1998).

[9] Pravila za rabota na nodotraslov syvet za tristranno sytrudnichestvo (Regulations for the Work of a Sectoral Council for Tripartite Cooperation) (Sofia: Ministry of Industry, March 1998).

production had guaranteed markets in the CMEA countries, mostly the USSR. After 1989, the disintegration of its international markets severely hurt Bulgarian electronics. In addition, high interest rates and increasing intercompany indebtedness hampered any attempts by the electronics companies to restructure.

Of all sectors, electronics was the one most severely hit by the economic crisis. While in 1988 the industry contributed almost 17 percent of GDP, in 1994 it produced not more than 4 percent, and in 1997 only 3.2 percent.[10] In 1992, losses in electronics accounted for 22 percent of the total decline in the Bulgarian economy, and electronics suffered the deepest drop in production of any industrial sector. In 1994, when national industrial sales increased 4 percent over 1993, sales of electronics production decreased almost 10 percent. Employment in electronics was also drastically reduced, from about 120,000 to 130,000 people in 1989 to only 40,000 in 1995 (excluding the electrotechnical industry). Wages and remuneration in the sector are delayed for long periods and are at least 10 to 15 percent lower than in other sectors.[11]

The slow pace of privatization (a total of sixty-four enterprises in the electronics and electrotechnical industry were selected by the government for liquidation, but they had not been privatized at the end of 1997) and the impoverishment of the Bulgarian population were the backdrop for the increased social and economic tensions among electronics employees. Such tensions arose mainly between the unions and the state, since the Branch Chamber of employers in electronics has been relatively weak and the unions prefer to negotiate directly with the Ministry of Industry.

The sectoral council for electronics and informatics – "Electronics and Informatics" – was formed in August 1992, with representatives from the Ministry of Industry, the Branch Chamber in Electronics of the Bulgarian Industrial Association, Podkrepa's Federation "Electronics, Electrotechnics, and Informatics" (3,000 members), and three CITUB trade unions: the Federation of Trade Union Organizations from Electronics and Machine-Building (18,000 members), the Trade Union Federation of the Organizations from Electronics, Machine-Building and Informatics (5,600 members), and the small Electrotechnical Trade Union. The Sectoral Council held seven sessions in the year of its founding, thirty-eight in 1993, five in 1994 before the breakup of social dialogue,[12] four in 1995 after its renewal in October, and eight in 1996.[13] The work of the council was interrupted in

[10] *Statisticheski spravochnik, 1998* (Sofia: National Statistical Institute, 1998), 97.

[11] Ibid., 52.

[12] "Sotsialnoto partnerstvo e fiktsija" (Social Partnership Is a Fiction), *Elektroshok*, no. 2 (June 1995), 3.

[13] Archive data: minutes of the sessions of the Sectoral Tripartite Council in Electronics and Electrotechnics.

1997 when the social partners could not agree on a sectoral contract. After the conclusion in March 1998 of the industry-wide agreement regulating the terms and conditions of tripartite cooperation at the Ministry of Industry, the social partners in the electronics and electrotechnical industry held four meetings in the remainder of that year.

The work of the council has focused on three major topics: (1) resolution of concrete problems and conflicts in the companies within the sector, especially those concerning union demands for replacement of company directors and board members; (2) negotiation of collective agreements regulating wages and work conditions in the sector; and (3) discussions of the parameters of economic reform in electronics.

Enterprise Conflicts. Concrete problems in companies comprised the most common topic of discussion. Out of 186 cases concerning local social tension that were discussed in the council, ninety involved the replacement of company directors and members of management boards. Problems with corporate restructuring and analyses of the financial and economic conditions in local enterprises were the basis for sixty-seven of the 186 cases; layoffs and the implementation of local collective contracts accounted for ten cases each; and nine cases involved strikes and other protest action. The overwhelming focus on personnel issues was the reason for the high politicization of the Tripartite Council.

Compared with tripartite councils in sectors experiencing less severe restructuring problems, such as telecommunications, the electronics council was much more politicized and held greater and more direct decision-making responsibilities. Thus, the Minister of Industry, Rumen Bikov, reached an agreement with the trade unions that company managers would not be replaced without the consensus of the sectoral council. In return, the unions agreed to a six-month moratorium on strikes in all the companies where new directors had been appointed with the council's consent. This "bargain" was targeted against illegal privatization and the frequent replacement of company directors for purely political reasons (such as changes in government after political elections). About one third of all company directors in the country (that is, approximately 500 of 1,500) had been replaced, while 430 of the 500 replaced were subordinate to (and hence replaced by) the Ministry of Industry. A great number of these dismissals occurred in the electronics industry. The tripartite council tried to work out a scheme for the replacement of old directors and the appointment of new ones.

Collective Bargaining. Another major area of negotiations has concerned the signing of collective agreements regulating wages and the employment relationship in electronics. An agreement signed in November 1992 by the social partners set the minimum wage in the sector, prescribed how wages were to be adjusted for inflation, and fixed additional payments from employers for education, night work, and overtime. The agreement also regulated work conditions and premiums, employment and professional development, health and safety, work time and holidays, social insurance, and the relations between the social partners.[14] The 1994 conflict over the signing of collective contracts reverberated in this sector. The Sectoral Chamber of Employers in Electronics and the Ministry of Industry insisted that the agreement that was in process of renegotiation should be signed only by the employers, while the unions demanded the direct involvement of the ministry. The collective agreement was renewed in 1995, after the restoration of social dialogue at the national and lower levels.

Economic Reform. The macroparameters of restructuring in the electronics industry were also discussed at the Sectoral Council in 1993–95. The government program for restructuring sought to liquidate the old marketing monoculture, optimize the utilization and management of the huge investments in electronics, regulate the indebtedness of companies, and seek foreign investments. The unions and employers criticized the analysis of the Ministry of Industry for envisaging a reduction in employment in electronics and electrotechnics to 30,000. The unions also criticized the strikingly slow pace of privatization in the sector and opposed the transformation of some enterprises into limited liability, rather than stock, companies, as the structure of the former offers much greater opportunities for corruption and illegal privatization.

The continuing economic decline of the Bulgarian electronics industry and the government's unclear policy and strategy for restructuring have led to increased tension and frequent strikes and other protest actions. In 1993 Podkrepa protested officially to the Bulgarian parliament, the Council of Ministers and the Ministry of Industry, demanding the quick adoption of a comprehensive strategy for the development of the sector, and legislative protection for domestic production. Other demands focused on the resolution of the problem of bad debts, the fulfillment of the sectoral agreement concerning electronics and electrotechnics, the payment of all overdue wages, and the creation of an employment program in the sector.

Efforts to resolve local problems through social dialogue have been tightly linked with lower-level company bargaining mechanisms in Bulgarian electronics. The case of the ELPEM electrotechnical company discussed below exemplifies how local enterprise problems have been jointly discussed by local and upper-level actors. In the process, company-level bargaining about the terms of economic transition has become an important part of the multitier bargaining structure that has emerged in Bulgaria.

As privatization has finally advanced, and especially since the new parliamentary elections in April 1997 and the creation of the currency board in July 1997, the emphasis on concrete issues in concrete companies has

[14] Otraslovo sporazumenie (Sectoral Agreement), *Informatsionen bjuletin* (Sofia: Federation of Trade Union Organizations from Electronics at CITUB), no. 1 (1993), 2–19.

dropped. The focus of discussion has shifted to the social issues of privatization, and the ministry created specialized consultative committees involving representatives of the social partners. The consultative committees extensively discussed the new government Strategy for the Development of the Electrotechnical and Electronics Industry until 2005, adopted in December 1998.[15] Trade unions, in particular, the Podkrepa Federation "Electronics, Electrotechnics and Informatics," had by far the greatest hand in elaborating the social aspects of the strategy.

Reflecting the preparations of the country for accession to the EU and the accession requirement for the creation of tripartite social and economic councils, the program envisioned the strengthening of sectoral social dialogue through the establishment of a social and economic council. Five specialized expert commissions to facilitate its work were also to be created: on work force, employment, and training; incomes and social protection; restructuring and privatization of the sector; health and safety at work; and monitoring the implementation of international labor standards and requirements, especially EU and ILO directives.

Following the legal requirement for the creation of specialized sectoral councils on health and safety at work issues,[16] a specialized Sectoral Council on Work Conditions in Electrotechnics, Electronics and Poligraphy was also created in early 1999.[17] The unions, especially the Podkrepa federation, worked out a special program for identification and monitoring of the priority issues in regard to work conditions in these sectors.[18] The program was approved by all social partners during the first session of the Sectoral Council on Work Conditions in Electrotechnics, Electronics and Poligraphy in March 1999, and was further presented and approved by the National Council on Work Conditions.[19]

The Case of ELPEM

The sectoral tripartite council of the "Electronics and Electrotechnical Industry" considered disputes at ELPEM, a Sofia-based producer of

[15] Strategija za razvitie na druzhestvata ot podotrasyl "Elektrotehnicheska i elektronna promishlenost do 2005 godina" (Strategy for the Development of the Units in the Electrotechnics and Electronics Sector until 2005) (Sofia: Ministry of Industry, December 1998).

[16] Law on Health and Safety at Work, *State Gazette*, no. 12, 23 December 1997.

[17] "Sindikati i rabotodateli za podobrjavane uslovijata na trud v elektronikata, elektrotehnikata i v spetsialnoto proizvodstvo" (Trade Unions and Employers for the Improvement of Work Conditions in Electronics, Electrotechnics and Special Production), *Informatsionen bjuletin* (Podkrepa CL), no. 2 (1999), 6.

[18] Programa za monitoring i opredeljane na prioritetnite problemi po uslovija na truda v elektrotechnicheskata, elektronna i poligraphicheska promishlenost (Program for the Monitoring and Determination of the Priority Problems Concerning Work Conditions in the Electrotechnical, Electronics, and Poligraphics Industries) (Podkrepa archives, 1999).

[19] "Otraslov syvet" (Sectoral Council), *Informatsionen bjuletin* (Podkrepa CL), no. 3 (1999), 2.

electrical machines, several times in 1996, each time at the request of the Podkrepa organization. In each case, local issues in the yet-to-be privatized company could not be resolved at the company level and were pushed upward for resolution at the sectoral level.

Before 1989, ELPEM, then part of a power-engineering unit of the huge ELPROM industrial agglomerate, was one of the most renowned companies in Bulgaria. As part of a process of decentralization and demonopolization in 1990–92, ELPROM was reformed and only a few of its units remained. The power-engineering company survived and was divided in September 1991 into two smaller companies: ELPROM-TRAFO, producing transformers; and ELPROM-ZEM (ELPEM), producing electrical machines. The two companies are in a relatively good economic shape, at least compared with other companies in the industry. The bulk of their production is exported, mainly to the countries of the former USSR and the Arabic world. The company was expected to be privatized through mass privatization.

ELPEM is beginning to overcome the calamitous production decline that began after 1989. Comparing the first seven months of 1996 with the same period in 1995, ELPEM has one of the best growth rates among Bulgarian electrotechnical companies. Now producing electrical engines, synchronous generators, and hydrogenerators, ELPEM has markets in Italy, Greece, Iran, Russia, Uzbekhistan, Ukraine, Turkhmenistan, Thailand, and Malaysia and exports in small quantities to Germany, the Netherlands, Finland, Belgium, and Austria. ELPEM works without credits, wages are paid regularly, and there have been no big layoffs in the company beyond one mass layoff, of eighty people, in 1994. In 1996 the company employed 780 people.

Within the company are organizations of CITUB with 200 to 300 members, and of Podkrepa CL with seventy members. In the spring of 1996 a new union organization belonging to the autonomous trade union "Independence," which is not nationally recognized, was created.

The 1996 campaign for conclusion of a collective contract for ELPEM resulted in the creation of a Commission for Collective Bargaining, which met frequently in January. According to the Labor Code an employer can conclude a collective contract with at most one representative body. In situations where more than one union has members in a firm, either they have to agree on a joint representative body to participate in collective bargaining or, if they cannot agree, a general meeting of the employees has to vote for one of the competing unions. When the branches of Podkrepa and the CITUB within ELPEM did not reach an agreement on a joint representative, the Podkrepa branch asked the sectoral council for tripartite cooperation to mediate the conflict and to extend negotiations for a contract.

The problem was discussed in the Sectoral Council in January 1996. The council reached consensus on four basic issues, and recommended (1) that the two union organizations in the company, Podkrepa and CITUB, collaborate on a joint representative body; (2) that the company's management disclose necessary information to the trade unions; (3) that the Podkrepa branch in the company deliver its own draft collective contract to the Commission on Collective Bargaining; and (4) that the company director postpone an upcoming scheduled general meeting of the company (meeting of representatives).

As no consensus between the two union organizations in the company was reached, the director of the company convened a general meeting of the employees on 19 February 1996. The workers voted for CITUB's proposal (80 percent) and the management of the company concluded the contract with CITUB on 26 Februar 1996. After the contract's conclusion the other two unions also joined in it, according to the legal procedure.

With guidance from the sectoral council for tripartite cooperation, a commission for social partnership was created at ELPEM after the signing of the company's 1996 collective contract. Social partnership commissions, found in some Bulgarian companies, are not mandated by law, as are their counterparts at upper levels. Although only the CITUB branch was a party to the collective contract, all unions were allowed to participate in the commission. There are six representatives in the commission: each union received one representative/vote, against the three representatives/votes of management.

Important as the process of negotiating the annual contract is, it lasts only a few months, and the commission on social partnership is supposed to function continuously. The commission meets once a month and discusses predominantly social issues, such as summer holidays, rest and recreation facilities, and the distribution of social aid to needy employees from the company's Social Fund. After reaching consensus on an issue, the members sign a protocol of agreement and prepare a draft ordinance on behalf of the director.

The second time ELPEM came to the attention of the sectoral tripartite council was in May 1996, and it again concerned the nature of social partnership in the company. The sectoral level social partners agreed to visit ELPEM and meet with representatives of its management and unions.

A third discussion concerning ELPEM took place in the sectoral council in early September 1996. This discussion concerned social tensions in the company caused by large and variable wage increases in violation of ELPEM's collective contract. According to the contract, wages were to be increased by 20 percent across the board by 1996, but by June 1996 the wage increase was much higher and varied: 33 percent for production workers and 47 percent for administrative personnel. As a result, there were 150 appeals from workers to the director of the company as well as to the union organization of Podkrepa. Based on these appeals, representatives of the sectoral tripartite council from the Ministry of Industry (the Chief of the Electronics and Electrotechnical Industry Department), CITUB and

Podkrepa, and the Bulgarian Industrial Association (including the author as an observer), visited the company to investigate the case. They found a violation of the company's collective contract, because the June 1996 increase had produced a wage differential much higher than the 1:3 limit specified in the contract. An agreement in principle was reached with the company management that the next wage increase would raise the wages of production workers by 45 percent and those of administrative personnel by 20 percent, in order to preserve the initial (pre-July 1996) wage relationship. As a result of this visit, the Sectoral Council's delegation began to consider the possibility of preventing similar tensions in the industry through much more detailed agreements over the basic/starting wages in the sectoral collective agreement to be negotiated for 1997.

Social Dialogue in Bulgarian Communications

In the socialist past the Bulgarian communications network and the services it offered were owned by the state. After 1989 the aim became to use communications as one of the bases of market development of Bulgaria (Mirski 1993; Markov 1994; Dragostinov 1994).[20] The first step of the structural reforms was the separation of state functions from economic functions, which was accomplished in mid-1991. State functions were assigned to the Committee of Posts and Telecommunications, while economic activities were taken up by Bulgarian Posts and Telecommunications Ltd. The second step was the separation, in January 1993, of postal communications from telecommunications. As a result, Bulgarian Posts and Telecommunications Ltd. was transformed into two companies: Bulgarian Posts Ltd. and Bulgarian Telecommunications Company Ltd. (BTC). The third basic thrust of communications reform has been demonopolization, by transforming construction companies into joint-stock companies to accomplish certain activities. The fourth basic trend is the liberalization of communications, the introduction of a market economy in communication activities, and the attraction of private capital to establish networks and provide services.

Communications was the only Bulgarian industry that has increased its production, in terms of revenue, after 1989. In 1994 communications services increased 76 percent over 1993 levels. There were no layoffs in communications; on the contrary, by 1996 some 2,000 new jobs were created.

[20] See also "Otchet za dejnostta na KPD pres 1994 godina" (Report on the Activities of the Committee of Posts and Telecommunications during 1994), *KPD Informatsionen bjuletin*, no. 3 (1995); "Programme for Development of Telecommunications in the Republic of Bulgaria until 2010. Summary," *Committee of Posts and Telecommunications Newsletter*, vol. 4, no. 4 (1996), 1–8; Council of Ministers Resolution no. 570 of 29 October 1998 for Approval of the Telecommunications Sector Policy of the Republic of Bulgaria, *Committee of Posts and Telecommunications Newsletter*, Special Issue no. 2 (1998).

In 1996 the national communication system had approximately 46,000 employees, of which 26,000 were at the BTC, 18,000 at the Bulgarian Posts, and 2,500 in the construction companies. Employment in communications increased to 47,100 in 1997, of which only some 1,900 positions were in the private sector.[21] Employment in communications trails only that in finance, credit, and insurance. Communications escaped mass layoffs in part because its technology did not need to be changed, but credit must also go to its high social potential and an early retirement strategy. Although privatization of the telecommunications services was delayed, telecommunications has been potentially attractive to foreign investors, because, compared with the other sectors, the sector is relatively efficient.[22]

In 1990 there were only three social partners in communications: the state organ Committee of Posts and Informatics, the Trade Union Federation in Communications at CITUB, and Podkrepa Federation in Communications. In 1992, following structural reform, the social partners were increased to four: the state organ, the Committee of Posts and Informatics; the Bulgarian Posts and Telecommunication Company; and the two unions, Podkrepa Federation in Communications and the Trade Union Federation in Communications at CITUB. As a result of further structural transformation, the social partners increased to thirteen in 1993: the state organ, the Committee of Posts and Telecommunications; the ten trade entities (the Bulgarian Telecommunication Company Ltd., the Bulgarian Posts Ltd., and eight construction companies in communications); and the two trade unions.

Of the two nationally recognized union organizations in communications that participate in the work of the tripartite forums, CITUB's federation claims 38,000 members, and Podkrepa's, 5,300 members. With 47,000 employed in communications, the unionization of the industry stood at an impressive 92 percent in 1995.

In 1990 the Sectoral Chamber of Telecommunications was established at the Bulgarian Industrial Association, by the general director of the Sofia division of the Bulgarian Telecommunication Company. As a member of the nationally recognized Bulgarian Industrial Association, the sectoral chamber had a right to participate in the work of the tripartite forums in communications as an employer representative. In July 1993 the chamber officially requested such participation in the industry-wide tripartite council. However, there was strong opposition by both unions and the leadership of the BTC. They objected that the chamber represented only some of the employers – the Sofia division of BTC – while all the other regional

[21] *Statisticheski spravochnik, 1998* (Sofia: National Statistical Institute, 1998), 40.

[22] "Privatizatsijata na BTK i nejnite sotsialni posleditsi. Materiali ot Natsionalnata konsultativna sreshta ot 30. VII.1998 godina" (Privatization of the BTC and Its Social Consequences. Materials of the National Consultative Meeting from 30 July 1998), *Informatsionen bjuletin* (Sofia: Trade Union Federation in Communications at CITUB), no. 4 (1998).

divisions of the BTC remained outside the social dialogue. At present the Sectoral Chamber of Telecommunications is still a member of the Bulgarian Industrial Association but has no access to the social partnership forum in telecommunications.

The division of the Bulgarian Posts and Telecommunications Ltd. into post and telecommunications companies affected the structure of social partnership in the sector as well as the nature of discussions within the social dialogue bodies. As a result, three levels of social partnership within the communications industry were established: (1) industry-wide, or social dialogue at the level of the state organ, the Committee of Posts and Telecommunications; (2) sectoral, or social dialogue at the level of the three communications branches – posts, telecommunications, and communications construction; and (3) social dialogue/collective bargaining at the level of the communications establishments and units.

A total of four social dialogue forums were set up in communications: an industry-wide tripartite council and three sectoral councils for coordination of interests: in telecommunications, in postal services, and in communication construction. The state organ – the Committee of Posts and Telecommunications – participates in the work of the four social dialogue forums and acts as a mediator and arbitrator. The employers participate in the industry-wide social dialogue as well as in their relevant sectoral forums: The Bulgarian Telecommunication Company Ltd. participates in the work of the Sectoral Council for Tripartite Cooperation in Telecommunications; the Bulgarian Posts Ltd. participates in the work of the Sectoral Council for Tripartite Cooperation in the Postal Industry; and the construction companies are jointly represented in the work of the Sectoral Council for Tripartite Cooperation in Communication Construction.

Industry-Wide Council for Tripartite Cooperation in Communications

The archetype of social partnership in communications is the Industry-Wide Council for Tripartite Cooperation in Communications. Created in June 1991,[23] it held six sessions in 1991, twenty-nine sessions in 1992, and ten sessions in 1993,[24] when the social partnership was decentralized into three sectoral tripartite councils. There were two major accents in the work of the council: conclusion of collective bargaining agreements and economic reform in the industry.

In sharp contrast to the case of Bulgarian electronics and electrotechnics, problems and conflicts at local communications units occurred very rarely

[23] Pravila za rabota na Otraslovata komisija za syglasuvane na interesite kym Komiteta po Poshti i dalekosyobshtenija (Regulations for the Work of the Industry-Wide Council for Coordination of Interests at the Committee of Posts and Telecommunications) (Sofia: Committee of Posts and Telecommunications, 1991).

[24] Archive data: minutes of the sessions of the Industry-Wide Council for Coordination of Interests at the Committee of Posts and Telecommunications.

and did not prevail in the discussions at the industry council. That silence may have been the result of the specificity of communications activities, with special requirements of national security and defense. Bulgarian labor legislation prohibits strikes in communications and encourages continuous negotiations among the social partners for the resolution of industrial conflicts. More important, however, there was lack of major social discontent that followed from high wages and, especially, high social benefits and regular and almost 100 percent adjustments of wages for inflation, particularly in the telecommunications sector. Besides, the communications sector was not shaken by the wave of mass dismissals of company "old nomenklatura" directors. Led by Stefan Sofijanski, a UDF technocrat (who subsequently became prime minister and then mayor of Sofia), the Committee of Posts and Telecommunications, despite Podkrepa's requests that it speed up reforms in communications through personnel changes, avoided dismissing managers.

Collective Bargaining. The conclusion of collective bargaining agreements regulated terms of employment and layoffs, wages, social benefits, conditions for trade union activities, and trade union control in local communications units. Important collective agreements and collective contracts – seventeen up to 1993 – were concluded within the industry-wide forum. Of the seventeen agreements, five concerned wages, six addressed other important issues, and four were complex in scope (Bochev 1993).[25]

Questions of employment and layoffs were at the center of discussions in the industry-wide tripartite forum, and those discussions produced important agreements, such as one making layoffs a last resort and another guaranteeing union control and participation in the processes of layoffs and new appointments.[26] The social partners further agreed to preserve a union's right to give approval/consent to layoffs, even after the new Labor Code of 1993 abolished that right. To prevent unemployment in the industry, unions insisted on the introduction of a temporary moratorium on layoffs and new appointments until a comprehensive concept for the structural reform of communications had been elaborated with an assessment of future

[25] See also Kolektiven trudov dogovor na otrasyl "Syobshtenija" za 1993 godina (Collective Labor Contract for the Communications Industry for 1993).

[26] Sporazumenie mezhdu sindikalnata federatsija na syobshtenijata i Komiteta po syobshtenija i informatika za reshavane na osnovnite problemi, zasjagashti interesite na sindikalnite chlenove pri preminavaneto na Natsionalnata syobshtitelna sistema kym pazarna ikonomika (Agreement Between the Trade Union Federation in Communications at CITUB and the Committee of Communications and Informatics for the Resolution of the Major Problems Concerning the Interests of Trade Union Members during the Transition of the National Communications System Toward a Market Economy) (Sofia: Committee of Communications and Informatics, 11 June 1991); Sporazumenie mezhdu Sindikata na syobshtenijata "Podkrepa" i Komiteta po syobshtenija i informatika (Agreement between the Podkrepa Union in Communications and the Committee of Communications and Informatics) (Sofia: Committee of Communications and Informatics, June 1991).

personnel needs. The moratorium was introduced in 1992 and lasted for about five months. However, technological reform in the industry, including the construction of a new telecommunication infrastructure on the basis of modern digital technologies (the Digital Overlay Network (DON) project), is expected to bring layoffs of at least 35 percent of the present work force. The unions, accepting the inevitability of these layoffs, demanded the creation of a comprehensive training and retraining program to fit present employees into the DON project.[27]

To protect wages against inflation, the social partners in communications agreed to renegotiate wage increases every three months, in accordance with the rate of inflation. Thus for the period 1991–93, wages in communications were increased ten times, and communications have moved from one of the lowest places in the scale of sectoral wages into the top ranks.

Collective bargaining in communications also covers social benefits and facilities. The 1993 industry-wide contract included several new social provisions, such as setting a higher rate of financial aid for retirement than envisaged by the Labor Code, providing Christmas and Easter aid for children and aid for socially weak families, and strengthening the Medical Treatment Abroad Fund created by the employers in communications.

Economic Reform. In addressing issues of employment, wages, and social benefits, social dialogue in Bulgarian communications resembled traditional collective bargaining practices in the developed market economies, but discussions of structural and technological reforms in communications represented a significant departure.

The trade unions were actively consulted about structural reforms in communications.[28] They had representatives in the commissions on the division of Bulgarian Posts and Telecommunications into Bulgarian Posts and Bulgarian Telecommunications, and unions gave their opinion on the reappointment of personnel in these companies. Union participation resulted in the division being made by reorganization rather than liquidation. In this way the jobs of more than 40,000 workers were preserved. The unions also negotiated a more equitable distribution of the social funds and benefits after the division, between the telecommunications workers (working in a much more profitable sector), and postal service workers (working in a subsidized sector).

Another concern of the council on economic reform concerned privatization issues. In December 1992 the government elaborated a program for

[27] Discussion Draft: Bulgarian Telecommunications Company Sector and Operator Restructuring Training Plan, 1993–97.

[28] Trade Union Federation in Communications at CITUB: "Stanovishte po srednosrochnata i dylgosrochnata programa za razvitieto na dalekosyobshtenijata v Bulgaria i otgovor ot BTK" (Opinion on the Medium- and Long-Term Program for the Development of Telecommunications, and Response from the Bulgarian Telecommunications Company), *Informatsionen bjuletin* (Federation of Trade Unions in Communications at CITUB), no. 1 (1996).

the privatization of Bulgarian communications that would privatize construction companies while postponing action on the Bulgarian Telecommunications Company. The unions insisted on their right under the industry-wide collective agreement to consultations, especially on the social aspects of the program, and in 1993 the unions and the state signed an agreement that there would be no privatization for five years. However, in March 1995, the Videnov government decided to begin privatization in telecommunications after 1995. As Bulgaria's most important service industry and the backbone of the emerging private businesses in Bulgaria, privatized telecommunications could speed up the process of economic restructuring. Unions feared, however, that illegal privatization would dominate, and they wished to delay the process until the new laws began to function properly.

The unions also negotiated several clauses in the industry-wide contract to protect workers from the negative consequences of restructuring and privatization. More than 50 percent of the stock of a privatizing enterprise was to be controlled by its workers and the state, and workers were guaranteed the most favorable conditions allowed by law. An additional agreement was signed between the trade unions and the Committee of Posts and Telecommunications concerning the restructuring and privatization of the trade companies and their units.

The industry-wide tripartite forum in communications has held sessions very rarely since the 1993 division: five in 1994 and one in 1995. Social dialogue occurs chiefly in the three branch forums. The activities of one of these – the Sectoral Council for Tripartite Cooperation in Telecommunications – are discussed below.

The Case of Telecommunications

Established in June 1993, the Sectoral Council for Tripartite Cooperation in Telecommunications held seven sessions in 1993, twenty-seven sessions in 1994, twenty-six sessions in 1995, seventeen sessions in 1996, twenty sessions in 1997, thirty-two sessions in 1998, and five sessions in the winter of 1999.[29]

Among the issues discussed at the sessions of the Sectoral Council for Tripartite Cooperation in Telecommunications are: the reform of the industry, discussed at thirty-five separate sessions; social issues such as distribution of the social fund, social development, sports, rest and recreation, and social payments to pensioners, at twenty-eight sessions; work conditions, at twenty-eight sessions; spending from the Medical Treatment Abroad Fund, at nineteen sessions; wages, at fifteen sessions; work time and vacations, at thirteen sessions; and concrete problems in the regional

[29] Archive data: protocols of the sessions of the Sectoral Council for Tripartite Cooperation in Telecommunications; interview data.

establishments and units of the national telecommunications structure, at thirteen sessions.

The program for the restructuring of telecommunications has been a major area of discussion. The employer, the BTC, agreed that restructuring would not lead to layoffs or a decrease in real wages. The agreement specified that reductions should be by natural attrition, and that existing personnel should be retrained for the new digital technology.

The social partners further negotiate the starting wage, and all social payments are set as a percentage of the starting wage. The social program in telecommunications has a long history and institutions such as the Social Development of Communications Department. In 1995 the Center for Social Policy was created at the Committee for Posts and Telecommunications, and a separate tripartite consultative council also was established to deal with issues arising from the BTC's social program.[30] Each of the committee's units has the right to form a special social fund, amounting to 10 percent of the wage fund. One percent of the social funds of each unit goes to the centralized Medical Treatment Abroad Fund.

The most difficult issues in the BTC's tripartite forum concerned disciplinary firings. The collective contract stipulated that firing can occur only with union consent, and management has made several attempts to abolish this requirement.

5.2. Sectoral Tripartism in Poland

Solidarity's predominantly regional structure and the 1991 labor legislation, which effectively excluded the state from the bargaining process below the national level, blocked the emergence of institutionalized tripartism in Poland's industries and sectors. The 1991 legislation assumed that the state should not be a direct party in labor relations and supported its involvement in sectoral social dialogue only as it related to the public sphere (e.g., education, health care, and culture). Sectoral social dialogues were typically bipartite union-employer engagements with the main purpose being the regulation of the employment relationship.

The legislative exclusion of the state from lower-level social dialogue was, however, premature, as long as employers had not established structures at lower levels and the state remained the dominant employer in Polish industry. Under strong social and political pressure, the state could not help but become directly involved in worker disputes. In most cases, protests led to negotiations with the direct participation of government representatives. Zygmund Gadaj, director of the Department for Cooperation with Trade Unions at the Ministry of Labor and Social Policy, estimated that in

[30] Pravila za ustrojstvo i dejnost na Konsultativen syvet pri Tsentyra za sotsialna politika na BTK-EAD (Regulations for the Composition and Activities of a Consultative Council at the BTC's Center for Social Policy).

1991–93 there were on average 200 meetings per year (Morawski and Hausner 1994).[31]

As in the Bulgarian case, in the conditions of unfinished privatization most cases of industrial protest spawned centralized tripartite arrangements, encompassing government sectoral programs and numerous local initiatives of the various professional, economic, and social actors. The result in Poland has been informal, issue-specific tripartite bargaining at Polish industries and sectors that found themselves in difficult restructuring situations. Increasingly, various ministries in Poland began to orchestrate issue- and region-specific social dialogues. But such meetings were not regular and institutionalized, as they have been in Bulgaria. Moreover, from its establishment in 1994, Poland's National Commission on Socio-Economic Issues did not develop close links with the tripartite meetings held at some ministries. The Ministry of Labor acted as an organizer and mediator of such sectoral meetings.

Sectoral-regional meetings were organized in regions facing difficult restructuring problems, such as Upper Silesia's mining industry. The social dialogue in Upper Silesia focused on the construction, under the initiative of Solidarity, of the so-called Regional Contract for the Katowice Province, and concerned the entire complex of social and economic relations. The contract was concluded in January 1995 between local governments and the state administration of the Katowice province, on the one hand, and Solidarity, Kadra, and OPZZ unions, on the other. The dialogue for miners in Silesia operates at two levels: one concerning the national government and the region, and the other concerning the local governments, organizations, and institutions. The negotiations focus on social insurance benefits, public infrastructure, the reconstruction of the regional economy, the restructuring of existing enterprises, and the creation of new ones. The dialogue represents an attempt to unify the programs proposed for the various sectors in the region and to carry out regional restructuring according to a rational plan (Wojtyla 1995).

Similar tripartite initiatives have emerged in other industries – mining, light industry, steel and metallurgy and military production – in response to efforts to restructure them and make them more competitive. Programs for the activation of local labor markets are prepared for these sectors, and special funds are diverted from the state budget for the implementation of such programs. In metallurgy, for example, which is not as troubled as coal mining, a tripartite team was created to elaborate a restructuring policy for the industry. It enunciated the principles of employment policy, the criteria for employment termination, employers' obligations during the restructuring period, and the principles for determining employment in metallurgy plants in the event of layoffs (Wojtyla 1995). Government

[31] Also, interview with Zygmund Gadaj, Warsaw, 1996.

authorities established other ad hoc sectoral tripartite bodies, such as the Tripartite Group for Miners' Social Security, the Tripartite Group on the Social Aspects of the Restructuring of the Steel Industry, and the Tripartite Group for the Textile Industry.

The case of the restructuring of Polish light industry demonstrates in greater detail these tendencies in Polish sectoral tripartism, while the case of the INTEX company, from that same industry, shows how company bargaining in industries in distress is tightly linked to upper-level tripartite bargaining.

The Case of Light Industry

After the Second World War, Poland's light industry was 80 percent export-oriented, mostly toward the CMEA markets, but since 1989 the enormous Soviet market has been lost. Despite union attempts to preserve employment in the industry, more than 350,000 workers have lost their jobs since the mid-1980s, and some 400 enterprises in the sector have been liquidated or privatized.[32] All Polish governments since 1989, including SLD, have had liquidation strategies for light industry, with significant reductions in employment.

To discuss the situation and prospects for light industry and textiles, in particular, there were irregular meetings between the Ministry of Industry, the Ministry of Labor, the Economic Chamber, the Chamber of Textile Industry, KPP, Solidarity, and OPZZ.[33] The first meeting was held in May 1995. There was a prospect for the creation of a standing tripartite commission for light industry, and an agreement was reached with the government to discuss in this forum the special government program for the development of light industry through 1997. Although the trade unions could not, in the end, enforce their demand for the creation of such a tripartite commission, they had extensive input into the elaboration of the Industrial Policy of the Government for the Period 1995–97.[34] The program, which derived from the government blueprint "Strategy for Poland," was adopted in December 1994.

In the fall of 1998, light industry workers in Warsaw initiated actions protesting the Buzek government's failure to proactively defend the industry,

[32] Report on the State of Polish Industry in 1993. Federation of Light Industry at OPZZ, No. 8, 1994. See also in "Polish Textile Industry in 1994 and Its Requirements in Respect of Technological Restructuring" (Interfashion Seminar, Polish Chamber of Textile Industry, Lodz, October 1994); Marszal 1991.

[33] Interview with Zbigniew Kaniewski, chairman of OPZZ Federation of Trade Unions in Light Industry, Parliament member, and member of the Regional Council for the Restructuring of Lodz Region and the Lodz Employment Council, Lodz, May 1995.

[34] Program on Industrial Policy for 1995–97 "International Competitiveness of Polish Industry," *Biuletyn Informacyjny Federacja NSZZ Przemyslu Lekkiego*, no. 6, 1995.

which allegedly had led to the industry's decay and, among other things, mass layoffs, liquidation of enterprises, and cessation of wage increases.[35] In December 1998 the OPZZ Federation of Light Industry urged the government to design – together with the industrial chambers – a program for the development of light industry, in accord with the requirements of the market and the processes of restructuring of the sector.[36] In this program the government should grant light industry the status of a strategic sector with key potential for development. The government should also consult with trade unions on anticipated mass layoffs in light industry, and should consider opportunities for early retirement after thirty-five and forty years of service.

The national leadership of Solidarity did not officially support the demonstrations and claimed they were political in character. Solidarity's sectoral unions in light industry were, however, supportive of the demonstrations. In January 1999, Solidarity–Lodz Region protested the lack of any government policy on light industry over the previous ten years, and asserted that the sector had the potential to be one of the leading sectors in the Polish economy. The union emphasized the need to develop a program for the restructuring of light industry and further insisted on the organization of government and parliamentary initiatives and activities for the resolution of the problems in the sector, such as recession, declining employment, and unfair foreign competition.[37]

The union protests continued in January 1999, with meetings organized in many enterprises.[38] On 21 January 1999 the workers organized protests in front of the Polish Sejm and the Council of Ministers.[39] About 2,500 workers traveled to Warsaw to demonstrate against the Buzek government for its passivity in regard to the restructuring of light industry, the worsening social and economic situation of the industry's establishments, and the layoffs of more than 10 percent of those employed in the sector, with an additional 15 to 20 percent of the work force, or some 80,000 to 100,000 workers, expected to be laid off in the future. The demonstrators decried the import of textile products and the lack of proexport and protectionist policies to defend the interests of national producers.

As a result of these increasing union pressures, and following a meeting between the labor minister Longin Komolowski and the leadership of

[35] "We Protest the Inactivity of the Buzek Government – the Reason for the Decline of Light Industry," *Biuletyn Informacyjny Federacja NSZZ Przemyslu Lekkiego*, no. 1, 1999.

[36] Resolution of the National Council of the Federation of Light Industry regarding Workers' Protest in Warsaw Light Industry Plants.

[37] Position of the Council of the Regional Secretariat for Light Industry of the Lodz Area.

[38] Interview with MP Zbigniew Kaniewski, "The Worse and Worse Situation of Light Industry: The Protest Has Begun," *Wiadomosci*, 2, 3 January 1999; "In Defense of Light Industry: Protest Until We Get Results," *Trybuna Lodzka*, 12 January 1999.

[39] "Light Industry, Heavy Scandal," *Trybuna*, 23–24 January 1999.

Solidarity–Lodz Region in December 1998, the Ministry of Labor established a working interinstitutional group for consultations with the trade unions and the Union of Employers from Light Industry. A more or less permanent tripartite group/unit for light industry was formed, and it started functioning between the end of 1998 and early 1999. On the trade union side, the tripartite unit included representatives from the OPZZ Federation in Light Industry, the National Commission of Solidarity, its National Secretariat of Light Industry, and Solidarity–Lodz Region. On the employers' side, participants included the KPP and its chambers of cotton, wool, and leather, and the Polish Chamber for Textile Industry. Participants on the government side included representatives of the Ministry of Economy, the Ministry of Finance, the Ministry of Labor and Social Policy, the Ministry of Environmental Protection, the Ministry of Health Care, the Chief Customs Office, the Polish Committee for Normalization, the Chief Trade Inspectorate, the General Customs Inspectorate, and the Agency for the Protection of Competition and Consumers.

Meetings held on 27 January, 12 and 24 February, and 3 March 1999 considered a program prepared by the Ministry of Economy, entitled "Strategy for Light Industry."[40] At these meetings, the Main Customs Office reported on its latest activities concerning increased control of cotton and textile turnover. The Polish Chamber for Textile Industry, with headquarters in Lodz, and the Main Customs Office agreed to prepare a joint opinion on textile prices. Discussion also focused on some foreign trade issues affecting light industry. Under pressure from the other social partners, the Ministry of Economy accepted the task of quickly reducing the import of secondhand clothes. In light of the preparation of the country for EU accession, such radical protectionist policies needed, however, preliminary consultation with the EU, and the Ministry of Economy agreed to consult with the EU on this issue.

In addition to these tripartite meetings, representatives of trade unions and employers in light industry, together with government representatives, attended a special symposium entitled "Light Industry: Chances and Challenges," organized by the parliamentary club of the Solidarity Electoral Action (AWS). Following symposium discussions, the Polish government and the Parliament jointly decided to take seven steps for the modernization of the industry: (1) work out a strategy for light industry; (2) create the normative basis and institutions of regional policy for regions in the country where light industry is dominant; (3) implement all instruments for the protection of the domestic market against foreign goods and harmonization of Polish legislation with the EU directives concerning light industry; (4) activate protective mechanisms for laid-off workers; (5) implement a system of state guarantees for the exporters in light industry;

[40] Archive data: protocols of meetings of the Tripartite Group for Light Industry.

(6) use existing research institutes to elaborate programs for the restructuring of light industry; and (7) implement normative regulations for the processes of liquidation and bankruptcy during this restructuring. Complete privatization of light industry was expected by 2000.

The Case of INTEX

INTEX is Poland's leading producer of cloth for suits, holding about 5 percent of the Polish domestic market. Until 1989, it included three spinning mills, two weaving mills, and one finishing mill, and produced 160 different kinds of cloth. The political and economic upheaval of 1989–90 put the enterprise in an extremely vulnerable situation. It had neither working capital of its own nor channels of distribution for its production, while at the same time its market partners disappeared. Production dropped to only eight kinds of cloth, mostly cotton and cotton-like varieties. Employment crashed: from 10,000 in the 1960s to 4,400 in 1989 to only 2,435 in 1996.

Protest activities were organized within the company in an attempt to draw government support for its survival. The unions, both Solidarity and OPZZ, organized a strike in 1993. They demanded the appointment of a government plenipotentiary who would deal with the restructuring of the enterprise. The strike continued for two days, with more than 2,000 workers – almost the entire work force – participating. Unions' main demand was fulfilled. Wage increases were also negotiated with the striking workers. A government plenipotentiary – the Lodz *voivod* – was also appointed to monitor the restructuring of the enterprise.

The restructuring program included liquidation of unprofitable parts of the company to secure a quick financial turnover and development of products that are competitive in new markets. In 1993, the enterprise was divided. The basic part continues to be INTEX and includes the spinning mill, one of the weaving mills, the finishing mill, the electric-power station, a shop, storage places, and the auto park. With the remaining assets, a separate enterprise was created: WESTER, which includes 30 percent of the mainly nonproductive assets of the former enterprise and about 50 percent of its land. In 1994 restructuring was completed, and in the first quarter of 1995, INTEX realized a profit. Part of this success was due to a 1993 law liquidating the old pre-1989 loans to state enterprises. The enterprise owes 25 percent of its assets to the state. Of this amount, 5 percent was allocated to the Privatization Fund, to compensate the former owners for their losses, and 20 percent was to be bought by the workers, at 50 percent of the price. In the interest of its survival, INTEX became a joint stock company at the State Treasury.

After 1989, the company had to develop its own marketing policy, the success or failure of which would largely determine its survivability.

INTEX's markets are now mainly domestic. Direct, unmediated exports represent only 5 to 8 percent of the production cost of the exported textiles. INTEX exports mainly to Scandinavia and Germany. Also, about 40 percent of its production is indirectly exported to the Czech Republic, Germany, and Romania as finished clothing. The enterprise's production is increasing: In 1994 it produced around 600 billion zloty, or $25 million; for 1995 the projected sales were 800 billion zloty, or $32 million.

INTEX is not a member of the Confederation of Polish Employers (KPP) but has been a member of the Textile Chamber from the creation of that institution in 1993, and of Club 500 since that group formed at the end of 1993. These memberships provide valuable marketing information and facilitate the distribution of the company's products. There are two unions in the company: a Solidarity organization with around 500 members, and an OPZZ organization with 720 members. The relations between the two unions have varied depending on the situation. They tend to agree on work conditions, economic issues, and financing, but to differ with regard to political demands. An informal balance of union power is maintained within the company: If in a certain department the manager sympathizes with Solidarity, his deputy will be an OPZZ sympathizer, and vice versa.

A collective agreement was concluded in 1993 and renewed in 1995. It was signed by the management and the two unions, as is required when two unions participate in the collective bargaining process. The unions are legally bound to collaborate; no collective agreement can otherwise be signed. The management considers the unions to be an important partner and a link between managers and workers. There are regular meetings each week among the management, the works council, the staff of the company's newspaper, and the unions. The initiative for these meetings came from the director. Other meetings are also held on an ad hoc basis, depending on specific problems. The discussions predominantly concern wages and wage levels in the company, but also include social issues, work conditions, and some economic issues and newly adopted labor legislation.

My examination of tripartism in Poland and Bulgaria reveals the emergence of two distinct paths of sectoral postcommunist adjustments: institutionalized in Bulgaria, and informal and noninstitutionalized in Poland. While both the Bulgarian and the Polish cases demonstrate that tripartism developed in response to the need to alleviate social tension arising from economic and organizational restructuring problems, these critical cross-national differences are rooted not in the different speed of economic restructuring or the depth of economic problems but, rather, in the different levels of commitment to social dialogue and tripartism by the state and the emerging new civil societies in these countries. A greater commitment to social dialogue and tripartism by the Bulgarian social partners, as exemplified by the 1993 legal endorsement of social dialogue at the national and lower levels of governance, led to the institutionalization and routine functioning of social dialogue even in industries that were not facing heavy restructuring problems and social tension, such as communications.

The cases of Bulgarian electronics and some of the Polish sectors in distress, such as light industry and coal mining, demonstrate that postcommunist tripartism evolved as a complex multitiered bargaining structure bringing together national social partners, lower – sectoral and regional – decision-making bodies and tripartite social dialogue forums, and representatives of local companies in an indivisible, systemic organ for conflict resolution.

6

The Politics of Regional Tripartism

6.1. Regional Social Dialogue in Bulgaria

To reduce their overwhelming involvement in the resolution of locally based social problems and protests, in 1990 the Bulgarian national social partners negotiated the development of social dialogue at the regional level. Tripartite regional agreements were to be signed, replicating the national General Agreement in its major areas. Regional tripartite bodies were to be established with the task of monitoring the implementation of the regional agreements.

The first regional tripartite agreement and tripartite forum emerged in early 1990 in the small city of Razlog.[1] Created spontaneously to combat social tension resulting from the collapse of the city's major employer – an electronics company – which caused unemployment in the region to rocket 50 percent, the Razlog forum involved extensive participation of upper-level ministerial and union structures.[2] Similar forums followed in other regions.

A regional tripartite commission typically included representatives of the local government (the mayor or deputy-mayor), local unions (Podkrepa CL and CITUB), and the local employers' structures. Initially, the lack of regional structures in both Podkrepa and some of the employers' organizations retarded the development of regional social dialogue. Thus, while the Statute of the National Tripartite Commission recommended the formation of regional commissions in 242 of the 273 municipalities in

[1] Agreement among the Municipal Council of Bulgarian Trade Unions, the Executive Committee of the Municipal People's Council and the Council of Employers in Razlog, Razlog, 1990; "Regionalnoto sporazumenie za bezrabotitsata v Razlog" (The Regional Agreement on Unemployment in Razlog), *Sindikalna praktika*, no. 10 (1990), 35–43.

[2] I was personally involved in the negotiations between the Razlog social actors and representatives of upper-level government and union structures for the conclusion of the Razlog Regional Agreement on Unemployment.

Bulgaria, by the end of 1991 only about fifty municipal tripartite commissions had been established.

Local conflicts mainly arose from acute industrial disputes in different state and municipal enterprises of a region, rising regional unemployment caused by the collapse of local enterprises, and various social problems in the region. Whenever, as was usual, a problem could not be resolved at the local level, often because the local social partners lacked the needed authority to bring about a resolution, the problem had to be transferred from regional forums to the national level.

After 1993, with the strengthening of the Professional Training and Unemployment Fund and the adoption of the National Program on Temporary Employment of the Ministry of Labor and Social Affairs,[3] single-issue forums – regional tripartite consultative committees dealing with employment issues – began to be created as part of the policy-making process in the area of employment. The Program attempted to combat unemployment by creating jobs, each lasting up to five months, for a region's registered unemployed in the main communal activities of the region. Four major institutions were involved in the program: the Ministry of Labor and the National Employment Agency, as well as local employment agencies; local "self-government" (the municipal council) and local state administration; organizations of local employers; and tripartite consultative committees.

Each tripartite consultative committee comprised two representatives of local self-government, two representatives of the unions (one from CITUB and one from Podkrepa CL), and two representatives of regional employers' organizations. The tripartite consultative committees focused on proposals of the local administration for job openings within the Program on Temporary Employment and had the right to approve or reject such proposals, according to certain criteria. The main outcomes of these regional tripartite deliberations were protocols of agreement that the National Employment Agency had to refer to in determining its subsidy for the region. In addition, the tripartite consultative committees were periodically informed by the local state administration and the local labor office about the fulfillment of the Program on Temporary Employment.

The new social legislation enacted in 1997–98 strengthened regional tripartite structures in two areas: promotion of employment, and health and safety at work. The December 1997 Act on Protection Against Unemployment and Employment Promotion mandated the participation of regional tripartite forums in employment promotion programs, to complement the activities of the three national tripartite structures: the National Council on Unemployment Protection and Employment Promotion, the National

[3] National Program on Temporary Employment (in Bulgarian), 1994 (Sofia: Ministry of Labor and Social Affairs).

Council on Vocational Training, and the Supervisory Board of the National Employment Office. The regional tripartite forums are most active in cases involving mass layoffs. Employers are required to provide two months' notice of mass layoffs (defined as layoffs of more than 10 percent of personnel) to the forums, as well as to the local administration and the National Employment Office. The regional tripartite structures, together with the local administration, the National Employment Office, and the employer, are charged with setting up special employment programs to provide professional retraining for laid-off workers.

The Act on Health and Safety at Work, adopted in December 1997, mandated the creation of specialized regional councils on work conditions, to complement the work of the two national tripartite bodies in this area: the National Council on Work Conditions and the Managing Board of the Work Conditions Fund. The regional councils on work conditions adopt regional programs for improvements in work conditions, to be financed by the Working Conditions Fund. They also discuss and implement activities aimed at improvements in health and safety at work in separate companies or the region as a whole.

The 1999 Law on Regional Development further broadened regional tripartism. It mandated the creation of district development councils, with representatives of local government, social partners, NGOs, and other civil society organizations. These councils are to perform consultative functions in the elaboration and fulfillment of a seven-year District Development Program for the development of each of the twenty-eight districts in Bulgaria. The plan includes initiatives at the district and local levels, such as activities stemming from the district employment programs, most of which are financed by the state budget.

Two case studies of regional social dialogue are further discussed in this section: Vratza and Blagoevgrad. In Vratza, and some other regions, the tripartite consultative committees were incorporated into already existing tripartite "social dialogue" forums, and the local social partners were committed to maintaining social partnership. In other regions, such as Blagoevgrad, which had UDF-dominated local self-government and mayors committed to drastic neoliberal restructuring, tripartism developed with more difficulty, as a rule. Tripartite "social peace" forums generally did not develop in such regions, but the law required the creation of tripartite consultative committees on employment issues. Their activities, however, were reduced to the procedures that were stipulated in national legislation or government decrees, such as the formal signing or rejection of the local administration's proposals within the Program on Temporary Employment.

Social Dialogue in Vratza

Vratza is a midsized city in northwest Bulgaria with a population of about 100,000 and a legacy of several huge heavy industry complexes that, since

1989, have been difficult to restructure or privatize. These included a military plant, a cast-iron foundry, a producer of metal-cutting machines, a cement company, and huge chemical and meat-processing companies. The accent in the restructuring policy of the region naturally fell on the demonopolization and restructuring of these huge state companies. Foreign investment was scarce, however, and the region has had to rely mainly on its own resources.[4]

Although by 1995 the region had begun a gradual recovery from its economic crisis, the average rate of growth was still low: the growth rate in March 1995 was only 70 percent of that registered in 1994.[5] Since 1989, unemployment has been the major source of increasing social tension in the region. Employment, including the private sector, dropped from 56,000 in 1987 to 41,500 in 1995. The number of those unemployed began to decrease, however, with the development of the private sector and the opening of trade services. While 14,000 to 15,000 unemployed were officially registered at the end of 1990, by June 1995 their number had fallen to 6,236. Around 6,000 to 7,000 private companies have absorbed some of the unemployed in the region. By January 1998 the number of unemployed in Vratza again had increased, to 8,471, while in January 1999 their number decreased to 7,620.[6]

Vratza's regional social partners are the municipal council, the local structures of Podkrepa and CITUB, and the local structures of several employers' organizations. After the 1995 local elections, the municipal council had twenty-eight counselors from the UDF and twenty-six from the BSP, while the rest (eleven) were from the political center (the Agrarian Party, social democrats, and independents). Since 1989, union coverage in the region fell drastically from the levels under state socialism, but remained relatively high, about 62 percent. The regional organization of CITUB has 42,000 members, including pensioners and unemployed, while Podkrepa's has about 4,000 to 5,000. Employers were initially represented in the region by NUEM, which existed only in the first few years after 1989, and had sixty-five members – economic managers – from Vratza. Later, the Union of Private Economic Enterprising, the Bulgarian Industrial Association, and the Regional Chamber of Commerce and Industry created regional structures.

When the national recommendations for the development of social dialogue at lower levels were issued in 1990, the unions in Vratza began to pressure economic managers in the territory to form themselves into an organization that could serve as a legitimate counterpart for the conclusion of a

4 See in Stomanjarski 1998.

5 Data from the Vratza Regional Statistical Office.

6 Vratza Labor Office, *Information Bulletin*, 1999; "Opityt na Bjuro po truda-Vratza v rabotata pri masovo osvobozhdavane i prerazpredelenie na rabotnata sila" (The Experience of the Vratza Labor Office in Mass Layoffs and the Relocation of the Work Force) (mimeo, 1999).

regional tripartite agreement and the creation of a regional tripartite commission. The Regional Council of CITUB called on its enterprise union organizations to refuse to engage in enterprise bargaining or sign collective agreements on layoffs in enterprises until the managers organized themselves into a regional employers' structure. At that time, union approval was a legal precondition for layoffs, and the refusal to sign agreements on layoffs forced the enterprise directors to organize a regional structure, of NUEM, and to sign a regional tripartite agreement with unions and local government. As with national developments, the regional structure of Podkrepa was initially reluctant to engage in tripartite talks with the official unions and the local BSP dominated government. The Vratza regional tripartite agreement was prepared mainly by representatives of CITUB, and only during the second round of negotiations did Podkrepa CL become involved.

The Vratza Regional Tripartite Agreement was signed in April 1991 by the Vratza Provisional Executive Committee (local self-government), the regional structures of CITUB and Podkrepa CL, and the regional structures of NUEM and the Union of Private Economic Enterprising.[7] The regional agreement put special emphasis on two sets of issues: employment and unemployment, and the resolution of certain social problems in the region. In terms of employment, the social partners agreed to facilitate research on the local labor market and new job openings in the region and to guarantee control over the implementation of the procedure for layoffs in companies and enterprises, adopted in March 1991 by the National Tripartite Commission. They agreed that mass layoffs should be discussed in the regional tripartite commission. The Union of Private Economic Enterprising was tasked with combatting regional unemployment through several projects that provided employment in the newly opened private companies. The local government, the local labor office, and the employers in Vratza negotiated to organize retraining for laid-off workers, to encourage and initiate early retirement, to create conditions for employee capital privatization, and to create special facilities for the disabled. The second part of the agreement, on the resolution of some social problems in the region, provided for increased production of consumer goods and communal services, development of private initiatives in agriculture, effective price control in the private sector, and control over prices observed by the Council of Ministers. The local government further agreed to facilitate housing and new home construction in Vratza. For their part, the unions agreed to control strike tensions in local companies and enterprises.

The Vratza regional tripartite agreement provided for the formation of a *Regional Commission for Coordination of Interests* to monitor im-

[7] Sporazumenie (Agreement) (Vratza, April 1991).

plementation. The commission was made up of the signatories of the agreement. Its goals focused on the establishment of dialogue and negotiations in the region as the basic elements of social partnership, on the coordination of the activities of the social partners for the fulfillment of the regional tripartite agreement, and on consultations about the social and economic policy of the local government.

Regional tripartism in Vratza developed alongside national tripartism. With each new national tripartite body, a corresponding regional tripartite body was founded in Vratza. In 1992, following the creation of the National Council for Social Partnership by the UDF government, a *Regional Council for Social Partnership* replaced the Regional Commission for Coordination of Interests. The resolution of local problems concerning work conditions, social insurance, and living standards remained the major focus of the renewed social dialogue in Vratza. The regional council was closely linked with the national tripartite council. It had to submit opinions to the National Council for Social Partnership regarding draft normative documents and changes in labor legislation on problems of labor, social insurance, and living standards, as well as proposals for stabilizing the social and economic conditions in the country and preserving social peace. The council was chaired by the deputy mayor of Vratza. Standing commissions and temporary working groups were created covering the same range of issues as those of the National Council. In 1992 the Regional Council for Social Partnership held twelve sessions over a period of approximately four months. The need to conclude collective agreements covering the public sphere and municipal companies accounts for the higher level of commitment to social dialogue shown by the Vratza social partners, compared with national tripartism.

Following the Berov government's creation of the National Council for Tripartite Cooperation in 1993, a new tripartite agreement was signed[8] and a new tripartite forum was set up in Vratza: *the Vratza Regional Council for Tripartite Cooperation.* Its goals included consultations and cooperation in resolving conflicts stemming from labor and labor relations, inadequate social insurance, and poor living standards in the region.[9] Five working commissions were formed, on (1) Employment, Unemployment, Training and Retraining; (2) Privatization; (3) Prices and Incomes; (4) Health Care; and (5) Education. When national social dialogue broke down in April 1994, the regional social partnership in Vratza continued to function with no interruption, because of the need to negotiate salaries in the public sphere – health care, education, and culture – half of which are secured by the local budget.

[8] Sporazumenie (Agreement) (Vratza, 19 October 1993).

[9] Pravila za rabota na Obshtinskija syvet za tristranno sytrudnichestvo – Vratza (Regulations for the Work of the Regional Council for Tripartite Cooperation – Vratza), Vratza, 1993.

Eight social dialogue meetings were held in Vratza in the year of its emergence, 1991; eight in 1992; twenty-four in 1993; six in each of the next three years; four in 1997; and ten in 1998.[10] In an attempt to reduce industrial and social tensions in the region arising from the processes of regional and national restructuring, the social partners have addressed several big issues, including problems in specific local companies, regional unemployment and employment issues, and collective bargaining in municipal companies and the public sphere (health, education, and culture). Issues of local regional restructuring were also discussed, though not so intensely.

Enterprise Conflicts

Most negotiations have been concerned with concrete problems in the local companies, both state and municipal. Of the forty-one companies whose problems were discussed in the council in the years 1991–98, fourteen were municipal and twenty-seven state. The most frequent issues in municipal companies were requests for the replacement of management, reorganization, and concrete financial and economic issues. While the state companies were in principal subordinate to their respective ministries, they sometimes initiated meetings and discussions with the local government for the resolution of specific problems. Tripartite discussions concerning state companies focused most frequently on financial-economic issues, reorganization and labor problems, union requests for the replacement of directors and changes in the management boards of companies, and health and safety issues. The Vratza regional tripartite forum is reported to have played a considerable role mediating many strike-alert situations in these companies.

Broad public consensus was needed for the dismissal of company directors and members of management boards, and the polarization in Bulgaria, particularly in Vratza, between excommunists and pro-UDF parties, institutions, and organizations has forced such personnel and cadre issues onto the agenda of the tripartite council. Such discussions were most frequent in 1993, when many company directors (old *nomenklatura*) were replaced by the UDF government, and in 1995, with the formation of a BSP government and a new round of management replacements. To avoid accusations of political purges, the political parties and the local government in Vratza refused to replace managers directly and used the Vratza tripartite council instead. The council worked out criteria for the replacement of directors, and when the social partners could reach consensus they submitted proposed dismissals to the government.

As transformation succeeded, the focus of activities shifted from personnel replacements to more creative local initiatives that could speed up the process of regional reform. In November 1998, the CITUB trade unions

[10] Minutes of the Sessions of the Vratza Tripartite Council; interviews with members of the council, 1995–99.

in the region, with support from CITUB's central leadership, formed a non-governmental organization – the so-called Civic Initiative for the Salvation of Himko Company-Vratza – to engage the Vratza population in activities to speed up the privatization of Himko.[11]

Regional Employment

The second major area of interest and collaboration among the social partners has been regional unemployment and employment. The 1991–98 discussions, which have included the regional labor office, focused on trends in regional unemployment and the regional labor market and on the 1993 National Program on Temporary Employment.[12] In 1994, some 2,900 people were offered new jobs through the labor office.[13] In 1998–99, this trend has stabilized.[14] In September 1998 the Vratza municipality concluded a separate agreement with the National Employment Office for joint activities in the realization of the National Program on Temporary Employment.[15] While in some other regions the Program on Temporary Employment has led to the creation of specialized tripartite forums on employment issues, in Vratza, the existing tripartite forum took on this additional function.

The social partners discussed the formation of an alliance for employment and the implementation of the Program for Temporary Employment. The social partners have been particularly concerned to assure that the program does not produce layoffs of permanently employed persons and their replacement with temporary workers; that new jobs are not linked to public works, which have to be financed by the budget; and that the jobs produced improve municipal activities and the environment in Vratza.

In the fall of 1998, the social partners worked to create an Alliance for Employment. Under an initiative of the German government and with the aid of German experts, two regional alliances for unemployed persons – for professional training and retraining, public works, and encouragement of self-employment – were created in the Rhodopes region, in the cities of Madan and Rudozem, in the mid-1990s. Encouraged by the success of these alliances, the government issued a resolution/decision for the creation of

[11] Interview data.

[12] Ministry of Labor and Social Policy: Metodichesko rykovodstvo za razrabotvane na regionalna programa za zaetost (Recommendations for the Development of a Regional Employment Program), 1998.

[13] Programa za osigurjavane na zaetost na bezrabotni litza v region Vratza (Program for the Provision of Employment for Unemployed in the Region of Vratza); interview data.

[14] Explanatory Note to the Request for the Creation of New Jobs under the Program for the Creation of Temporary Employment for Unemployed during the Winter Months of December 1998–30 April 1999, of Vratza Municipality.

[15] Contract for Joint Activity with Regard to the National Program for Temporary Employment, Sofia, 28.09.1998.

such alliances in all regions with unemployment problems. The law on employment later regulated the creation of such alliances, with funding from EU programs.

After discussing the experience of employment alliances in Pleven, Madan, and other cities, the Vratza Regional Council for Tripartite Cooperation decided to form a local alliance in September 1998, and the company was registered in early 1999.[16] The local self-government, companies from the region (state, municipal, and private), banks, regional trade union organizations of CITUB and Podkrepa, local/company trade union organizations, regional employers' organizations, and municipal councils from the region all assisted. The Vratza Alliance for Employment gathered initial capital of more than 5 million leva (some $2,800), provided by the Vratza municipality, Podkrepa, and CITUB. It is further financed from the Professional Training and Unemployment Fund, from the municipal budget, and from resources provided by some employers, mainly municipal companies. The alliance, according to guidelines from the National Employment Office, could function as a limited liability company providing employment to some 190 unemployed from the region. It worked out a Program for Securing Employment for Unemployed Persons in the municipality, which was approved by the Ministry of Labor and Social Policy, and the National Employment Office.

Collective Bargaining in Municipal Firms and the Public Sphere

A third major area of activity and negotiation among the social partners in Vratza concerned the employment relationship in municipal companies, and in this respect the regional social dialogue represents a typical collective bargaining process, with the local government acting as an employer. The process ends with the conclusion of a collective agreement, such as the one signed on 19 October 1993 by the local administration and the two trade unions. The aim of that agreement was to create a framework for the conclusion of contracts between unions and employers in municipal companies. A consensus was reached that conflicts arising over collective agreements in municipal companies should be resolved in the tripartite council. The regional agreement regulated wages and inflation adjustments, work conditions (especially health and safety), social and cultural services, social insurance, privatization policy, and other issues. It was renewed in January 1995.

Wages in the public sphere are 50 percent subsidized from the municipal budget, and this involves the conclusion of annual collective agreements. The tripartite council created two specialized commissions to address problems and negotiate agreements concerning health care and educational

[16] Archive data; interview data.

units. Local self-government and the unions sign the agreements, which create frameworks for the conclusion of collective contracts in local schools and health-care units. Pluralization on the union side has created some problems in the process.

Regional Restructuring

Some more specific issues of economic restructuring were also discussed in the regional tripartite council, such as the municipal budget deficit and concrete problems of the local infrastructure. The privatization of municipal enterprises emerged as an issue in June 1993. Despite the elaborate regional program for privatization of municipal enterprises, the privatization process has advanced slowly in Vratza.[17]

The decisions and networkings of the regional tripartite body in Vratza point to the broader civic character of local tripartism. In addition to the regional social partners, the work of the tripartite forum has involved management and unions of local, state, and municipal firms through joint discussions of their concrete problems and some entrepreneurial initiatives. The regional council has also referred concrete problems of the region to higher state organs and the national tripartite council. These problems have most often involved requests by local unions for the replacement of directors in state firms, but have also included regional unemployment, the deteriorating financial situation of local companies, and health and safety issues.

Social Dialogue in Blagoevgrad

Under state socialism more than 30 percent of Blagoevgrad's jobs were in electronics. With the dissolution of the CMEA markets, the industry collapsed, and 80 to 90 percent of the employees in electronics were laid off. Unemployment in the Blagoevgrad region was among the highest in the country and produced serious conflicts between company directors and the trade unions.

A tripartite commission was established in Blagoevgrad in 1990, during the period when local power was controlled by temporary executive committees made up of representatives of the major political forces. Functioning until 1992, it involved the regional union organizations, the local government, and an alliance of twenty to thirty enterprise directors representing local employers.

Initially, the commission focused on rising social tensions and conflicts in the region arising from management dismissals and illegal privatization

[17] Programa za privatizatsija na obshtinskite predprijatija v obshtina Vratza (Program for the Privatization of Municipal Enterprises in the Vratza Region), Vratza, November 1993; Information Regarding the Fulfillment of the Municipal Program for Privatization in 1994 and the Measures Undertaken by the Municipal Council, Vratza 1994.

activities. In 1990 and 1991, the unions, mainly Podkrepa, called for dismissals of company directors, and many of the problems discussed were personnel and cadre issues. State executives and trade unions were intertwined in a political unity for supervision and control over local companies. The tripartite commission in Blagoevgrad ceased to exist as soon as the UDF government, with its firm neoliberal and antiunion policies, took power, in November 1991.

Tripartite dialogue was restored in Blagoevgrad at the beginning of 1993, in response to the Program on Temporary Employment. The dialogue was reduced, however, to formal signings of protocols about new job openings for temporary employment. *The Blagoevgrad Council on Temporary Employment Issues* comprised six members: two local counselors from the local self-government, representatives of Podkrepa and CITUB, and representatives of the Bulgarian Industrial Association and the Union for Private Economic Enterprising. The major concern of the unions was that the temporary openings not replace permanent jobs.

The unions demanded the creation of a permanent tripartite organ in place of the temporary employment council, which did not offer substantial opportunities for local tripartite contacts and negotiations. While their demand was not met, the unions were invited to participate in the sessions of the local self-government organ, mainly when election procedures for managers of municipal firms and privatization of municipal companies were discussed, and were able to submit their own proposals at these sessions. Thus, local initiative could compensate, to a degree, for the lack of a permanent tripartite organ in the region.

6.2. Regional Social Dialogue in Poland

Regional social dialogue in Poland emerged in response to employment/unemployment issues. The December 1989 law on employment regulated the creation of a national corporatist body, the Main Employment Council, as well as the establishment of provincial and municipal employment councils. These territorial employment councils complemented the efforts of the national Main Employment Council to deal with unemployment. Relatedly, local commissions for labor protection were created to complement the activities of the National Council for Labor Protection. These commissions include representatives of local government administration, self-government, the state labor inspection, trade unions, and employers' organizations. The commissions discuss mostly labor safety issues but also some broader issues. Such commissions existed in thirty-seven of the forty-nine *voivod*ships (provinces) that existed under the old territorial administrative structure. As the new administrative-territorial structure moved to sixteen *voivod*ships, changes in the structure of these commissions were also initiated.

Second, the Enterprise Pact, which was concluded by the social partners in 1992, stipulated the creation of regional social dialogue forums to negotiate regional collective agreements governing wages and the employment relationship in the public sector (education, health care, culture). And finally, in some regions with particularly difficult restructuring and unemployment problems, local actors instituted social dialogues to address difficult problems in situations of rising social tensions. The experience of Lodz, one of Poland's main industrial centers, illustrates how all three forms of regional social dialogue can help to alleviate economic and social problems.

Emergence of Social Dialogue in Lodz

The smallest of the forty-nine provinces (*voivod*ships) in Poland, at least until the administrative-territorial reform of 1999,[18] Lodz is a major industrial center, concentrated on textiles, mainly wool and cotton. During state socialism its textiles and clothing dominated textile markets in the CMEA. The collapse of these markets created severe economic problems for textile producers.[19] Of all the branches of Poland's economy, textiles suffered the biggest decline – 40 percent in 1989 – and Lodz experienced regional unemployment of 17 to 20 percent, among the highest in Poland. The 300,000 jobs remaining in the textile sector in 1996 were only 40 percent of the pre-1989 employment, and Lodz faced extraordinarily difficult restructuring problems.

There are four major local actors in Lodz: political authorities, or local state administration, local self-government, and political groupings; trade unions; organizations of employers and entrepreneurs; and professional and academic communities. At the regional level, representation is not specified by law, but since the 1991 Trade Union Act requires that local governments consult *all* union and employer organizations on local legislative documents, any union or employer organization can participate in regional social dialogue.

Following a reform in 1990, local administration in Poland was split, and functions were divided between the *voivod* (provincial governor) and the president of the city council (local self-government). As a result, two

[18] The administrative-territorial reform from early 1999 enlarged the Lodz *voivod*ship: Now Lodz is one of sixteen larger *voivod*ships, absorbing parts of Mazowsze and Piotrkowsk *voivod*ships. So-called *powiaty* were created as administrative-territorial units of the sixteen *voivod*ships.

[19] The Polish economy began to shift its exports from the former CMEA markets to the EC countries. In 1992 Poland's export to Czechoslovakia declined by some 20 percent, and to Hungary by about one third; Czechoslovakia participated with only 4 to 5 percent and Hungary with less than 1 percent in the Polish foreign trade. See in Gorzelak 1994: 88. The economic recession in the first years of Polish transformation was increased by the opening of Polish economy to foreign competitors, price liberalization, and restrictive monetary and fiscal policies.

different administrations at two different levels emerged: state administration at the level of *voivod*ship, and self-government at the municipal level (*gmina*). The *voivod* and his administration act as representatives of central state administration. The *voivod* is directly appointed by the prime minister and has considerable powers. In June 1996 the Polish Sejm (Parliament) approved a reform limiting the government's role in the economy, streamlining decision-making, and strengthening the position of provincial governors. Control over most state firms was to be transferred from ministries to provincial governors, leaving only some 200 strategic, large companies under direct central government supervision.[20]

The position of local government in the social dialogue has further shifted as political parties have exchanged power in both local and national elections. In the first local elections, in 1990, the pro-Solidarity parties such as LPO (Lodzkie Porozumenie Obywatelskie) prevailed. But the next local elections, in 1994, marked a shift toward the left, and in Lodz the ruling SLD-PSL coalition in association with Nowa Lodz (Unia Wolnosci and others) and LPO-Lega Lodzka (National and Christian Union (ZChN) and others) was victorious. The 1993 parliamentary elections marked a similar shift in the local state administration as well. The 1997 parliamentary elections, the November 1998 local elections, and the new administrative territorial reform implemented from 1 January 1999 also changed the structure of Lodz's government. A so-called self-government parliament (*sejmik samorzandowy*) governs the new Lodz *voivod*ship. It comprises fifty-five councilors: nineteen from AWS, twenty-four from SLD, eight from PSL and four from the Freedom Union (UW).[21] At the level of *powiat*, the so-called Municipal Council (*Rada Miasta*) is made up of eighty councilors: forty-four from SLD, and of them nine from OPZZ; twenty-six from AWS; and ten from the UW. The president of the Lodz Municipal Council is from SLD.

The professional communities in the dialogue include societies of engineers, economists, managers, and other professional and academic groups. They are not unified locally in a single organization but play a prominent role as individual or group consultants, especially to the *voivod*'s office.

The two biggest unions in the country, Solidarity and OPZZ, have regional offices in Lodz. Solidarity–Region Lodz claimed 60,000 members in 1996, with seventeen branch sections and union organizations in 700 enterprises. In 1999 it claimed 45,000 members in 565 enterprises. The headquarters of Solidarity's Branch Secretariat for Textile Industry are also in Lodz. In 1996, OPZZ–Region Lodz claimed 200,000 members united in twenty-three branch sections and in more than 200 enterprises. In 1999, its membership had dropped to 65,000, including 8,500 pensioners in the

[20] *OMRI Daily Digest*, 24 June 1996.
[21] "The Assembly Has Been Elected," *Wiadomosci Dnia*, 21 October 1998.

pensioners' section. The headquarters of OPZZ's Federation of Trade Unions from Light Industry are also in Lodz. In 1999 the federation had members in 220 enterprises – some 40,000 out of a total of about 140,000 employed in light industry.

Relations between the OPZZ and Solidarity unions, on the one hand, and the local government, on the other, are politicized and depend on the composition of the latter. Thus, OPZZ leaders say that relations were much better with the SLD *voivod* before the victory of the AWS in the 1997 parliamentary elections. Solidarity–Region Lodz, in contrast, met more frequently with the Lodz *voivod* before 1993 and after 1997.

Employers are represented by the Lodz Regional Union of Employers at the Confederation of Polish Employers, created in August 1991, which, at the end of June 1994, united fifty-two member organizations with 32,264 employees.[22] Unlike unions, employers of the Lodz region have no representatives in the Polish Parliament or in the local self-government. However, they have worked with the unions to force the local government to speed up the process of local restructuring. Employers even supported Solidarity's protest against the excess wage tax (*popiwek*), and for four months in 1993 they increased wages in their enterprises and refused to pay the tax.[23]

In the process of formulating programs for the development and restructuring of the Lodz region, gaps and conflicts of authority have developed between these local actors over decentralization of power and the extent of state intervention in restructuring (Buchner-Jeziorska and Kulpinska 1994). Tensions within the elite have been joined with direct pressure from employees. In March 1993, the Solidarity Regional Board organized a forty-eight-hour general strike with the support of the OPZZ to mark the culmination of several weeks of protest. The strike was the first in Poland in which workers demanded an acceleration of economic change and local restructuring. In the spring of 1993 it resulted in the creation of various specialized agencies (administrative and "market-oriented") and forums for periodic public discussions. Local tensions and initiatives in Lodz have led to national parliamentary debates and the appointment of a Government Plenipotentiary for Restructuring the Lodz Region and the creation of a corporatist-like Regional Council for Restructuring the Lodz Region, which advises and consults with the government plenipotentiary to facilitate the process of regional restructuring.

[22] Regional Union of Employers in Lodz: Information Bulletin no. 2, Lodz, December 1994, p. 1; Statute of the Union of Employers in Lodz.

[23] The exccess wage tax was abolished in 1994, as a result of negotiations in the National Tripartite Commission for Socio-Economic Issues and the adoption of the Law on the Increase of Average Wages through a System of Negotiations. The excess wage tax was an important element of the Balcerowicz plan, and in the very beginning of transformation it was necessary to control inflation.

Protest actions were thus a significant factor in the emergence of spontaneous – not regulated by national legislation or government directives – local tripartism. In addition to issues of regional restructuring, the regional social dialogue covers the more normatively regulated issues of employment and unemployment, and collective bargaining over the employment relationship in municipal enterprises and the public sphere.

Combatting Unemployment

Following the collapse of the textile industry, Lodz was officially recognized as a region particularly hard hit by unemployment, and the right to unemployment benefits was extended from twelve to eighteen months locally. Additional resources from the state budget were also directed to Lodz for the development of active employment policies, including retraining and support for small businesses initiated by the unemployed (Borkowska and Bohdziewicz 1994; Gorzelak 1994). Since 1994 the number of unemployed has gradually decreased. In June 1996 the rate of unemployment dropped to 18 percent. The drop lost the Lodz region its right to extended unemployment benefits, but under pressure from trade unions, the benefits were kept until the end of December 1996. At the end of December 1998 unemployment in Lodz had already dropped to 11 percent.[24]

The Lodz Provincial Employment Council was formed in 1991. The provincial (*voivod*ship) and regional (*rejon*) employment councils in Poland were developed as advisory-consulting bodies to the *voivod* and the provincial and regional administration, respectively. They track employment trends in their area closely, assess the efficacy of the Labor Fund's expenditures, and advise on financial plans drawn up by provincial and regional labor offices. The law of 14 December 1994 on Employment and Prevention of Unemployment enlarged the legal basis of these councils and specified their role in achieving full and rational use of the labor force. The provincial employment councils have sixteen members, drawn equally from the provincial organizations of unions, employers, the state administration, and the self-governing communes. The 1994 Law on Employment and Prevention of Unemployment gives the opportunity to organizations, such as scientific associations, that are not represented in the employment councils to participate in their sessions. The chair of the provincial employment council is the *voivod*. The members of the provincial employment councils are appointed by the Minister of Labor and Social Policy, and their mandate is four years.

The Lodz Provincial Employment Council comprised sixteen members, four each from the local government administration, including the *voivod*; the territorial self-management; the trade unions – Solidarity and OPZZ; and employers, represented by directors from the biggest local companies.

[24] Voivodship Labor Office in Lodz: Early Warning Report of the Labor Market, 1991; Voivodship Labor Office in Lodz: Analysis and Evaluation of the Situation in the Voivodship Labor Market in 1998 (Lodz, March 1999).

Initially, OPZZ and Solidarity each had two representatives out of a quota of four; after 1994, following the change in local power, three members from OPZZ and one from Solidarity sat on the Lodz council.

Representatives of organizations, organs, and institutions dealing with the problems under discussion can be invited to the plenary sessions. For example, the *voivod* has invited members of trade unions and employers from big, medium-sized, and small enterprises to participate in the work of the Lodz Provincial Employment Council. Experts from Lodz University and representatives of banks have also been invited to attend. The council has four working groups: one oversees the employment of foreigners; another controls the activities of the local and provincial labor office; a third looks at education and professional improvement of employees in the labor offices; and the last discusses interventions. The working groups meet every two weeks.

The Lodz Provincial Employment Council holds regular meetings at least once in three months, but it was most active immediately after its creation and during the most acute period of labor market and unemployment problems in the region: It had eight meetings in 1993, compared with four in 1994, six in 1995, three in 1996, four in 1997, and three in 1998.[25] The labor market situation in the Lodz region was discussed at every meeting of the provincial council. The distribution of resources from the Labor Fund, in accordance with a Program for Active Forms of Combatting Unemployment, has been another major area of deliberations.[26] These issues were discussed at more than twenty sessions, and included activities such as the financing of the Fifth Students' Labor Fair in Lodz, a Labor Newspaper, and a vocational training center in one of the local cities. The provincial council worked out criteria for the allocation of work certificates to foreigners and loans to unemployed persons seeking to start a small business, and adopted a program for the retraining of unemployed persons.

The use of resources from the State Rehabilitation Fund and the Guaranteed Workers' Benefits Fund are another major subject of deliberations in the provincial employment council. According to the Act of 29 December 1993, concerning the protection of workers' claims in the event of insolvency of their employers, workers' claims that are not satisfied should be paid by the Guaranteed Workers' Benefits Fund, administered by the Central Labor Office. The fund's board, which approves the financial

[25] Archive data: minutes from the sessions of the Lodz Employment Council.

[26] The Labor Fund is administered by the Minister of Labor and Social Policy, and pays for unemployment benefits, the costs of training and retraining unemployed workers, social insurance contributions, loans for the creation of new jobs, vocational training programs for apprentices, and other projects. The regional labor offices can grant loans from the fund to establishments for the creation of additional jobs for the unemployed and to unemployed individuals to start a business. Each year, the employment councils decide on the distribution of resources from the Labor Fund, focusing especially on programs for the promotion of active forms of employment.

plan for the fund and reports on its implementation, is composed of representative employers' organizations (two thirds) and of representative trade union organizations appointed by the Minister of Labor and Social Policy and discusses the distribution of resources to alleviate the pain of enterprise closures in Lodz region.

According to its members, the Lodz Provincial Employment Council functions well. The *voivod*s, regardless of their political affiliation, have considered it a very effective consultative organ. The council has, however, gone beyond simple consultation to acquire control through its active distributive policies. Some tensions and conflicts of interest have arisen between the provincial and the regional levels, since councils on both levels may create independent programs to deal with unemployment.[27]

The administrative-territorial reform in effect from 1 January 1999 led to changes in the structure and organization of labor offices and the tripartite employment councils. Now the employment councils operate at three levels: national (Main Employment Office), provincial (provincial employment councils), and municipality (*powiat*, where municipal employment councils replaced regional employment councils). The provincial councils became consultative-advisory organs not to the *voivod* but to the *marszal* of the *voivod*ship who chairs the employment council and is directly appointed by the Minister of Labor. From 1 January 2000 the provincial councils are to have fifteen members, representative of five, rather than four, major groups: organizations of trade unions, organizations of employers, the *voivod*ship administration, the territorial self-government organs at the lower levels of *powiat* and *gmina*, and all agricultural chambers acting on the territory of the *voivod*ship. Members of the provincial employment councils are appointed by the *marszal* of the *voivod*ship. The employment councils at the level of *powiat* from 1 January 2000 will have twelve members: an equal number from the organizations of trade unions and employers' organizations, the territorial self-government at the level of *powiat* and *gmina*, and the agricultural chambers. The chairman of the employment council at the level of *powiat* is appointed by the *voivod*, while the members of the council are appointed by its chairman, from among the organizations specified above.

Regional Restructuring

The restructuring potential of Lodz is dominated by both constraints and opportunities.[28] The collapse of the textile industry brought a structural

[27] Interview with Krzysztof Kaczmarek, director of Labor Market Department at the Lodz Provincial Labor Office, Lodz, May 1995; interview with Marek Kostanek, deputy director of the Lodz Provincial Labor Office, Lodz, March 1999.

[28] "The Lodz Voivodship: Now and in the Year 1999" (Regional Council of Solidarity – Lodz Region).

crisis that made any action difficult. Unemployment rates were very high, and earnings were low. Despite the crisis, industry still dominates Lodz. At the end of 1994, manufacturing activities, with power, gas, and water supply systems, yielded over 78 percent of the total revenue of all enterprises, and industry accounted for 66 percent of total employment. In 1997, light industry (dominated by textiles) produced 38 percent of total manufacturing revenue and an average of 57 percent of manufacturing employment.[29]

With the gradual recovery of its dominant textile enterprises (and the development of underground textile production), Lodz was able to recover from its crisis. The survival and restructuring of individual enterprises varies depending on their specific situations, on how big the decline in the enterprise production was, and on the specific strategies for survival developed by the individual enterprises. Lodz has also been helped by a high level of urbanization and development and good proximity to the capital. The region also has a flourishing private sector, especially in the area of services and small-scale manufacturing. The private sector accounts for 58 percent of industrial revenues and 57 percent of employment, and Lodz had the fourth fastest pace of privatization in the country, 14 percent, for the period 1989–91 (Gorzelak 1994: 86). In terms of foreign capital, Lodz has a relatively large number of international and joint venture companies (second and sixth, respectively, in Poland). Strategic location and human capital, as well as development projects, are the basis for the regional transformation of Lodz into a European transport and communications junction.

To summarize, Lodz is a typical urban agglomeration with a high potential for restructuring. However, the old dominant industry, still in trouble, is a heavy burden on the region. Massive unemployment, overrepresentation of narrowly educated workers, and a worn-down urban infrastructure jeopardize the city's chance to take full advantage of its potential. That is why any restructuring program for Lodz has an inherent contradiction: It is desirable to preserve the textile sector, but the perpetuation of a monoindustrial structure is a source of regular economic crises and social tension.

A draft of a regional program for restructuring was jointly written by the local administration and Solidarity, with the assistance of the Department of Economics at Lodz University.[30] The project was presented to the national government in December 1992, and most of it was accepted in the spring of 1993. The program later became a pattern for restructuring other cities in Poland.[31]

[29] Voivodship Labor Office in Lodz: Analysis and Evaluation of the Situation in the Voivodship Labor Market in 1998 (Lodz: March 1999).

[30] Regional Council of Solidarity–Lodz Region: Notes on the Restructuring Program of Lodz Region Proposed by the Vice-Voivod Boguslaw Grabowski, Lodz, 30.06.1993; Office for Restructuring the Lodz Region: Program for Restructuring the Lodz Region: Synthesis (Lodz: June 1993).

[31] Interview with Waldemar Bohdanowicz, former *voivod* of Lodz, Lodz, May 1995.

An important accent in the Program for Economic Restructuring of Lodz was an attempt to change the branch structure of industry. The program emphasized the development of other industries and sectors, such as food processing, construction, and equipment. It also stressed training for new professions and job openings. The OPZZ Federation of Trade Unions in Light Industry, with headquarters in Lodz, had a very strong textile lobby nationwide and opposed the reduction of textile jobs in the region.[32] Solidarity favored the restructuring plan, but demanded bigger structural changes, such as balancing a loss of 1,000 jobs in textile with a gain of 800 jobs in other industries.[33]

With living standards plummeting, unemployment rising past 20 percent, and the city's light industry approaching death, Solidarity–Region Lodz realized in 1993 that the problem could not be resolved with local effort alone. It asked the Suchocka government for a regional program for the restructuring and development.[34] The Polish government attended to the model of EU countries that had developed regional programs for the equalization of levels of development, and in January 1993 started talks with Solidarity–Region Lodz to elaborate a regional program for restructuring. While the government emphasized that existing legislation recognized no regional policies, Solidarity persuaded the government to put local state enterprises under the governance of the *voivod* on the grounds that it would be much easier to hold discussions at the local level than in the central ministries. There was no discussion of funding centers of modernization and modernization of the industry because the state budget had no resources available. The union did, however, demand the restructuring of the debts of the local enterprises so that they could continue to operate, if on a reduced level.

When the government refused to restructure debt, the union decided to strike communications and transport. Fearing that the government could use a general strike as an excuse to close those enterprises that were in difficult financial situations, the union opted for a forty-eight-hour step-by-step strike. The government initiated negotiations with Solidarity–Region Lodz,[35] and on 8 January 1993, Jacek Kuron, the Minister of Labor, organized a round table for the restructuring of Lodz region at the Ministry of Labor and Social Policy, with participants from the *voivod*ship, local self-government, employers in Lodz, and the two unions, Solidarity and OPZZ.

[32] Interview with Zbigniew Kaniewski, chairman of OPZZ Federation of Trade Unions in Light Industry, Parliament member, and member of the Regional Council for Restructuring the Lodz Region and the Lodz Employment Council, Lodz, May 1995.

[33] Interview with Marek Kostanek, chairman of the NSZZ Solidarity Branch on Light Industry, Lodz, May 1995.

[34] Interview with Janusz Tomaszewski, chairman of NSZZ Solidarnosc–Region Lodz, Lodz, May 1995, August 1996.

[35] Interview with Waldemar Krenc, chairman of NSZZ Solidarnosc–Region Lodz, March 1999.

The round table produced a consensus that the government should appoint a plenipotentiary responsible for the restructuring of the region. The plenipotentiary was to prepare a program for restructuring the region and develop a strategy for the next ten years and was to seek resources in the state budget to pay for initiatives in Lodz.

The Regional Council for Restructuring the Lodz Region was founded in March 1993, following the Solidarity-led forty-eight-hour strike and the government's decision of March 1993 to appoint a plenipotentiary for the restructuring of Lodz Region.[36] It was intended as an advisory-consultative organ to the plenipotentiary in the development of plans for the implementation of the plenipotentiary's program. Its main tasks are to facilitate the restructuring of the Lodz region and to resolve problems arising as restructuring progresses.[37] More specifically, the council is responsible for working out a regional strategy as it relates to the central government, developing proposals for intervention, facilitating the creation of institutional and legal conditions for the resolution of systemic problems arising from the regional process of restructuring, and creating small working groups for the implementation of the program.

The council is a broad civic body. Its thirty members are appointed by the *voivod*[38] and represent important socioeconomic spheres of the *voivod*ship. In addition to its core members (local government, unions, and employers), the council also includes representatives of the central administration (the Antimonopolistic Department, Ministry of Property Transformation, Regional Planning Office of the Central Planning Office, and the territorial branch of the Agency for Agrarian Property), Parliament members elected from Lodz, representatives of the Provincial Labor Office, mayors of local municipalities, bankers, representatives of research centers and scientific academies, and all of the local institutions that deal with restructuring issues, such as the Lodz Agency for Regional Development, the Foundation for Restructuring the Lodz Region, the Lodz Regional Development Bureau, the Lodz Chamber of Commerce and Industry, the

36 Resolution #19/93 of the Council of Ministers from March 1, 1993, regarding the appointment of a Plenipotentiary for Restructuring the Lodz Region.

37 Regulation of the Regional Council for Restructuring the Lodz Region.

38 Order No. 235/94 of the Lodz Voivod from December 30, 1994, regarding the Establishment of a Regional Council for Restructuring the Lodz Region, named hereafter Regional Council; Order No. 162/96 of the Lodz Voivod from October 7, 1996, regarding the organization and mode of work of the Regional Council for Restructuring the Lodz Region; Order No. 4/97 of the Lodz Voivod from January 8, 1997 changing the order regarding the organization and mode of work of the Regional Council for Restructuring the Lodz Region; Order No. 23/98 of the Lodz Voivod from February 24, 1998, regarding the organization and mode of work of the Regional Council for Restructuring the Lodz Region; Order No. 19/99 of the Lodz Voivod from March 4, 1999, regarding the organization and mode of work of the Council for Regional Development and European Integration.

Lodz Economic Chamber, the Foundation "Inkubator," the Foundation for the Development of Entrepreneurship, the Fund for Protection of Environment and Water Supply in Lodz, the Chamber of Craftsmen in Lodz, the Polish Chamber of Textile Industry, and the Lodz office of the Polish Chamber of Foreign Trade.

The council holds quarterly meetings and takes decisions by a simple majority vote. It has a five-member presidium, comprising chairman, vice-chairman, two members, and a secretary. With the exception of the chair, who is appointed by the *voivod*, the council elects the presidium from among its members. The council also has a supervising body, or collegium, comprising the chair, the vice-chair and the secretary of the council. At first the council was organizationally serviced by the Bureau for Restructuring the Lodz Region, but later the Regional Development and European Integration Department in the *voivod*ship took on that responsibility. To develop projects, the council has created seven standing or temporary working groups on regional policy, financing restructuring, institutions of the regional economy, gathering data about the processes of restructuring, utilization of aid funds, organization of health care in the region, and entrepreneurship.

Following the parliamentary elections of 1993, the Ministry of Labor and Social Policy organized a meeting with the representatives of Solidarity–Region Lodz, the Ministry of Labor and Social Policy, the Ministry of Industry and Trade, the Ministry of Ownership Restructuring, and the government plenipotentiary for the restructuring of Lodz region. The aim was to negotiate the continuation and realization of the government program for restructuring the Lodz region, adopted by the previous Solidarity government. The new government decided to continue the program and keep the institution of government plenipotentiary for restructuring the region. Moreover, the Council of Ministers decided to create a commission for restructuring Lodz chaired by the prime minister. The Ministry of Labor and Social Policy, for its part, agreed to support the request of the Lodz *voivod* for the allocation of financial resources from the state budget to finance the program.

The new Lodz *voivod*, Andrzej Peczak, and his administration preserved the main elements of the old program.[39] Both programs sought to reduce the influence of the textile industry and strengthen other industrial branches. Both also supported changing the structure of ownership in industry through the privatization of enterprises in industry and trade. And both envisioned the creation of conditions favorable to foreign investment as a strategic precondition for the success of the privatization program.

[39] Interview with Andrzej Peczak, *voivod* of Lodz and chairman of the Regional Council for Restructuring the Lodz Region, Lodz, May 1995; interview with Pawel Jankiewicz, chairman of OPZZ–Region Lodz and Senator from Lodz, Lodz, May 1995.

Solidarity, however, staged many protests against the diversion of funds to infrastructure projects and the general politicization of the program.

Since its creation in 1993, the council has discussed important questions of regional policy and European integration and has given opinions and taken stands on problems of restructuring and development of the region.[40] Bringing together professionals from diverse areas, the council has facilitated the exchange of information and ideas. It has gone beyond consultation and created new jobs, with the help of the Agency for Regional Development. The council has also attempted to develop small business through a variety of companies, agencies, and institutions in Lodz. The council has also focused on the utilization of funds from the EU's STRUDER program for financial assistance, and divided its attention equally among the restructuring of state enterprises, the development of private enterprises, the development of communal infrastructure, and the development of the agricultural-food processing sector.

The council was very active, especially in 1993 and 1994, when it held ten meetings – two in 1993 and eight in 1994, before lapsing in 1995 after convening only twice.[41] In the fall of 1996, under pressure from Solidarity–Region Lodz, including a protest in June 1996, and a petition to the government,[42] negotiations to restore the council were held at the Ministry of Labor. The meeting was attended by representatives of the Ministry of Labor, all unions from the region, the local employers' organization (KPP–Region Lodz), and representatives of local governments in the Lodz region. An agreement was reached to renew the activities of the Council for Restructuring the Lodz Region in September 1996. As part of this agreement, the government agreed to provide additional subsidies to facilitate restructuring.[43]

The council held two sessions in 1996, and five each in 1997 and in 1998. Most of its deliberations focused either on the principles of the government policy for the region and the instruments for the realization of this policy or on the concrete activities of the local actors for the realization of the Program for Restructuring the Lodz Region. The council addressed the financial situation and restructuring, commercialization, and privatization of state enterprises in the region and the distribution of budget resources for restructuring. A long-term development strategy – "Lodz – Center of Tomorrow: Strategy for the Development of Lodz Region 1998–2002" –

[40] Interview with Wlodzimierz Mielczarek, secretary of the Regional Council for Restructuring the Lodz Region and director, Department for the Restructuring of Lodz Region, Lodz *Voivod*ship, Lodz, May 1995, August 1996.

[41] Archive data: minutes from the sessions of the Regional Council for Restructuring the Lodz Region.

[42] Petition of Solidarity–Lodz Region to the Prime Minister of the Polish Republic. Lodz, 4 June 1996.

[43] Interview with Waldemar Krenc, chairman of NSZZ Solidarnosc–Region Lodz, March 1999.

was discussed in early 1998. The strategy was developed with PHARE funds as part of Poland's EU accession efforts, and integrated proposals for the development of Lodz as a free economic zone, the creation of a local banks' council, and the establishment of a regional guaranteed credits fund and a loan fund. The latter was created in 1996 by the Lodz Regional Development Agency. Some forty local enterprises were given credits from this fund, and the investments created about 100 new jobs.

Following the administrative-territorial reform and the deepening of processes of accession to the EU, the council was recreated, on the basis of the June 1998 law on administrative governance in *voivod*ships, in March 1999 and renamed the Council for Regional Development and European Integration. The new council is to mobilize and stimulate the activities of the local self-government (Parliament). Meanwhile, as accession has accelerated, the program for regional restructuring received 75 percent of its funds from the EU, while the remaining 25 percent come from the state budget.

Collective Bargaining in Municipal Companies and the Public Sphere

Another tripartite initiative at the local level is the conclusion of agreements with the local self-government regarding wage levels in the municipal companies and the transformation of municipal ownership. Lodz's municipal enterprises and property are supervised by the municipal office as an agency of the local self-government. By the terms of the 1991 law on trade unions, local governments must consult unions on price increases in transport, rent, and water supply, as well as on other communal issues. With its strong territorial structure, Solidarity initiated negotiations on the conclusion of local agreements for the transformation of municipal property.

In the public sphere (culture, health care, and education), a joint commission was created to prepare collective contracts on employment relationships in these fields.[44] Although decentralized and managed by the local government, these activities receive subsidization from the central budget. The greatest local tensions arose between the local government and OPZZ's teachers' union. The union demanded centralization of decision-making in education and an increase in the responsibilities of the Minister of Education, thus undermining the municipality's local efforts to resolve education-related problems in Lodz. For example, in 1990 most of the local kindergartens were deteriorating. Factoring in Lodz's declining birth rate, the local government concluded that about 25 percent of the kindergartens had to be closed. This spawned conflicts between the local authorities and the Federation of Teachers at OPZZ, since around 1,000 kindergarten teachers would lose their jobs. After long negotiations between the local authorities and the federation, an agreement was signed providing for the

[44] Interview with Elzbieta Hibner, deputy mayor of the City of Lodz, Lodz, May 1995.

organization of courses for training and retraining. A similar situation occurred in January 1996, when a low education budget and school debt threatened the positions of teachers in elementary schools. In May 1995, both OPZZ and Solidarity organized protests in Lodz, and the Minister of Education resolved the problem by securing additional financial resources for Lodz teachers.

To summarize, restructuring in Lodz has been given much attention by political elites and the national government, which have kept informed through both a government team and a plenipotentiary specially appointed to assume responsibilities related to that subject. International organizations like the EU have also favored Lodz with attention, and the region is an important part of the 60 million ECU STRUDER Program, which is devoted to regional restructuring in Poland. In addition, Lodz is more ready for restructuring than are other troubled regions in Poland, such as Silesia, because much smaller investments are needed to restructure the textile industry than to restructure mining and other industries. The economic revitalization of the Lodz *voivod*ship points to the emergence of a civic tripartite cartel managing the implementation of government programs and also numerous local initiatives of local governments and various professional, economic, and social actors.

Tripartite cooperation at the regional level, I have shown, emerged in both Bulgaria and Poland, and the two countries did not differ substantially in the patterns of its establishment or context. The Bulgarian and Polish cases of regional tripartism demonstrate that social dialogues among the local actors were established to help cope with problems of unemployment and regional restructuring, as well as to facilitate the conclusion of collective agreements for the public sphere and municipal companies. In both countries, tripartite forums dealing with employment issues were institutionalized in the early years of transition: provincial and regional employment councils in Poland, and tripartite consultative committees on employment issues in Bulgaria. Regional tripartism remained politicized in both Bulgaria and Poland, and – when not normatively regulated – largely depended on the good will of the social partners to maintain it. The case of Blagoevgrad in Bulgaria, where a neoliberal UDF local government successfully blocked the development of regional tripartism, as well as tripartism's politically impelled ups and downs in both Poland's region of Lodz and Bulgaria's region of Vratza, confirm this broad intercountry trend in the development of postcommunist tripartism.

7

Conclusions:

Transiency and Continuity

> When in danger the sea-cucumber divides itself in two:
> one self it surrenders for devouring by the world,
> with the second it makes good its escape.
> It splits violently into perdition and salvation,
> into fine and reward, into what was and what will be.
> In the middle of its body there opens up a chasm
> with two shores that are immediately alien.
> On one shore death, on the other life.
> Here despair, there hope.
> If a scale exists, the balance does not tip.
> If there is justice, here it is.
> To die as much as necessary, without going too far.
> To grow back as much as needed, from the remnant that survives. . . .
>
> Wislawa Szymborska, *Autotomy*

In the aftermath of the 1989 breakthrough, two important trends, one harking to the past and one to the future, shaped the emerging new relationship between a politically discredited state and a politically disillusioned, economically choked working society.

First, a confused history of almost half a century cast its long shadow. The year 1989 marked the collapse of the "dictatorship of labor" and the outpouring of decades-old worker aspirations for greater input in enterprise and upper-level governance that erupted in spectacular worker protests against the party-state. The corporatist-like links between a reforming state and the working society that began to develop after 1989 were historically facilitated by these worker aspirations. State socialism also left a highly communitarian culture that generally fostered corporatist linkages among the state and social groups. However, decades-old "transmission-belt" institutions and the politics of authoritarian and hypocritical corporatism under state socialism had left workers and their interest representation organizations generally reluctant to collaborate with a still reforming state.

Second, the formation of those links was also affected by the multifarious prospects and options for the future that suddenly opened up for the CEE countries. Awakening from their long, troubled sleep, and still groggy with a deeply ingrained Cold War mentality, they beheld an increasingly borderless world that presented them, among other things, with examples of three distinct species of capitalism, each linking the state and social groups in its own way. In the early years of transition, a succession of Western models, roughly corresponding to the brands of capitalism associated with three economic blocs – the United States, Europe, and Japan/Asia – offered alternative solutions to the problems of postcommunist restructuring.

The "burden" of history and the "blueprint" of the future narrowed the choices on the road but did not decisively determine the road per se. The legacies of transition and transformation – the powerful twin necessities to preserve, under great uncertainty, social peace, and guarantee legitimacy of newly emerging actors and transforming old ones – led to the spectacular mushrooming of corporatist-like institutions across the CEE region. In the ten years since the Cold War, the CEE countries have all used tripartite corporatist adjustments to dispel uncertainty and facilitate the process of political and economic reform. This concluding chapter attempts to compare and analyze the empirical evidence presented in Chapters 3 to 6. It addresses two major questions: First, to what extent are these characteristics varying across countries, regions, sectors and time, and, second, to what extent are they losing relevance versus becoming permanent?

7.1. Variation in Tripartism

Convergence has been evident in some important aspects of postcommunist tripartism as it has unfolded throughout the region. Across the CEE countries, tripartism focused on more fairly distributing the burden and rewards of transformation among the population at large, and it included multiple participants at national and lower levels of governance and bargaining. As a dynamic institutional hybrid, with the balance of compromise fluctuating among the interests of all social partners, postcommunist tripartism – imperfect though it has been in various ways – sought to combine the economic efficiency of self-generating markets with the creative power of government intervention, while neutralizing the destructive chaotic tendencies of unregulated markets and the rigidities of a planned economy.

Within the framework of tripartite coordination, the political pressures exerted by state officials and emerging business and employer organizations have engendered policies favoring liberal markets, market efficiency, and profits; simultaneously, trade unions' input has resulted in plans that help guarantee adequate wages and, at a minimum, hold open the door for a socially responsible redistribution of publicly owned assets by involving the public and the emerging private sectors in processes of bargained exchange. In addition, when the demands of international creditors and lending institutions have induced governments to adopt starkly antiprotectionist state policies, postcommunist tripartism has sometimes stepped in to speak for and protect the interests of the CEE domestic actors.

Yet, as the Bulgarian and Polish cases demonstrate, tripartite coordination varies considerably across countries, regions, and sectors and in the course of transition and transformation. I outline and analyze below these variations.

National Variation

In the immediate aftermath of 1989, different paths of extrication from state socialism and, in particular, different levels of organizational restructuring and differentiation among the social partners have resulted in the emergence of different types of tripartite coordination in Bulgaria and Poland. The relative mildness of Bulgaria's economic crisis, the weakness of its civil society prior to 1989, and the preservation of the Communist party as a major force in the political process contrasted with a decades-long extrication from state socialism in Poland that created a civil society that was highly united, monolithic, and powerful but largely undifferentiated. The monobloc known as Solidarity produced four Solidarity-led governments, Solidarity trade unions, and a Solidarity-rooted employer organization, the Confederation of Polish Employers. Whereas Poland's extrication from state socialism was relatively consensual, Bulgarian politics and, consequently, Bulgarian tripartism, have been dominated by a "perpetual flux" of political life between two camps and two organizations: the former Communist party, which reconstituted itself into the Bulgarian Socialist Party in April 1990, and the democratic opposition, the Union of Democratic Forces.

Bulgarian tripartism emerged and began its consolidation within one complex, multiple-issue forum – the National Commission for Tripartite Coordination – and with the dual task of coping with the social explosions that might be produced by anticipated political and economic reforms and legitimating old organizations: the former communists and the old trade unions. Bulgarian tripartism, while maintaining a single institutional form, changed its institutional face with each change in government cabinet, before being given legal form by the new 1993 labor code. Thus, under the Popov government, the National Commission for Coordination of Interests was replaced in 1991 by the National Standing Tripartite Commission for Coordination of Interests; in 1992, with the formation of the Dimitrov cabinet, the National Council for Social Partnership was set up; and finally, in 1993, the formation of the Berov cabinet resulted in the National Council for Tripartite Cooperation. By 1993, Bulgarian tripartism, three times forced by political warfare and polarization to change its institutional form, emerged consolidated, highly institutionalized, and normatively regulated by law. Since then the national dialogue has broken off only relatively rarely.

From quite early on, Bulgarian tripartism was more inclusive than the Polish version. At first, the need to preserve social peace and legitimate all parties to negotiations dictated that both countries include a broad range of groups to share the responsibilities and burdens of transition. Indeed, in the early stages of the transition (between 1989 and 1990), the political round tables in both Poland and Bulgaria included almost all interest groups. Political agreements and pacts spelling out plans for a peaceful exit from state socialism were signed by all identifiable interest groups, including unions.

In Bulgaria, the initial consensus agreements were followed by two major political pacts on economic restructuring signed by the government and a broad variety of political parties and social organizations, including unions. The Bulgarian tripartite commissions of 1990 and 1991 were constituted on the basis of these pacts. The commissions included government, union, and employer representatives, but also admitted any other interested organizations or institutions. Thus, representatives of the Bulgarian National Student Confederation regularly attended sessions of the Bulgarian tripartite commission in 1991 and held consultative rights. Representatives of various political parties were also present as observers.[1]

In the initial days of high political and economic uncertainty, the Bulgarian tripartite organ often had decision-making powers and dealt with some purely political issues. Prior to the June 1990 elections for Grand National Assembly, the council discussed some politicized issues in an effort to avoid political passions in enterprises. Before 1993, a special government decree in April 1991 transformed the tripartite commission into a decision-making body, whose decisions were mandatory for the lower levels of state administration.

From this impressive starting position, the shift to the more inconclusive consultation schemes that followed seemed a backward step. Nevertheless, Bulgarian tripartism opened the way for unions and employers to share government responsibility for the negative consequences of macroeconomic stabilization and transformation such as surging unemployment and declining

[1] Similarly in Hungary, negotiations to forge a social and economic agreement in 1994 as a "historic compromise" between the government and society at large went far beyond the labor market actors. While the agreement had to be negotiated within the tripartite institutional framework, the social partners were responsible for considering input from groups outside the council as well (Lado 1997: 16). No finished pact was ratified, however, largely because the politicians invited numerous players to the game even as the social partners greatly widened the agenda, so that extraction of a compromise within a reasonable time seemed impossible.

real wages. The tripartite councils jointly decided many employment issues, especially those involving allocation of central funds to depressed regions and sectors to alleviate unemployment.[2]

Bulgaria's legal-institutional developments occurred within a single tripartite forum, while Poland produced a more informal and diversified tripartism. One might suspect that Poland had less need for tripartite coordination as a tool for maintaining social peace, because Poland entered the reform process with a stronger political and moral consensus on the necessity of radical change. Bulgaria, however, also enjoyed a broad socio-political consensus on the need for radical change. The critical difference was the relatively retarded organizational differentiation and restructuring among the social partners in Poland. As a result, no group had a strong commitment to creating an institutionalized body to articulate its (presumably different) interests, as happened in Bulgaria and everywhere else in the region.

Due to this peculiarity, Poland's tripartism emerged, in 1990, in three distinct forms: (1) informal government-union talks aimed at the resolution of pressing social and industrial conflicts, most often wage-related following the introduction of neoliberal economic reforms; (2) legally endorsed institutionalized social dialogue (the Main Employment Council, formed in early 1990), targeted at a single issue, namely, the prevention of unemployment, which had emerged as the greatest social challenge to economic restructuring and social peace and could not safely be ignored in the hope that an informal truce over economic reform would somehow produce a resolution; and (3) "parliamentarian" tripartism through Solidarity's and OPZZ's direct representation in Parliament, where they could voice political concerns.

Poland's informal arrangement survived the first pains of shock-therapy adjustment with impressive sangfroid. Meanwhile, other tripartite forums emerged for the coordination of interests in particular areas, such as labor protection, social assistance, minimum payments, and rehabilitation of disabled people. However, rapidly dropping living standards, increasing unemployment, and other negative consequences of reform eventually

[2] In that connection, a survey of participants in the Hungarian Interest Reconciliation Council in the early 1990s showed that both labor and business were very satisfied with their influence over policy-making. Some 71 percent of employers' groups and 68 percent of trade unions saw themselves as either active or very active in attempting to influence national policy; 67 percent of trade unions and 92 percent of employers' groups were firmly of the view that as a result of their contacts they had been able to persuade the government to change its legislative proposals to accommodate their concerns. The main policy areas in which trade unions felt they were effective were economic and industrial legislation (15 percent), labor and trade union legislation (37 percent), and legislation on education (15 percent). For employers' groups, the main areas were economic and industrial legislation (50 percent), agricultural legislation (9.1 percent), and legislation on administrative matters (9.1 percent) (Cox and Vass 1998: 9–10).

undermined the consensual acceptance of rapid change. In February 1994 tripartite talks – after a series of negotiations over an Enterprise Pact dealing with the social consequences of ownership transformation – were institutionalized in the National Tripartite Commission on Socio-Economic Issues.

The tripartite organ that emerged in Poland in 1994 was open to all interested actors in the industrial arena. It was largely constructed by the mere political acceptance of the social partners, with no official criteria for membership beyond signing the Enterprise Pact.[3] The pact was signed in February 1993 by the two major unions, Solidarity and OPZZ, seven branch unions, and one employer organization, KPP. However, in September 1992 the government had invited a broader spectrum of interested organizations: fifteen unions, professional and cooperative organizations, three employer organizations, and the national organization of local self-government. Some voluntarily withdrew from participation or joined the talks only as observers. The Main Employment Council, founded in early 1990 under the employment law, also included national representatives of the local self-governments, in addition to those of the three major actors: the government, unions, and employers.

In 1994, Poland belatedly joined Bulgaria and the rest of the postcommunist countries in creating more clear-cut interest-based institutionalized arrangements linking the state with the working society. Considering the weak institutionalization of tripartism in Polish labor law and the distinctly neoliberal policies of the governments, it may have been the EU's PHARE Social Dialogue Project that was most responsible for the shift toward more standard, institutionalized tripartism in Poland. Completed in 1992–93, the Social Dialogue Project inculcated norms of social dialogue and compromise among social partners and played a decisive part in conciliating the politically strained relations between Solidarity and OPZZ unions and in the shift toward negotiated compromise in concluding the Enterprise Pact. As J. Kulpinska has concluded, the corporatist model has been fostered in Poland not by domestic forces but mostly by international organizations such as the EU (Kulpinska 1998: 23).

While Poland lagged in the formalization of tripartism, it had been relatively precocious in developing tripartite functions with variety and breadth. It was not until 1997–98 that Bulgaria joined Poland in forming additional single-issue tripartite forums and even in giving tripartism an institutionalized "stretch" to Parliament.

With the development of civil society in Bulgaria – which placed increasing pressure on the National Council for Tripartite Cooperation to discuss a broad range of issues concerning its consolidation – and following a

[3] In Hungary, the government left it to the workers' and employers' sides of the interest reconciliation council to determine their own representation. Participation was extended to include all seven trade union confederations and nine employers' associations.

drastic economic downturn in the winter of 1996–97, Bulgarian tripartism expanded its scope through the creation of a well-elaborated web of eight additional institutions and five specialized social funds, governed with the broad participation of the social partners. A total of thirteen different tripartite institutions included additional social actors, mostly from the third, nongovernmental, sector. This meant the direct, institutionalized participation of various civic organizations: organizations of producer cooperatives, the national organization of local self-government, and charitable/humanitarian organizations active in social assistance and social security, health and safety, and the social rehabilitation of disabled people. The trend toward expanded civic tripartism was strengthened as part of the efforts to move toward accession to the EU. The formation of the Council for the Ratification of the European Social Charter (Revised) at the end of 1998 marked the inclusion of some forty different institutions and organizations in deliberations to harmonize Bulgarian labor legislation with the EU social *acquis*.

In sharp difference with the Polish form, however, tripartism in Bulgaria has included international lending institutions such as the IMF and the World Bank – despite their basic neoliberal philosophies – from its very early formation. The IMF was the invisible, "shadow," but permanent, partner in Bulgarian tripartism (Petkov 1996), laying down the framework within which governments could negotiate with unions and employers. In contrast to countries such as Poland, the Czech Republic, and Hungary, where advanced economic transformation and large foreign capital inflows fulfilled the borrowing needs of the government, Bulgaria relied on the IMF's assistance programs. The Czech Republic used IMF credits only in 1994, and managed to clear its debt to the IMF in the following year. A year later, in 1996, Poland followed suit, while Hungary settled its bills with the IMF in 1998 (Minassian 1999: 7). In Bulgaria, the 1996–97 financial crisis and the relatively low inflows of foreign capital resulted in a continued need for IMF credits in the process of economic restructuring.

On the one hand, the IMF policies required the maintenance of social partnership as a condition for preserving social peace in the face of unpopular economic reforms, especially drastic wage restraints. As international lenders, the IMF and the World Bank have been deeply interested in securing social peace to assure the successful implementation of their stabilization and general assistance programs. In negotiations and agreements with the Bulgarian government, the IMF has insisted that the governments involve the social partners in dialogues over the major parameters of reform. It was thus only after the interference of the IMF that Bulgarian tripartism was restored in mid-1992 and legally endorsed in the new 1993 labor code, following the abandonment of social dialogue by the neoliberal government of F. Dimitrov. On the other hand, the IMF has also set clear limits to the economic and social parameters of social dialogue, especially after the introduction of a currency board, in 1997, significantly diminished the policy efficacy of the tripartite bargaining by imposing drastic wage ceilings.

Bulgarian tripartism further differed from Poland's in its relations with Parliament. Even after a "parliamentary" element was introduced in the 1997–98 institutional expansion, it substantially differed from Poland's parliamentary corporatism. Influenced by Poland's unique mixture of union and political party and direct union representation in Parliament (Solidarity as part of the Solidarity-rooted political parties, OPZZ as part of the SLD's parliamentary caucus), Poland's variant of tripartism includes the "transfer" of part of the tripartite function to the Parliament. Through its direct participation in Parliament, the Solidarity union accomplished two major parliamentary-political initiatives: a separate project of mass privatization, and amendments to the Polish constitution. Poland's "corporatist" Parliament is one-sided, however, because employers, and the KPP in particular – though possessed of strong parliamentary lobbies – were hardly represented at all, and the rivalries that emerged between Parliament and the tripartite commission after its formation in 1994 have diminished the "parliamentarian" stretch of Polish tripartism.

In Bulgaria, a specialized, more formalized institutional structure – the Consultative Council for Legislative Initiatives – was formed at the National Assembly in October 1997 as a tripartite extension toward Parliament. One of the council's goals is to improve the quality of social dialogue in the country, with special reference to initiatives in the area of social legislation, and the council developed into the widest institutional structure for interest coordination in Bulgaria. It confirmed a trend toward expansion of social dialogues to the third sector, through the inclusion of a wide variety of interest groups, professional and consumer organizations, social movements, foundations, and charitable groups. On average, nearly thirty different organizations, in addition to the classic three partners and Parliament members, participate in each session of the Council on Legislative Initiatives.

To summarize, by the late 1990s Bulgaria and Poland have consolidated their tripartisms along converging lines. Three distinct forms of tripartite arrangements are now evident in each country: (1) one central multiple-issue tripartite forum as the major agent of interest articulation and policy-making initiatives: the National Council for Tripartite Cooperation in Bulgaria, and the National Tripartite Commission for Socio-Economic Issues in Poland; (2) a similar constellation of smaller, single-issue tripartite forums around the major tripartite institution: on employment and vocational training, social security and social aid, work conditions, and health and safety; and (3) a tripartite stretch to Parliament: more direct but informal in Poland, and more narrowly channeled and institutionally formalized in Bulgaria.

In both countries, tripartism is now consolidated as a civic-political hybrid, relatively stronger in Bulgaria, and weaker in Poland, due to the different social commitments of currently empowered governments. Although both governments' policies are right-of-center, the more neoliberal AWS-UW coalition in Poland has marginalized tripartism to some extent, while in Bulgaria the Kostov government's greater friendliness toward social-market reforms and, more important, the legal endorsement of social dialogue has accounted for the more active involvement of Bulgarian tripartism in social and employment aspects of transformation.

By the end of 1999, the tripartite institutions in both Poland and Bulgaria were open to the participation of various political parties (through the parliamentarian stretch of tripartisms), local self-governments, professional and academic communities, and various nongovernmental organizations. The purely political elements of their tripartisms, however, have been gradually abandoned: In Bulgaria, political parties have ceased to monitor the activities of the tripartite forums closely, while the latter have abandoned discussion of some purely political issues, and are no longer influenced by political changes in cabinets.

Overall, the consolidation of tripartism in both Poland and Bulgaria has brought more organizations from the third sector – not just trade unions and employer associations – into tripartite talks to protect particularistic interests, meet needs not met by government, promote citizen participation, and, overall, ensure a democratic society.[4] The participation of NGOs in tripartite negotiations was secured separately or on a par with trade unions and employers' organizations – thus partly mimicking similar trends in western Europe[5] and, in particular, the emerging trend toward "enlargement" and "loosening" of the "corporatist triangle," a shift that occurred in Western Europe in the beginning of the 1990s as a revival of corporatist schemes.[6] This shift is often described by adding the concepts of "networks" and "communities" of various sorts to the corporatist analysis,[7] indicating less structured and close-knit, informal, and decentralized access of inter-

[4] Third-sector organizations, occupying a distinctive social space outside both the market and the state, flourished worldwide beginning in the mid-1970s as a response to the "crisis of the welfare state" (Heidenheimer et al. 1990). They provided an alternative to government as a provider of quasipublic services and as organizational vehicles for citizen participation (Kuhnle and Selle 1992; Kramer et al. 1993). Neoliberals on the right have seen voluntary organizations as a bulwark against further government intervention, while those on the left often view these organizations nostalgically, as a means of recovering a lost sense of community through voluntarism, self-help, and other forms of citizen participation (Janowitz 1976; Clayre 1980; Hadley and Hatch 1981). Some authors smitten with the promise of these organizations have even talked about a global "association revolution" (O'Neil 1989; Gidron et al. 1992; Salamon 1995; Salamon and Anheier 1997).

[5] See in Edwards and Hulme 1992; Smillie and Helmich 1993; Heinelt and Smith 1996.

[6] See the spring–summer 1999 issue of *Transfer: European Review of Labour and Research*, which explores trends in state intervention in Europe; also Ferner and Hyman 1998.

[7] See in Rokkan 1969; Marin and Mayntz 1991; Marsh and Rhodes 1992; Rhodes 1997.

est groups to the policy-making process (Richardson and Jordan 1979; Jordan 1990; Marin and Mayntz 1991).

Another shift in focus in both Poland's and Bulgaria's tripartism is the move away from predominantly social-peace functions toward policy-oriented functions and participation in the policy-making process along socio-economic lines. That trend is less evident in Poland, where the emerging tripartism was more policy-oriented from the start: in 1990, on employment issues, and in 1994, with the tripartite commission's focus on the negotiated formation of wages and other aspects of incomes and social policies. In Bulgaria, all tripartite forums were constituted with the single task of maintaining social peace. Thus, the creation of the second tripartite forum in 1991 followed the conclusion of two agreements among the social partners, on the preservation of social peace (the Agreement on Preservation of Social Peace of January 1991 and the Agreement on Further Course of Economic Reform and Preservation of Social Peace, signed in August 1991). In a similar fashion, social dialogue at the industry level emerged as a conflict-resolving, mediating, rather than policy-making, institution. Social dialogue forums in sectors were convened only at the request of partners from lower levels for the resolution of major conflicts within the sectors.

It was at a much later stage, when the ministries inserted tasks and issues urgently facing their respective sectors into the social dialogue agenda, that these forums acquired some purely policy-making functions. This shift in focus also emerged nationwide, with the creation of more policy-oriented tripartite arrangements, as in the 1993 expansion of social dialogue to employment policy-making. With the 1997–98 institutional reform of the Bulgarian tripartite system, Bulgarian tripartism, like Poland's, became more or less equally oriented toward organizing and controlling conflicting interests and making and implementing public policy. Notably, however, in Poland and Bulgaria, as well as Hungary and the Czech Republic, the shift toward policy-making was accompanied by a reduction of tripartite consultations on purely economic issues, and a focus on social and employment issues and wage and income regulation.[8]

[8] While in the Slovak Republic the Council for Economic and Social Agreement's responsibilities have basically remained unchanged up to the present, in the Czech Republic they were restricted to the areas of labor-law relations, collective negotiations and wages, payments and related issues, safety at work, and social issues. Economic issues are no longer on the agenda, a fact reflected in the new name of the Czech "Tripartite": the Board for Dialogue between Social Partners. See in Cambalikova and Mansfeldova 1997. In early 1999, Hungary's government acceded to a major restructuring of its system of tripartite social dialogue. The National Council for Interest Reconciliation was split into five councils: three on economic, social, and labor coordination, and two devoted to international consultation on matters related to EU membership and the International Labor Office, respectively. Admittedly, the split led to the marginalization of social dialogue on purely economic issues, as the Economic Council was granted very restricted consultative functions.

The trends toward more flexibility and civic and policy-making expansion of social dialogue have also moved the stage from the national level to the subnational sectoral, regional, and firm levels, as those arenas increasingly become key to understanding the detail of state-society policy formation and the success of policy implementation (Nielsen 1993). In both countries tripartism has developed at lower levels of interaction, albeit with some significant variation in timing and focus.

Sectoral Variation

In both Bulgaria and Poland, tripartite coordination at the sectoral level developed to alleviate social tension arising from the economic restructuring of particular sectors. Tripartite social dialogue in the Bulgarian electronics industry and the restructuring of Polish textile industry further reveal that national responses to these pressures could vary. While in Bulgaria the sectoral adjustments became heavily institutionalized, in Poland sectoral responses developed into informal and noninstitutionalized, ad hoc tripartite "teams." The different legal-institutional frameworks of tripartism in these countries – legal endorsement of social dialogue in all Bulgarian industries and the legal withdrawal of the Polish state from direct participation in social dialogue and collective bargaining at the industry level – largely account for these different institutional forms. The different legal bases for social dialogue in the two countries reflect different levels of commitment to social dialogue and tripartism by governments and emerging civil societies.

The legal endorsement of Bulgarian social dialogue at national and lower levels led to the institutionalization and routine functioning of social dialogue even in industries that were not facing heavy restructuring problems or social tension, such as telecommunications. The focus and accent of tripartite talks varies considerably in such sectors, however. In industries with heavy restructuring problems, as is the case with Bulgarian electronics, tripartite coordination focuses predominantly on the resolution of local enterprise problems and industry-wide restructuring problems; it plays the role of a mediating, conflict management institution. Tripartism's more "classic" function in the area of collective bargaining (conclusion of annual industry-wide collective agreements regulating the terms of the employment relationship for the industry) becomes the predominant function only in industries with minimal restructuring problems, such as telecommunications.

As transformation advanced – revealed by the Bulgarian case with tripartism in electronics – a shift from conflict resolution to policy-making occurred. Initially, the tripartite council in electronics convened only as a response to local enterprise conflicts and problems raised by local social partners; later, the social partners were directly involved in the drafting of a strategy for the restructuring of the sector. Trade unions, in particular the

Podkrepa union, had by far the greatest hand in elaborating the social aspects of the government Strategy for the Development of the Electrotechnical and Electronics Industry until 2005. As far as the direct involvement of local enterprises in the tripartite multilevel bargaining system is concerned, the development of a new system of labor mediation and arbitration is likely to result in the disappearance of enterprise tripartism.

Regional Variation

Social dialogue at the regional level emerged in both Bulgaria and Poland, but, unlike sectoral tripartism, it did not differ substantially in context or patterns of establishment. In both countries, social dialogues among the local actors performed three major functions: handling unemployment, facilitating regional restructuring, and securing the conclusion of collective agreements for the public sphere and municipal companies.

In both countries, tripartite forums dealing with issues of employment were institutionalized in the early years of transition: provincial and regional employment councils in Poland, tripartite consultative committees on employment issues in Bulgaria. In Poland, social dialogue over these three major tasks was diversified and concentrated in separate institutional forums, while in Bulgaria the predominant practice favored their consolidation in a single, multipurpose tripartite body.

Regional tripartism remained politicized in both Bulgaria and Poland, and – when not normatively regulated – largely depended on the good will of the social partners, especially, as the case of regional tripartism in the Bulgarian region of Blagoevgrad demonstrates, on the commitment of local governments to social dialogue and local policy-making that includes inputs from local unions and employers.

7.2. Toward European Social Dialogue

With the EU's historical decision in December 1997 to open accession negotiations with five CEE applicants (among them, Poland) and its decision in December 1999 to extend the same opportunity to an additional five applicants (including Bulgaria), EU members and EU candidates have embarked on a new and more challenging future. The road to EU accession is open to the countries of CEE and their social partners, but they can travel its length only if they complete difficult processes of transformation and cope with two major challenges of accession: complying with the EU's *acquis communautaire* and meeting the standards of "European" social dialogue.

Among the thousands of *acquis*, the norm for social dialogue was not well elaborated until in 1998. It was strengthened in 1999 when the commission, in its October 1999 Composite Paper on Progress Toward Accession, advised candidate countries to continue targeted reform of the existing regulatory environment, "including through close contacts with the business community and enhanced social dialogue." The commission also reaffirmed its commitment to urging candidates to step up their efforts in the area of the social *acquis*, particularly with respect to the development of social dialogue, "in view of the negative consequences" the slow pace of social reform "could have for social cohesion."[9]

Although the EU accession norm on the establishment and maintenance of "social dialogues" is mostly with reference to bipartite labor-business cooperation, the norm is nonetheless viewed by the social partners as important for defending tripartism against potential attempts by neoliberal governments to abolish it. Tripartite institutions and arrangements, which in many countries decreased in strength as the transformation advanced, may gain new potency and vigor as a result of accession to the EU, since the maintenance of such arrangements is a precondition for EU entry.

European transnational networks further contribute to the development of social partnership across Europe. One such institution – the Economic and Social Committee of the European Union – seeks to advocate the EU's social *acquis* and the development of social partnership in CEE.[10] Established under the Treaty of Rome (1957), it comprises national representatives of economic and social groups in member countries, such as employers, workers, and particular interests including agriculture, transport, local government, and consumer groups. Although the Economic and Social Committee has not been seen as a powerful EU institution, it has played a visible role in enforcing social dialogue and tripartism in the CEE region. The Economic and Social Committee has organized meetings in Brussels and elsewhere that brought together social partner representatives from the EU and from the applicant countries to discuss the importance of developing social dialogue structures and activities in the applicant countries so that they can take part in the various social dialogue structures at the European level. The latter play a triple role: developing joint actions between workers' and employers' representatives, negotiating framework agreements, and assisting the EU institutions in their areas of responsibility.[11]

The Economic and Social Committee has also forged and consolidated bilateral links with groups from the applicant countries, by establishing joint consultative committees on economic and social issues between the EU and these countries. The first such committee, created in February 1997,

[9] Composite Paper, Regular Report from the Commission on Progress Toward Accession by Each of the Candidate Countries, October 13, 1999.

[10] Opinion of the Economic and Social Committee on the Enlargement of the European Union, *Official Journal of the European Communities*, 21 January 1998; Opinion on Reinforcing the Pre-Accession Strategy (Own-Initiative Opinion) (Brussels: Economic and Social Committee of the European Communities, 25–26 March 1998).

[11] "Padraig Flynn Encourages Development of Social Dialogue," *European Report*, no. 2393, 24 March 1999.

was the Joint Consultative Committee of the Economic and Social Committee of the EU and the Hungarian National Interest Conciliation Council (*Euro-East*, no. 55, 3 June 1997). The second, established in January 1999, is a joint body between the Economic and Social Committee of the EU and economic and social interest groups in Bulgaria.[12] The committee was set up to pave the way for enlargement of the EU by promoting dialogue and supporting the Bulgarian professional organizations in their efforts to create a functioning civil society, one in which their consultation by the government would be an integral part of the decision-making process.

European interest group organizations, especially the European Trade Union Confederation (ETUC), have been prominent advocates of the maintenance of social dialogue during accession. Trade unions from Western Europe, united in the ETUC, have developed a policy of active cooperation with trade unions in the ten associated countries. They are helping trade unions in the applicant countries to make themselves heard by their governments.

European integration is already producing demands for changes in the organizational structures of social dialogue throughout the applicant countries, at national and lower levels, that will make them more flexible in responding to the specific needs of accession adjustments. In 1998 and early 1999, the Bulgarian social partners initiated a reform of their tripartite system, an action that is viewed as crucial if future EU accession-related structural adjustments are to succeed.[13] Hungary's government, too, in early 1999 acceded to a major restructuring of its system of tripartite social dialogue that resulted in the creation of a separate tripartite body on matters related to EU membership.

Countries with greater commitments to neoliberalism and a free market economy, however, such as Poland, the Czech Republic, the Baltic states, and Slovenia, as well as prominent CEE neoliberals such as Poland's Leszek Balcerowicz and members of the Freedom Union, have been slightly more reserved toward the EU. In their public debates on accession, they have raised some concerns about the European "social model" and the social-democratic elements of its policies. A compromisal consensus on accession already exists, however. Even Balcerowicz, while raising concerns about the EU's imposition of its social standards in its eastward expansion, has acknowledged that little can be done to prevent that development, as long as the CEE applicants wish to become EU members (Balcerowicz 1999).

A major challenge to postcommunist tripartism is the fact that social dialogue, as practiced in most of continental Western Europe, is a moving target. EU member states are currently earnestly searching for "Social

[12] "EU/Bulgaria Joint Consultative Committee Inaugural Meeting" (Commission of the European Communities: RAPID, 26 February 1999).

[13] Data from the Bulgarian Ministry of Labor and Social Policy, March and July 1999.

Europe's" vitally needed adjustments to the pressures of global neoliberalism. As already discussed in Chapter 1, in the 1990s, Western European corporatism resurfaced as a means of adjustment to global pressures for more flexible markets and production patterns. Further pressure for structural readjustment of the Western European model has accompanied the move toward economic and monetary union (EMU). The primary "growth potential" for European corporatism thus lies in the efforts of national governments to comply with EU directives, meet product and professional standards, and satisfy the convergence criteria for EMU (Schmitter and Grote 1997). The double task now faced by European governments is to reform the model and to adjust social policies across Europe in such a way that they can boost employment without removing the generous safety nets, financed by social welfare spending that in 1997 claimed an average of 28 percent of GDP in EU member countries (Anderson 1997).

As privatization spreads and democracy is further consolidated in the CEE region, and as more countries near their goal of gaining admittance to the EU, CEE's tripartite arrangements will most probably begin to synthesize their constructive elements into a new democratic political and economic structure, integrated closely into European structures and globalized economics and politics.

Tables

TABLE 1. *Emergence of the Bulgarian National Council for Tripartite Cooperation (1990–93)*

	National Commission for Coordination of Interests (NCCI) 5 April–17 October 1990	**National Standing Tripartite Commission for Coordination of Interests (NSTCCI) 15 January–7 October 1991**	**National Council for Social Partnership (NCSP) 13 June–13 July 1992 4–30 September 1992**	**National Council for Tripartite Cooperation (NCTC) Since 19 February 1993**
Normative Grounds	* General Agreement for 1990 between the Government of Bulgaria, CITUB, and NUEM (15 March 1990) * Rules for the Work of the NCCI (5 April 1990) * Agreement between the Government of Bulgaria, CITUB, Podkrepa CL, and NUEM on Indexation of Incomes (14 August 1990)	* Agreement for Preservation of Social Peace between the Government of Bulgaria, Podkrepa CL, CITUB, NUEM, the Central Cooperative Union, the Union of Producer Cooperatives, the Vazrazhdane Union of Private Producers, the Union for Private Economic Enterprising, and the Bulgarian Industrial Association (8 January 1991) * Statute of the National Standing Tripartite Commission for Coordination of Interests (15 January 1991) * Agreement on the Further Course of Economic Reform and Preservation of Social Peace	* Regulations for the Functioning of the National Social Partnership System between the Government of Bulgaria, Podkrepa CL, CITUB, the Bulgarian Industrial Association, the Union for Private Economic Enterprising, the Vazrazhdane Union of Private Producers, and the Alternative – 2000 Association of Free Entrepreneurs (29 May 1992)	* New Labor Code, enacted on 1 January 1993 * Government Decree no.7 on Regulation of the Principles, Terms and Order of Recognition of Workers' and Employers' Organizations as Representative at the National Level of Tripartite Partnership (22 January 1993) * Government Decree no. 51 on Working Rules of the National System of Tripartite Partnership (15 March 1993)

Parties	* The Government of Bulgaria * Unions: CITUB Podkrepa CL (from 26 April 1990) * Employers' organizations: NUEM	* The Government of Bulgaria * Unions: CITUB Podkrepa CL * Employers' organizations: NUEM Bulgarian Industrial Association Union for Private Economic Enterprising Vazrazhdane Union of Private Producers Central Cooperative Union Union of Producer Cooperatives	* The Government of Bulgaria * Unions: CITUB Podkrepa CL * Employers' organizations: Bulgarian Industrial Association Union for Private Economic Enterprising Vazrazhdane Union of Private Producers Alternative – 2000 Association of Free Entrepreneurs	* The Government of Bulgaria * Unions: Podkrepa CL (22 February 1993) CITUB (22 February 1993) * Employers' organizations: Union of Private Economic Enterprising (22 February 1993) Bulgarian Chamber of Commerce (22 February 1993) Bulgarian Industrial Association (8 March 1993) Vazrazhdane Union of Private Entrepreneurs (21 May 1993)
Recognition of unions' and employers' organizations	No recognition from the government at national level required. Requirement for signing the General Agreement	No recognition from the government at national level required. Requirement for signing the Agreement on Social Peace. First recognition of unions and employers' organizations with the Agreement on the Further Course of Economic Reform and Preservation of Social Peace (no criteria specified)	No recognition from the government at national level required	Recognition from the government at national level required. Criteria specified with government decree

(continued)

TABLE 1 *(continued)*

	National Commission for Coordination of Interests (NCCI) 5 April–17 October 1990	National Standing Tripartite Commission for Coordination of Interests (NSTCCI) 15 January–7 October 1991	National Council for Social Partnership (NCSP) 13 June–13 July 1992 4–30 September 1992	National Council for Tripartite Cooperation (NCTC) Since 19 February 1993
Goals	(1) Establishment and development of dialogue, negotiations, agreements (2) coordination of the activities of the parties and resolution of conflicts arising from the fulfillment of the General Agreement (3) preparation of a new General Agreement, as well as other agreements on specific issues (4) proposals of coordinated stands for the resolution of nationally important labor conflicts	(1) Establishment of dialogue and negotiations for the resolution of basic issues concerning labor and labor relations (2) coordination of the activities of the parties and resolution of any possible conflicts during the fulfillment of the Agreement on Social Peace (3) coordinated stands on proposals from commissions for coordination of interests (4) joint stands on the major issues of the Agreement on Social Peace and on basic issues of the government social and economic policy	(1) Proposals for projects of normative acts on the issues of labor, social insurance, and living standards and the economic parameters of social partnership (2) resolution of labor and social conflicts (3) issues of collective bargaining at national level: social and living minimum, structure of consumption, minimum wage, and general level of employment (4) mechanisms of adjusting already reached agreements with respect to changing conditions (5) proposals for stabilization of the social anconomic situation in the country and preservation of social peace	Organ for consultations and cooperation for the resolution of problems of labor and labor relations, social insurance, and living standards at national level

Administration	Secretary of the Commission, from the government	Secretariat (Secretary of the NSTCCI and technical secretary), provided by the government	Secretariat, provided by the government	Secretariat (secretary of the NCTC and technical secretary), provided by the government
Organization of sessions	Not regular. Upon request of any of the member parties	Regular sessions, according to adopted schedule. Extraordinary sessions possible upon motivated request of any of the participants	Regular sessions, according to adopted schedule. Extraordinary sessions possible upon motivated request of any of the participants	Regular sessions, according to adopted schedule. Extraordinary sessions possible upon motivated request of any of the participants
Representation in sessions	Three representatives of each party, at the level of deputy prime minister and deputy leaders of union and employers' organizations	Four to five authorized representatives of each participant. Rank of representatives not specified	Not specified	Three representatives of each party, at the level of deputy prime minister and unspecified rank of representatives of union and employers' organizations. No more than two experts of each party can also participate
Chair	No chair; sessions chaired in consecutive order by the deputy eaders of participating members	Chair of the NSTCCI: deputy prime minister	Chair of the NCSP: deputy prime minister	Chair of the NCTC: deputy prime minister
Other participants	Interested political and other organizations can participate in the sessions. No requirements for participation specified	Interested organizations or institutions. No requirements for participation specified	Interested organizations, in case they meet some criteria for participation set up by the members of the NCSP	Interested organizations or institutions. No requirements for participation specified

(continued)

TABLE I *(continued)*

	National Commission for Coordination of Interests (NCCI) 5 April–17 October 1990	**National Standing Tripartite Commission for Coordination of Interests (NSTCCI) 15 January–7 October 1991**	**National Council for Social Partnership (NCSP) 13 June–13 July 1992 4–30 September 1992**	**National Council for Tripartite Cooperation (NCTC) Since 19 February 1993**
Principles of decision making	Consensus. If consensus is not reached on two consecutive sessions, issue is dropped from agenda	Consensus. Coordinated joint opinion of each party (with exception of unions)	Consensus. If consensus not reached, each party acts on its own, according to the laws	Consensus. If consensus not reached, each party acts on its own, according to the laws
Organizational structure	Working groups on: living standards unemployment wages privatization economic legislation labor and social legislation rest and recreation conditions of work safety at work	Standing subcommissions on: financial and credit policy and banking employment, redundancies, and requalification of labor force social minimum, wages and compensations of incomes industrial conflicts privatization, expert evaluation and autonomization of state and municipal property social insurance and social care labor and social legislation misuse of state property	Standing commissions on: labor force: labor, employment, qualification, and requalification incomes and prices collective labor disputes social insurance and social aid privatization and restructuring of economy financial, tax, and credit parameters of social partnership specific problems of employees in budget organizations	Standing commissions on: labor force: employment, unemployment, qualification, and requalification incomes, prices, and living standards collective labor disputes social insurance and social aid international labor legislation and work with the ILO conditions of work privatization and restructuring of economy financial, credit and tax relations specific problems of employees in budget organizations

Branch structures	None	Yes, upon initiative of any of the parties in the NSTCCI	Yes, upon request of branch structures of any of the social partners in the NCSP	Yes, upon request of branch structures of any of the social partners in the NCTC
Regional structures	None	Yes, upon initiative of any of the parties in the NSTCCI	Yes, upon request of regional structures of any of the social partners in the NCSP	Yes, upon request of regional structures of any of the social partners in the NCTC

TABLE 2. *Organizational Structure of Bulgarian Social Dialogue*

I. National Economy

1. **National Council for Tripartite Cooperation**
   - A. Plenary Sessions of the National Council for Tripartite Cooperation
   - B. Standing Expert Commissions of the National Tripartite Council:
     - labor force: employment, unemployment, training, and retraining
     - incomes, prices, and living standards
     - collective labor disputes
     - social insurance and social aid
     - international labor legislation and work with the ILO
     - work conditions
     - privatization and restructuring of the economy
     - financial, credit and tax relations
     - specific problems of employees in the public sphere
2. Supervisory Board of the National Employment Office
3. National Council on Unemployment Protection and Employment Promotion
4. National Council on Vocational Training
5. Managing Board of the Vocational Training and Unemployment Fund
6. National Council on Work Conditions
7. Managing Board of the Work Conditions Fund
8. Supervisory Board of the National Social Security Institute
9. Managing Board of the Social Security Fund
10. Council on Social Assistance
11. Managing Board of the Social Assistance Fund
12. National Council on Rehabilitation and Social Integration
13. Managing Board of the Rehabilitation and Social Integration Fund
14. Meeting of Representatives of the National Health Insurance Bank
15. Consultative Council for Legislative Initiatives at the Bulgarian Parliament
16. Council for the Ratification of the European Social Charter
17. Joint EU-Bulgaria Consultative Committee
18. Economic and Social Council (to be established)

II. Industries and Sectors

1. Industry-Wide and Sectoral Councils for Tripartite Cooperation at each ministry;

   Ministry of Industry
   - A. Departmental Council at all-industry level
   - B. Sectoral Tripartite Councils:
     - machine-building
     - electronics and electrotechnics
     - chemistry and mineral oil processing
     - metallurgy
     - timber, forestry, and furniture industry
     - light industry
     - mineral resources
     - special production

2. Tripartite Sectoral Councils on Work Conditions
3. Collective bargaining for each industry and sector

III. Regions

1. Regional Councils for Tripartite Cooperation, in most regions
2. Regional Tripartite Commissions on Employment Issues, in all regions
3. Regional Tripartite Councils on Work Conditions, in all regions
4. District Development Councils
5. Collective bargaining for municipal companies and for the local budgetary institutions

IV. Enterprises

1. Collective bargaining
2. Union–Management Commissions for Social Partnership

TABLE 3. *Organizational Structure of Polish Social Dialogue*

I. National Economy

1. **National Tripartite Commission on Socio-Economic Issues**
   A. Plenary Sessions of the National Tripartite Commission on Socio-Economic Issues
   B. Standing Working Groups of the National Tripartite Commission:
      pay and social security
      employment and prevention of unemployment
      social security
      health care
      housing
      culture and education
2. Main Employment Council
3. National Council for Labor Protection
4. Council for Social Assistance
5. Commission on Minimum Payments
6. Supervisory Board of the State Fund for Rehabilitation of Disabled People
7. Council of the Guaranteed Workers' Benefits Fund
8. Supervisory Board of the Social Security Institute
9. Commission on Collective Bargaining Issues
10. Tripartite Commission for Cooperation with the ILO
11. Commission for the Ratification of the European Social Charter (1992–97)
12. EU-Poland Joint Consultative Committee
13. Economic and Social Council (to be established)

II. Industries and Sectors

1. Industry-Wide and Sectoral Tripartite Groups for industries and sectors with heavy restructuring problems (steel, textile, coal mining)
2. Collective bargaining for each industry and sector;

(continued)

TABLE 3. *(continued)*

III. Regions

1. Employment Councils at the levels of province (*voivod*ship), region (*rejon*), municipality (*powiat*)
2. Councils for Regional Restructuring, in regions with heavy restructuring problems
3. Local Commissions for Labor Protection, in all regions
4. Collective bargaining in municipal companies and for the local budgetary institutions

IV. Enterprises

1. Collective bargaining
2. Union–Management Commissions for Social Partnership

References

Adam, Jan. 1999. *Social Costs of Transformation to a Market Economy in Post-Socialist Countries: The Cases of Poland, the Czech Republic and Hungary*. New York: St. Martin's Press.

Albert, Michel. 1993. *Capitalism vs. Capitalism*. New York: Four Wall Eight Windows.

Amsden, Alice H., Jacek Kochanowicz, and Lance Taylor. 1994. *The Market Meets Its March: Restructuring the Economies of Eastern Europe*. Cambridge, Mass.: Harvard University Press.

Anderson, Anthony. 1997. "Europe Faces Challenge of 18 M Unemployed." *European Dialogue* 6 (November–December 1997): 22–23.

Andrain, Charles F., and David E. Apter. 1995. *Political Protest and Social Change: Analyzing Politics*. Washington Square: New York University Press. Pp. 36–48.

Ararski, Vasil, and Ivan Chavdarov. 1990. "Trudovite konflikti i stachnata vylna pres zimata na 1989–1990 godina: Osnovni izvodi" (The Labor Conflicts and the 1989–90 Winter Strike Wave: General Conclusions). *Sindikalna praktika*, no. 5–6: 23–30.

Arato, A. 1981. "Civil Society against the State: Poland 1980–81." *Telos*, no. 47: 23–47.

1981/82. "Empire vs. Civil Society: Poland 1981–82." *Telos*, no. 50: 19–48.

Arato, Andrew. 1990. "Revolution, Civil Society and Democracy: Paradoxes in the Recent Transition in Eastern Europe." Ithaca, N.Y.: Cornell University, Center for International Studies, Cornell Project on Comparative Institutional Analysis.

Atanassova, Elena. 1994. "Contemporary Corporatist Developments in Eastern Europe: The Battle between Past and Future." Paper presented at the XIIIth World Congress of Sociology, University of Bielefeld, July.

Balcerowicz, Leszek. 1999. "Europe Growing Together." In Victoria Curzon Price, Alice Landau, and Richard G. Whitman, eds., *The Enlargement of the European Union: Issues and Strategies*. London and New York: Routledge. Pp. 3–9.

Bankov, Goran. 1994. "State and Problems of Social Dialogue in Bulgaria." Sofia: Ministry of Labor and Social Affairs, 20 September. Mimeo.

Bartlett, David. 1992. "The Political Economy of Privatization: Property Reform and Democracy in Hungary." *East European Politics and Societies* 6, no. 1 (Winter): 73–94.

Beleva, Iskra, Richard Jackman, and Mariela Nenova-Amar. 1995. "Bulgaria." In Simon Commander and Fabrizio Coricelli, eds., *Unemployment, Restructuring, and the Labor Market in Eastern Europe and Russia*. Washington, D.C.: The World Bank.

Bell, Janice, and Tomasz Mickiewicz. 1999. "EU Accession and Labour Markets in the Visegrad Countries." In Karen Henderson, ed., *Back to Europe: Central and Eastern Europe and the European Union*. London and Philadelphia: University College London Press. Pp. 129–50.

Bell, John D. 1986. *The Bulgarian Communist Party from Blagoev to Zhivkov*. Stanford: Hoover Instritution Press.

1998. "Introduction." In John D. Bell, ed., *Bulgaria in Transition: Politics, Economics, Society, and Culture after Communism*. Boulder, Colo.: Westview Press.

Bielasiak, Jack. 1980. "Modernization and Elite Cooptation in Eastern Europe, 1954–1971." *East European Quarterly* 14 (Fall): 345–69.

1997. "Substance and Process in the Development of Party Systems in East Central Europe." *Communist and Post-Communist Studies* 30, no. 1: 23–44.

Bieniasz, Dorota, and Gertruda Uscinska. 1999. *System ubezpieczen spolecznych po reformie*. Warszawa: Instytut Pracy i Spraw Socjalnych.

Blankert, Jan Willem. 1997. "Poland's Integration into the European Union: An Economic Perspective." In Peter-Christian Muller-Graff and Andrzej Stepniak, eds., *Poland and the European Union – Between Association and Membership*. Baden-Baden: Nomos Verlagsgesellschaft. Pp. 301–8.

Bloch, A. 1989. "Entrepreneurialism in Poland and Hungary." *Telos*, no. 79: 95–108.

Bloomfield, Jon. 1979. *Passive Revolution: Politics and the Czechoslovak Working Class, 1945–1948*. New York: St. Martin's Press.

Bochev, Georgi. 1993. "Po pytja na syvremennija sindikalism: Predstavjame vi Sindikalnata federatsija na syobshtenijata" (On the Road of Contemporary Trade Unionism: An Introduction of the Trade Union Federation of Communications). *Sindikalna Praktika* 6: 3–22.

Bogdanova, Rumjana. 1983. "The Political Platform of the 'Zveno' Popular Alliance and the People's Democratic Revolution (September 1944–September 1945)." *Bulgarian Historical Review* 2: 3–21.

Bogdanowicz-Bindert, Christine A., and Jan Czekaj, 1999. "Poland: A Privatization Model That Works." In Sue Faulkner, Jim McLoughlin, and Stanislaw Owsiak, eds., *Polish Transition Ten Years On – Processes and Perspectives*. Aldershot: Ashgate. Pp. 73–118.

Boll, Michael M. 1984. *Cold War in the Balkans: American Foreign Policy and the Emergence of Communist Bulgaria, 1943–1947*. Lexington: University Press of Kentucky.

Borkowska, Stanislawa, and Piotr Bohdziewicz, eds. 1994. *Rynek Pracy w makroregionie Lodzkim: Stan i Perspektiwy* (Labor Market in the Lodz Region: State and Perspectives). Lodz: Lodz University Press.

Bozoki, Andras. 1993. "Hungary's Road to Systemic Change: The Opposition Round Table." *Eastern European Politics and Societies* 7, no. 2: 276–308.

Brada, Josef C. 1991. "The Economic Transformation of Eastern Europe." Mimeo.
Brown, F. 1970. *Bulgaria under Communist Rule*. New York: Praeger.
Brown, J. F. 1988. *Eastern Europe and Communist Rule*. Durham and London: Duke University Press.
Bruszt, Laszlo. 1992. "Transformative Politics: Social Costs and Social Peace in East Europe." *East European Politics and Societies* 6, no. 1: 55–71.
Brzezinski, Zbigniew K. 1967. *The Soviet Bloc: Unity and Conflict*. Cambridge, Mass.: Harvard University Press.
Buchner-Jeziorska, Anna, and Jolanta Kulpinska. 1994. "Social Problems in Restructuring the City of Lodz." In Kazimiera Wodz, ed., *Transformation of Old Industrial Regions as a Sociological Problem*. Katowice: Uniwersytet Slaski and Friedrich Ebert Stiftung. Pp. 214–27.
Bunce, Valerie. 1983. "The Political Economy of the Brezhnev Era: The Rise and Fall of Corporatism." *British Journal of Political Science*, no. 13: 129–58.
1999. *Subversive Institutions: The Design and the Destruction of Socialism and the State*. Cambridge, Eng.: Cambridge University Press.
Bunce, V., and J. M. Echols. 1980. "Soviet Politics in the Brezhnev Era: 'Pluralism' or 'Corporatism'?" In D. R. Kelly, ed., *Soviet Politics in the Brezhnev Era*. New York: Praeger. Pp. 1–26.
Cambalikova, Monika, and Zdenka Mansfeldova. 1997. "Social Partnership in the Czech Republic and the Slovak Republic." *Sociologia* 29, no. 3: 301–14.
Cawson, A. 1985. "Varieties of Corporatism: The Importance of the Meso-Level of Interest Intermediation." In A. Cawson, ed., *Organized Interests and the State*. London: Sage.
Chirot, Daniel. 1980. "The Corporatist Model and Socialism." *Theory and Society* 9, no. 2 (March): 363–81.
Christensen, Paul T. 1999. *Russia's Workers in Transition: Labor, Management, and the State under Gorbachev and Yeltsin*. Dekalb: Northern Illinois University Press.
Clayre, Alasdair, ed. 1980. *The Political Economy of Co-Operation and Participation: A Third Sector*. Oxford, Eng.: Oxford University Press.
Commisso, Ellen. 1991. "Property Rights, Liberalism, and the Transition from 'Actually Existing' Socialism." *East European Politics and Societies* 5, no. 1 (Winter): 180–88.
Cook, Linda J., and Mitchell Orenstein. 1999. "The Return of the Left and Its Impact on the Welfare State in Russia, Poland, and Hungary." In Linda J. Cook, Mitchell A. Orenstein, and Marilyn Rueschemeyer, eds., *Left Parties and Social Policy in Postcommunist Europe*. Boulder, Colo.: Westview Press. Pp. 47–108.
Cox, Terry, and Bob Mason. 1999. *Social and Economic Transformation in East Central Europe: Institutions, Property Relations and Social Interests*. Cheltenham, Eng.: Edward Elgar.
Cox, Terry, and Laszlo Vass. 1998. "Hungary: The Politics of Unions and Employers' Associations." Paper presented at the 1998 Anual Meeting of the American Political Science Association, Boston, 3–6 September.
Crampton, Richard. 1990. "The Intelligentsia, the Ecology and the Opposition in Bulgaria." *World Today* (February): 23–26.
Crampton, R. J. 1997. *A Concise History of Bulgaria*. Cambridge, Eng.: Cambridge University Press.

Dahl, Robert A. 1998. *On Democracy*. New Haven and London: Yale University Press.

Daskalov, Roumen. 1998. "A Democracy Born in Pain." In John D. Bell, ed., *Bulgaria in Transition: Politics, Economics, Society, and Culture after Communism*. Boulder, Colo.: Westview Press. Pp. 9–38.

Daskalova, Nadezhda. 1999. "Ikonomicheskijat i sotzialen syvet – otvarjane na sotzialnija dialog kym grazhdanskoto obshtestvo" (The Economic and Social Council: Expansion of Social Dialogue Towards Civil Society"). *Trud – Information Newsletter of the CITUB*, 3 (May–June), 4–5.

Dawisha, Karen, and Bruce Parrott. 1997. *The Consolidation of Democracy in East-Central Europe*. Cambridge, Eng.: Cambridge University Press.

Deppe, Rainer, and Melanie Tatur. 1994. "Trade Unions in the Transformation Process: Comparative Observations on the Role of Trade-Union Representation in Poland, Hungary, Russia, and in the Territory of the Former GDR." *International Journal of Political Economy* (Summer): 7–38.

Diamond, Larry. 1999. *Developing Democracy: Toward Consolidation*. Baltimore and London: Johns Hopkins University Press.

Diamond, Larry, ed. 1992. *The Democratic Revolution: Struggles for Freedom and Pluralism in the Developing World*. New York: Freedom House.

Diamond, Larry, Juan J. Linz, and Seymour Martin Lipset. 1995. "Introduction: What Makes for Democracy?" In Larry Diamond, Juan J. Linz, and Seymour Martin Lipset, eds., *Politics in Developing Countries: Comparing Experiences with Democracy*. Boulder, Colo.: Lynne Rienner Publishers. Pp. 1–66.

Dimitrov, Mitko. 1996. "Privatization: Its Goals, Progress to Date and Prospects." In Iliana Zloch-Christy, *Bulgaria in a Time of Change: Economic and Political Dimensions*. Aldershot: Avebury. Pp. 107–18.

Dimitrov, Roumen. 1991. "March across the Institutions: Formation of the Bulgarian Opposition, 1989–1991." *Bulgarian Quarterly* 1, no. 2: 43–52.

Dimitrov, Roumen, ed. 1998. *Grazhdanskite organizatsii: definitsija i klasifikatsija* (Civil Organizations: Definition and Classification). Sofia: Development of Civil Society Foundation.

Di Palma, Giuseppe. 1990. *To Craft Democracies: An Essay on Democratic Transitions*. Berkeley: University of California Press.

Donath, Ferenc. 1982. "1956 and Self-Management." *Telos*, no. 53 (Fall): 160–63.

Done, Kevin. 1998. "Currency Board Is a Boost to Stability." *Financial Times*, 8 March, p. 11.

Dragostinov, Marian. 1994. "Reformata v Bulgarskite syobshtenija: S 'malki stypki' kym pazarno orientirani otnoshenija" (The Reform in Bulgarian Communications: With 'Small Steps' Toward Market Oriented Relations). *KPD Informatsionen bjuletin*, no. 3(7) (March): 1 and 6.

Dye, T. R., and H. Zeigler. 1988. "Socialism and Equality in Cross-National Perspective." *PS: Political Science and Politics* 21: 45–57.

Edwards, Michael, and David Hulme, eds. 1992. *Making a Difference: NGOs and Development in a Changing World*. London: Earthscan Publications Ltd.

Ekiert, Grzegorz. 1991. "Democratization Processes in East Central Europe: A Theoretical Reconsideration." *British Journal of Political Science*, no. 21: 285–313.

1998. "Legacies of Struggle and Defeat." In Richard F. Staar, ed., *Transition to Democracy in Poland.* New York: St. Martin's Press. Pp. 15–46.

Ekiert, Grzegorz, and Jan Kubik. 1997. "Collective Protest and Democratic Consolidation in Poland, 1989–93." Pew Papers on Central Eastern European Reform and Regionalism, no. 3. Princeton, N.J.: Center of International Studies, Princeton University.

Ekiert, Grzegorz, and Jan Kubik. 1999. *Rebellious Civil Society: Popular Protest and Democratic Consolidation in Poland, 1989–1993.* Ann Arbor: University of Michigan Press.

Elster, Jon. 1996. "Introduction." In Jon Elster, ed., *The Roundtable Talks and the Breakdown of Communism.* Chicago: University of Chicago Press.

Elster, Jon, Claus Offe, and Ulrich K. Preuss. 1998. *Institutional Design in Post-Communist Societies: Rebuilding the Ship at Sea.* Cambridge, Eng.: Cambridge University Press.

Faulkner, Sue, Jim McLoughlin, and Stanislaw Owsiak. 1999. "Polish Transition Ten Years On: An Introduction." In Sue Faulkner, Jim McLoughlin, and Stanislaw Owsiak, eds., *Polish Transition Ten Years On – Processes and Perspectives.* Aldershot: Ashgate. Pp. 1–4.

Ferner, Anthony, and Richard Hyman, eds. 1998. *Changing Industrial Relations in Europe.* Oxford: Blackwell Publishers.

Ficorov, Ivan. 1996. "Forming the Fatherland Front Policy Towards Private Initiative in Industry (September 1944–September 1945)." *Bulgarian Historical Review*, no. 1: 67–91.

Field, Mark G., ed. 1976. *Social Consequences of Modernization in Communist Societies.* Baltimore: Johns Hopkins University Press.

Fischer, Mary Ellen, ed. 1996. *Establishing Democracies.* Boulder, Colo.: Westview Press.

Fowkes, Ben. 1993. *The Rise and Fall of Communism in Eastern Europe.* New York: St. Martin's Press.

Freeman, Richard B. 1993. "What Direction for Labor-Market Institutions in Eastern and Central Europe?" In Robert Vogt, Bertram Silverman, and Murray Yanowitch, eds., *Double Shift: Transforming Work in Postsocialist and Postindustrial Societies (A U.S.–Post-Soviet Dialogue).* Armonk, N.Y., and London, Eng.: M. E. Sharpe. Pp. 95–125.

Gabor, Istvan. 1978. "The Second (Secondary) Economy." *Acta Oeconomica*, 21: 243–60.

Gerlich, Peter. 1992. "A Farewell to Corporatism." *West European Politics* 15, no. 1 (January): 132—46.

Gidron, Benjamin, Ralph M. Kramer, and Lester M. Salamon, eds. 1992. *Government and the Third Sector: Emerging Relationships in Welfare States.* San Francisco: Jossey-Bass Publishers.

Goodwyn, Lawrence. 1991. *Breaking the Barrier: The Rise of Solidarity in Poland.* New York: Oxford University Press.

Gorzelak, Grzegorz. 1994. "Regional Patterns of Polish Transformation, 1990–2005." In Kazimiera Wodz, ed., *Transformation of Old Industrial Regions as a Sociological Problem.* Katowice: Uniwersytet Slaski and Friedrich Ebert Stiftung. Pp. 70–107.

Gradev, Grigor. 1994. "Bulgaria: Tripartism and Social Pact." Paper presented at the conference "Negotiations as the Way to Social Pact: Experiences, Essence, Partners and Forms," Warsaw, 17–18 October.

Grote, Jurgen R., and Philippe C. Schmitter. 1999. "The Renaissance of National Corporatism: Unintended Side-Effect of European Economic and Monetary Union or Calculated Response to the Absence of European Social Policy?." *Transfer: European Review of Labour and Research* 5, nos. 1–2 (Spring–Summer): 34–63.

Grzymala-Busse, Anna. 1999. "The Dominance of the Weak: Political Party Weakness and Strength in East Central Europe after 1989." Paper presented at the Annual Meeting of the American Political Science Association, Atlanta, Ga., 2–5 September.

Hadley, Roger, and Stephen Hatch. 1981. *Social Welfare and the Failure of the State.* London: George Allen and Unwin.

Haggard, Stephan, and Robert R. Kaufman. 1995. *The Political Economy of Democratic Transitions.* Princeton: Princeton University Press.

Hall, Peter A., and Rosemary C. R. Taylor. 1996. "Political Science and the Three New Institutionalisms." *Political Studies* 44: 936–57.

Harding, Neil. 1984. "Socialism, Society and the Organic Labour State." In Neil Harding, ed., *The State in Socialist Society.* Albany: SUNY Press. Pp. 1–50.

Hart, Jeffrey A. 1992. *Rival Capitalists: International Competitiveness in the United States, Japan, and Western Europe.* Ithaca: Cornell University Press.

Hauslohner, Peter. 1987. "Gorbachev's Social Contract." *Soviet Economy* 31: 54–89.

Hausner, Jerzy, and Witold Morawski. 1994. "Tripartism in Poland." Paper presented at the Roundtable Conference on Tripartism in Eastern Europe, Budapest, 26–27 May.

Hausner, Jerzy, Bob Jessop, and Klaus Nielsen, eds. 1993. *Institutional Frameworks of Market Economies: Scandinavian and Eastern European Perspectives.* Aldershot: Avebury.

Havel, V., et al. 1985. *The Power of the Powerless: Citizens against the State in Central-Eastern Europe.* Armonk, N.J.: Sharpe.

Heidenheimer, Arnold, Hugh Heclo, and Carolyn Adams, eds. 1990. *Comparative Public Policy: The Politics of Social Choice in America, Europe and Japan.* New York: St. Martin's Press.

Heinelt, Hubert, and Randall Smith, eds. 1996. *Policy Networks and European Structural Funds.* Aldershot: Avebury.

Hethy, Lajos. 1994a. "Tripartism in Eastern Europe." In Richard Hyman and Anthony Ferner, eds., *New Frontiers in European Industrial Relations.* Oxford-Cambridge: Blackwell. Pp. 312–36.

1994b. "Tripartism in Public Policy Formulation in Hungary (The 1992 November CRI Agreement)." Paper presented at the Roundtable Conference on Tripartism in Eastern Europe, Budapest, 26–27 May.

1995. "Tripartism and Wage Determination in Hungary: Are Negotiated Wage Policies a Success or a Failure?" In Daniel Vaughan-Whitehead, ed., *Reforming Wage Policy in Albania.* United Nations Development Program, ILO, Ministry of Labor of the Republic of Albania. Pp. 251–69.

Hethy, Lajos, and Robert Kyloh. 1995. "A Comparative Analysis of Tripartite Consultations and Negotiations in Central and Eastern Europe." In Robert Kyloh, ed., *Tripartism on Trial: Tripartite Consultations and Negotiations in Central and Eastern Europe*. Geneva: ILO-CEET.

Holmes, Leslie. 1997. *Post-Communism. An Introduction*. Durham: Duke University Press.

Hristova, Ekaterina. 1961. *Kolektivnijat trudov dogovor v Narodna Republika Bulgaria* (Collective Labor Contract in the People's Republic of Bulgaria). Sofia: Nauka i izkustvo.

Huntington, Samuel. 1991. *The Third Wave: Democratization in the Late Twentieth Century*. Norman: University of Oklahoma Press.

Iankova, Elena A. 1998. "The Transformative Corporatism of Eastern Europe." *East European Politics and Societies* 12, no. 2: 222–64.

2000. "Multi-Level Bargaining in Bulgaria's Return to Capitalism." *Industrial and Labor Relations Review* 54, no. 1 (October): 115–37.

Iankova, Elena A., and Lowell Turner. 2000. "Building the New Europe: Western and Eastern Roads to European Social Partnership." Mimeo.

International Labor Organization (ILO), Central and Eastern European Team. 1994. *The Bulgarian Challenge: Reforming Labour Market and Social Policy*. Budapest: Commission of the European Communities PHARE Program.

Ionescu, Ghita. 1964. *Communism in Rumania, 1944–1962*. London: Oxford University Press.

Istorija na profsajuznoto dvizhenie v Bulgaria (History of Trade Union Movement in Bulgaria) 1973. Sofia: Profizdat.

Isusov, Mito. 1971. *Rabotnicheskata klasa v Bulgaria, 1944–1947* (The Working Class in Bulgaria, 1944–1947). Sofia: Bulgarian Academy of Sciences.

Ivanov, Vassil. 1969. *Sotzialisticheskata revoljutzija i rabotnicheskata klasa v Bulgaria* (Socialist Revolution and the Working Class in Bulgaria). Sofia: Nauka i izkustvo.

Jakubowicz, S. 1988. *Bitwa o samorzad 1980–1981* (The Battle for Self-Management 1980–1981). London: Aneks.

Janowitz, Moris. 1976. *Social Control of the Welfare State*. New York: Elsevier Scientific Publishing.

Jordan, A. G. 1990. "Policy Community Realism versus 'New Institutionalism' Ambiguity." *Political Studies* 38: 470–84.

Jowitt, K. 1971. "The Concepts of Liberalization, Integration, and Rationalization in the Context of Eastern European Development." *Studies in Comparative Communism* 4 (1971): 79–92.

Judt, T. R. 1988. "The Dilemmas of Dissidence: The Politics of Opposition in East-Central Europe." *East European Politics and Societies*, no. 2: 185–241.

Kabaj, Mieczyslaw. 1998. "Searching for a New Results-Oriented Wage Negotiation System in Poland." In Daniel Vaughan-Whitehead, ed., *Paying the Price: The Wage Crisis in Central and Eastern Europe*. New York: St. Martin's Press. Pp. 234–71.

Kamenov, Dimiter, Vassil Mruchkov, Jordan Bliznakov, Yuri Aroyo, Ivan Neikov, and Nedka Koleva. 1996. *Tristranno partnjorstvo* (Tripartite Partnership). Sofia: OKOM High School for Industrial Relations and Management and Plovdiv University "P. Hilendarski."

Kaplan, Frederick I. 1968. *Bolshevik Ideology and the Ethics of Soviet Labor. 1917–1920: The Formative Years*. New York: Philosophical Library.

Kaplan, Karel. 1981. *The Short March: The Communist Takeover in Czechoslovakia, 1945–1948*. London: C. Hurst and Company.

Karl, Terry, and Philippe Schmitter. 1991. "Modes of Transition in Latin America, Southern and Eastern Europe." *International Journal of Social Science* (May): 269–84.

Katzenstein, Peter J. 1978. "Introduction: Domestic and International Forces and Strategies of Foreign Economic Policy." In Peter J. Katzenstein, ed., *Between Power and Plenty: Foreign Economic Policies of Advanced Industrial States*. Madison: University of Wisconsin Press. Pp. 3–22.

1984. *Corporatism and Change: Austria, Switzerland and the Politics of Industry*. Ithaca, N.Y.: Cornell University Press.

1985. *Small States in World Markets: Industrial Policy in Europe*. Ithaca and London: Cornell University Press.

Kemp-Welch, A. 1991. *The Birth of Solidarity*. New York: St. Martin's Press. Pp. 188–99.

Kenney, Padraic. 1997. *Rebuilding Poland: Workers and Communists, 1945–1950*. Ithaca and London: Cornell University Press.

Kirichenko, Olga A., and Pavel M. Koudyukin. 1993. "Social Partnership in Russia: The First Steps." *Economic and Industrial Democracy* 14: 43–54.

Kitschelt, Herbert, Zdenka Mansfeldova, Radoslaw Markowski, and Gabor Toka. 1999. *Post-Communist Party Systems: Competition, Representation, and Inter-Party Cooperation*. Cambridge, Eng.: Cambridge University Press.

Kiuranov, Deyan. 1991. "Political Establishment of the Bulgarian Opposition (January 1988–April 1990)." Paper prepared for the Center for the Study of Constitutionalism in Eastern Europe at the University of Chicago Law School in partnership with the Central European University, April 25, 1991, cited in Juan J. Linz and Alfred Stepan, *Problems of Democratic Transition and Consolidation: Southern Europe, South America, and Post-Communist Europe* (Baltimore and London: Johns Hopkins University Press, 1996), 335.

Kloc, Kazimierz. 1992. "Polish Labor in Transition (1990–1992)." *Telos* 92 (Summer): 139–48.

Kolankiewicz, George, and Paul G. Lewis. 1988. *Poland: Politics, Economics and Society*. London and New York: Pinter Publishers, 1988.

Kolarska-Bobinska, Lena. 1999. "Completed Transformation: Integration into the European Union." Warsaw: Institute of Poblic Affairs.

Konrad, G., and I. Szelenyi. 1979. *The Intellectuals on the Road to Class Power*. Brighton, Sussex: Harvester.

Korbel, Josef. 1959. *The Communist Subversion of Czechoslovakia, 1945–1948*. Princeton: Princeton University Press.

Korbonski, A. 1975. "Liberalization Processes." In C. Mesa-Logo and C. Beck, eds., *Comparative Socialist Systems*. Pittsburgh, Pa.: University of Pittsburgh Center for International Studies.

Kornai, Janos. 1979. *The Economics of Shortage*. Stockholm: Institute for International Economic Studies.

Kovanda, Karel. 1977. "Works Councils in Czechoslovakia, 1945–47." *Soviet Studies* 29, no. 2 (April): 255–69.

Kovrig, Bennett. 1979. *Communism in Hungary: From Kun to Kadar.* Stanford: Hoover Institution Press.

Kramer, Ralph M., Hakon Lorentzen, Willem B. Melief, and Sergio Pasquinelli. 1993. *Privatization in Four European Countries: Comparative Studies in Government-Third Sector Relationships.* Armonk, N.Y.: M. E. Sharpe.

Kubicek, Paul. 1996. "Variations on a Corporatist Theme: Interest Associations in Post-Soviet Ukraine and Russia." *Europe-Asia Studies* 48: 1.

Kuhnle, Stein, and Per Selle, eds. 1992. *Government and Voluntary Organizations: A Relational Perspective.* Aldershot: Avebury.

Kulpinska, Jolanta. 1994. "Changes in Power Structure in the Polish Enterprises and the Process of Transformation Toward Market Economy." In Akihiro Ishikawa, ed., *Market Economy and Social Justice.* Tokyo: Chuo University Press. Pp. 209–16.

1998. "Stosunki przemyslowe w Polsce w perspektywie integracji Europejskiej" ("Industrial Relations in Poland in the Perspective of European Integration"). In Wieslawa Kozek and Jolanta Kulpinska, eds., *Zbiorowe stosunki pracy w Polsce: Obraz zmian.* Warszawa: Wydawnictwo Naukowe Scholar. Pp. 11–25.

Kulpinska, Jolanta, and Wielislawa Warzywoda-Krusynska. 1995. "Social Costs of Transformation," *Economic and Social Transformation in Poland.* Proceedings of the Conference on Econometric and Social Transformation in Poland, Lodz, 22–23 May.

Laba, Roman. 1991. *The Roots of Solidarity: A Political Sociology of Poland's Working-Class Democratization.* Princeton: Princeton University Press.

Lado, Maria. 1996. "Continuity and Changes in Tripartism in Hungary." Mimeo.

1997. "The Changing Role of Tripartism in Hungary." Paper presented at the workshop "Institution Building in the Transformation of Central and Eastern European Societies," Budapest, 5–7 December.

Landau, Luis. 1997. *Poland Country Assistance Review: Partnership in a Transition Economy.* Washington, D.C.: The World Bank.

Lash, Scott, and John Urry. 1987. *The End of Organized Capitalism.* Madison: University of Wisconsin Press.

Lehmbruch, Gerhard. 1979. "Consociational Democracy, Class Conflict and the New Corporatism." In Philippe C. and Gerhard Lehmbruch Schmitter, eds., *Trends Toward Corporatist Intermediation.* Beverly Hills and London: Sage Publications. Pp. 53–62.

1984. "Concertation and the Structure of Corporatist Networks." In John H. Goldthorpe, ed., *Order and Conflict in Contemporary Capitalism.* Oxford, Eng.: Oxford University Press. Pp. 60–80.

Linz, Juan J., and Alfred Stepan. 1996. *Problems of Democratic Transition and Consolidation: Southern Europe, South America, and Post-Communist Europe.* Baltimore and London: Johns Hopkins University Press.

Lipset, Seymour Martin. 1981. *Political Man.* Baltimore: Johns Hopkins University Press.

Lowenthal, Richard. 1970. "Development vs. Utopia in Communist Policy." In Chalmers Johnson, ed., *Change in Communist Systems.* Stanford: Stanford University Press. Pp. 33–116.

MacShane, Denis. 1994. "The Changing Contours of Trade Unionism in Eastern Europe and the CIS." In Richard Hyman and Anthony Ferner, eds., *New Frontiers in European Industrial Relations.* Oxford: Blackwell. Pp. 337–67.

Maier, Charles S. 1984. "Preconditions for Corporatism." In J. Goldthorpe, ed., *Order and Conflict in Contemporary Capitalism.* Oxford: Clarendon Press. Pp. 39–59.

Malle, Silvana. 1985. *The Economic Organization of War Communism, 1918–1921.* Cambridge, Eng.: Cambridge University Press.

March, J. G., and J. P. Olsen. 1984. "The New Institutionalism: Organizational Factors in Political Life." *American Political Science Review* 78: 738–49.

March, James G., and Johan P. Olsen. 1989. *Rediscovering Institutions: The Organizational Basis of Politics.* New York: Free Press.

Marin, Bernd, and Renate Mayntz. 1991. "Introduction: Studying Policy Networks." In Bernd Marin and Renate Mayntz, eds., *Policy Networks: Empirical Evidence and Theoretical Considerations.* Boulder, Colo.: Westview Press. Pp. 11–23.

Markov, Venko. 1994. "Reformata v Bulgarskite syobshtenija: Bulgaria – 3 godini sled nachaloto" (The Reform of Bulgarian Communications: Bulgaria – Three Years After the Beginning). *KPD Informatsionen bjuletin*, no. 7–8: 1 and 7–8.

Marsh, David, and R. A. W. Rhodes. 1992. *Policy Networks in British Government.* Oxford, Eng.: Oxford University Press.

Marszal, Tadeusz. 1991. "Szanse i mozliwosci rozwoju Lodzkiego przemyslu wlokienniczo-odziezowego na tle tendencji rozwojowych we wlokiennictwie swiatowym." Lodz.

Martin, Roderick, Anna Vidinova, and Stephen Hill. 1996. "Industrial Relations in Transition Economies: Emergent Industrial Relations Institutions in Bulgaria." *British Journal of Industrial Relations* 34, no. 1 (March): 3–24.

Mason, Bob. 1995. "Industrial Relations in an Unstable Environment: The Case of Central and Eastern Europe." *European Journal of Industrial Relations* 1, no. 3: 341–67.

Matey, Maria. 1995. "Approximating Polish Labour Law to European Community Standards." In Michal Sewerynski, ed., *Polish Labour Law and Collective Labour Relations in the Period of Transformation.* Warsaw: Ministry of Labour and Social Policy. Pp. 69–87.

Matuchniak-Krasuska, Anna. 1996. "Dylematy tozsamosci zwiazkowej" (Dilemmas of Trade Union Identity). In J. Kulpinska and A. Pilichowski, eds., *Strategie adaptacyjne spoleczenstwa polskiego.* Lodz: University of Lodz Press. Pp. 156–69.

Max, Stanley M. 1985. *The United States, Great Britain, and the Sovietization of Hungary, 1945–1948.* Boulder, Colo.: East European Monographs; New York: Distributed by Columbia University Press.

McCauley, Martin. 1977. *Communist Power in Europe 1944–1949.* New York: Barnes and Noble Books.

Meininger, Thomas A., and Detelina Radoeva. 1996. "Civil Society: The Current Situation and Problems." In Iliana Zloch-Christy, ed., *Bulgaria in a Time of Change: Economic and Politcal Consequences.* Aldershot: Avebury. Pp. 45–73.

Michta, Andrew A. 1997. "Democratic Consolidation in Poland after 1989." In Karen Dawisha and Bruce Parrott, eds., *The Consoldiation of Democracy in East-Central Europe.* Cambridge, Eng.: Cambridge University Press. Pp. 66–108.

Migev, Vladimir. 1997. "The Bulgarian Peasants' Resistance to Collectivization (1948–1958)." *Bulgarian Historical Review* 1: 53–71.

Mikolajczyk, Stanislaw. 1948. *The Pattern of Soviet Domination*. London.

Millard, Frances. 1994. "The Shaping of the Polish Party System, 1989–93." *East European Politics and Societies* 8, no. 3 (Fall): 467–94.

Millard, Frances. 1999. *Polish Politics and Society*. London and New York: Routledge.

Minassian, Garabed. 1999. "Bulgaria and the International Monetary Fund." Paper prepared for an international conference on Accession to the European Union, Sofia, 1 July.

Minchev, Mincho. 1985. "Sotzialnata politika na pyrvoto Otechestvenofrontovsko pravitelstvo, 9 septemvri 1944–mart 1946" (Social Policy of the First Fatherland Front Government, 9 September 1944–March 1946). *Bulletin of the Bulgarian Historical Society* 37 (Sofia): 243–66.

Mirski, Krastyu. 1993. "Reformata v Bulgarskite syobshtenija: Osnovni printsipi, problemi i etapi na razvitie" (The Reform in Bulgarian Communications: Basic Principles, Problems and Stages of Development). *KPD Informatsionen bjuletin* (Sofia: Committee of Posts and Telecommunications), no. 1 (May 1993), 1 and 6.

Morawski, Witold. 1994. "Emerging Patterns of Corporatist Industrial Relations in Poland: Contextual Mechanisms." Paper presented at the conference "Negotiations as the Way to Social Pact: Experiences, Essence, Partners and Forms," Warsaw, 17–18 October.

Morawski, Witold, and Jerzy Hausner. 1994. "Tripartism in Poland." National Reports: Roundtable Conference on Tripartism in Central and Eastern Europe, vol. 2. Budapest, 26–27 May 1994.

Moses, Joel C. 1987. "Worker Self-Management and the Reformist Alternative in Soviet Labor Policy, 1979–85." *Soviet Studies* 39, no. 2 (April): 205–28.

Mruchkov, Vassil. 1993. "Tristrannoto sytrudnichestvo za urezhdane na trudovite otnoshenija v Kodeksa na truda" (Tripartite Cooperation for the Regulation of Labor Relations in the Labor Code). *Syvremenno pravo* 1: 20–27.

Mruchkov, Vassil, Krasimira Sredkova, and Atanas Stoilov. 1993. *Komentar na Kodeksa na truda* (Commentary on the Labor Code). Sofia: CITUB.

Musil, Jiri. 1991. "New Social Contracts: Responses of the State and the Social Partners to the Challenges of Restructuring and Privatization." *Labour and Society* 16, no. 4: 381–99.

Myant, M. R. 1981. *Socialism and Democracy in Czechoslovakia, 1945–1948*. Cambridge, Eng.: Cambridge University Press.

Nemes, Dezso, ed. 1972. *History of the Revolutionary Workers Movement in Hungary, 1944–1962*. Budapest: Corvina Press.

Nielsen, Klaus. 1993. "Pluralism, Corporatism and the Negotiated Economy – Perspectives for Post-Communism." In Jerzy Hausner and Grzegorz Mosur, eds., *Transformation Processes in Eastern Europe: Western Perspectives and the Polish Experience*. Cracow: Institute of Political Studies, Polish Academy of Sciences. Pp. 199–242.

Ogrodzinski, Piotr. 1991. "The Four Faces of Civil Society." Unpublished manuscript, Warsaw, 1991 cited in Juan J. Linz and Alfred Stepan, *Problems of Democratic Transition and Consolidation: Southern Europe, South America, and Post-Communist Europe* (Baltimore and London: Johns Hopkins University Press, 1996).

O'Neil, Michael. 1989. *The Third America: The Emergence of the Nonprofit Sector in the United States*. San Francisco: Jossey-Bass Publishers.

Orenstein, Mitchell. 1996. "The Czech Tripartite Council and Its Contribution to Social Peace." In Attila Agh and Gabriella Ilonszki, eds., *Parliaments and Organized Interests: The Second Steps*. Budapest: Hungarian Center for Democracy Studies.

Osiatynski, Wictor. 1996. "The Roundtable Talks in Poland." In Jon Elster, ed., *The Roundtable Talks and the Breakdown of Communism*. Chicago and London: University of Chicago Press. Pp. 21–68.

Ost, David. 1989. "Toward a Corporatist Solution in Eastern Europe: The Case of Poland." *East European Politics and Societies*, no. 3: 152–74.

1990. *Solidarity and the Politics of Anti-Politics: Opposition and Reform in Poland since 1968*. Philadelphia: Temple University Press.

Panitch, Leo. 1979. "The Development of Corporatism in Liberal Democracies." In Philippe C. Schmitter and Gerhard Lehmbruch, eds., *Trends Toward Corporatist Intermediation*. Beverly Hills and London: Sage. Pp. 119–46.

Pankert, Alfred. 1994. "Preface." In Anne Trebilcock et al., eds., *Toward Social Dialogue: Tripartite Cooperation in National Economic and Social Policy-Making*. Geneva: ILO. P. viii.

Pasic, Najdan, Stanislav Grozdanic, and Milorad Radevic. 1982. *Workers' Management in Yugoslavia: Recent Developments and Trends*. Geneva: International Labour Office.

Pedersen, Ove, Karsten Ronit, and Jerzy Hausner. 1993. *Evolution of Interest Representation and Development of the Labour Market in Post-Socialist Countries*. Cracow: Cracow Academy of Economics.

Pelczynski, Z. A. 1988. "Solidarity and the Rebirth of Civil Society." In J. Keane, ed., *Civil Society and the State*. London: Verso. Pp. 361–81.

Pempel, T. J., and Keiichi Tsunekawa. 1979. "Corporatism Without Labor? The Japanese Anomaly." In Philippe C. and Gerhard Lehmbruch Schmitter, eds., *Trends Toward Corporatist Intermediation*. Beverly Hills and London: Sage Publications. Pp. 231–70.

Perez-Diaz, Victor. 1987. "Economic Policies and Social Pacts in Spain during the Transition." In Ilja Scholten, ed., *Political Stability and Neo-Corporatism*. London: Sage. Pp. 216–46.

Peters, B. Guy. 1999. *Institutional Theory in Political Science: The "New Institutionalism."* London and New York: Pinter.

Petkov, Krastyo. 1994. "Tripartism in Bulgaria: 1990–1994." National Reports: Roundtable Conference on Tripartism in Central and Eastern Europe, vol. 1. Budapest, 26–27 May.

1996. "Partnjoryt v sjanka: strukturnoto prisposobjavane i erosijata na trudovite standarti i sotzialnata zashtita v Tzentralna i Iztochna Evrope" (Shadow Partner: Structural Adjustment and the Erosion of Labor Standards and Social Protection in Central and Eastern Europe). Mimeo.

Petkov, Krastyu, and Grigor Gradev. 1995. "Bulgaria." In John Thirkell, Richard Scase, and Sarah Vickerstaff, eds., *Labour Relations and Political Change in Eastern Europe*. London: UCL Press. Pp. 31–59.

Petkov, Krastyo, and J. E. M. Thirkell. 1991. *Labour Relations in Eastern Europe: Organizational Design and Dynamics*. London and New York: Routledge.

Petkov, Krustyo, Maria Sotirova, Yuri Aslanov, Danail Danailov, Elena Tseneva, and Atanas Stoilov. 1987. *Prehodat kum samoupravlenie v sotzialisticheskite strani* (Transition to Self-Management in the Socialist Countries). Sofia: Profizdat.

Piotrowski, Bartlomiej. 1994. "Trojstronnosc w zarzadzaniu rynkiem pracy" (Tripartism in Administering the Labor Market). In Stanislawa Borkowska and Piotr Bohdziewicz, eds., *Rynek pracy w macroregionie lodzkim: stan i perspectywy (Labor Market in the Lodz Macroregion: State and Perspectives)*. Lodz: Wydawnictwo Uniwersytetu Lodzkiego. Pp. 15–18.

Pliszkiewicz, Marek, and Michal Sewerynski. 1995. "Problemy Reprezentatywnosci w Zbiorowych Stosunkach Pracy w Polsce" ("Representation Problems in Collective Labor Relations in Poland"). Paper presented at the Seminar on the Representativeness of the Social Partners in Industrial Relations, Warsaw, 23–24 May.

Pollert, Anna. 1996. "The Revival of Czech Social Democracy: A New Turn in Central Eastern Europe?" *Labor Focus on Eastern Europe*, no. 54 (Summer): 55–62.

1999. "Trade Unionsim in Transition in Central and Eastern Europe." *European Journal of Industrial Relations* 5, no. 2: 209–34.

Pollert, Anna, and Irena Hradecka. 1994. "Privatization in Transition: the Czech Transition." *Industrial Relations Journal* (March): 52–63.

Polonsky, Antony, and Boleslaw Drukier. 1980. *The Beginnings of Communist Rule in Poland*. London: Routledge and Kegan Paul.

Poznanski, Kazimierz Z. 1996. *Poland's Protracted Transition: Institutional Change and Economic Growth, 1970–1994*. Cambridge, Eng.: Cambridge University Press.

Pravda, Alex. 1973. "Some Aspects of the Czechoslovak Economic Reform and the Working Class in 1968." *Soviet Studies* 25, no. 1 (July): 102–24.

1981. "East-West Interdependence and the Social Compact in Eastern Europe." In Morris Bornstein, Zvi Gitelman, and William Zimmerman, eds., *East-West Relations and the Future of Eastern Europe*. London: Allen and Unwin. Pp. 162–90.

Przeworski, Adam. 1991. *Democracy and the Market*. Cambridge, Eng.: Cambridge University Press. Pp. 136–88.

Raikin, Spas T. 1998. "Bulgaria." In Sabrina P. Ramet, ed., *Eastern Europe: Politics, Culture, and Society since 1939*. Bloomington and Indianapolis: Indiana University Press. Pp. 224–50.

Ramet, Sabrina P. 1991. *Social Currents in Eastern Europe*. Durham and London: Duke University Press.

Ramet, Sabrina P., ed. 1998. *Eastern Europe: Politics, Culture, and Society since 1939*. Bloomington and Indianapolis: Indiana University Press.

Reynolds, Jaime. 1978. "Communists, Socialists and Workers: Poland 1944–48." *Soviet Studies* 30, no. 4 (October): 516–39.

Rhodes, Martin, and Bastiaan van Apeldoorn. 1997. *The Transformation of West European Capitalism?* EUI Working Papers, RSC no. 97/60.

Richardson, J. J., and A. G. Jordan. 1979. *Governing under Pressure: British Politics in a Post-Parliamentary Democracy*. Oxford: Martin Robertson.

Rhodes, R. A. W. 1997. *Understanding Governance: Policy Networks, Governance, Reflexivity, and Accountability*. Buckingham: Open University Press.

Rokkan, S. 1969. "Norway: Numerical Democracy and Corporate Pluralism." In R. A. Dahl, ed., *Political Oppositions in Western Democracies*. New Haven: Yale University Press. Pp. 70–115.

Rothschild, Joseph, and Nancy M. Wingfield. 2000. *Return to Diversity: A Political History of East Central Europe since World War II*, 3rd ed. New York and Oxford: Oxford University Press, 2000.

Rueschemetyer, Marylin, and Sharon L. Wolchik. 1999. "The Return of Left-Oriented Parties in Eastern Germany and the Czech Republic and Their Social Policies." In Linda J. Cook, Mitchell A. Orenstein, and Marilyn Rueschemeyer, eds., *Left Parties and Social Policy in Postcommunist Europe*. Boulder, Colo.: Westview Press. Pp. 109–44.

Salamon, Lester M. 1995. *Partners in Public Service: Government-Nonprofit Relations in the Modern Welfare State*. Baltimore and London: Johns Hopkins University Press.

Salamon, Lester M., and Helmut K. Anheier. 1997. *Defining the Nonprofit Sector: A Cross-National Analysis*. Manchester and New York: Manchester University Press.

Sally, Razeen, and Douglas Webber. 1994. "The German Solidarity Pact: A Case Study in the Politics of the Unified Germany." Manuscript.

Scheuer, Steen. 1998. "Denmark: A Less Regulated Model." In Anthony Ferner and Richard Hyman, eds., *Changing Industrial Relations in Europe*. Oxford: Blackwell. Pp. 146–70.

Schienstock, Gerd, and Franz Traxler. 1994. "Economic Transformation and Institutional Change: A Cross-National Study in the Conversion of Union Structures and Politics in Eastern Europe." *International Journal of Comparative Labour Law and Industrial Relations* (Winter): 313–38.

Schmitter, Philippe C. 1974. "Still the Century of Corporatism?" *Review of Politics* 36 (January): 85–96.

1979. "Modes of Interest Intermediation and Models of Societal Change in Western Europe." In Philippe C. Schmitter and Gerhard Lehmbruch, eds., *Trends Toward Corporatist Intermediation*. Beverly Hills and London: Sage.

1990. "Sectors in Modern Capitalism: Modes of Governance and Variations in Performance." In R. Brunetta and C. Dell'Aringa, eds., *Labor Relations and Economic Performance*, proceedings of the International Economic Association Conference, Venice, Italy. New York: New York University Press.

Schmitter, Philippe C., and Jurgen R. Grote. 1997. *The Corporatist Sisyphus: Past, Present and Future*. European University Institute Working Paper no. 97/4. Badia Fiesolana, Florence: European University Institue.

Schopflin, George. 1977. "Hungary." In Martin McCauley, ed., *Communist Power in Europe, 1944–1949*. New York: Barnes and Noble Books. Pp. 95–110.

Seleny, Anna. 1999. "Old Political Rationalities and New Democracies: Compromise and Confrontation in Hungary and Poland." *World Politics* 51 (July): 484–519.

Seton-Watson, Hugh. 1951. *The East European Revolution*. New York: Praeger.

Sewerynski, Michal. 1995. "Evolution of Polish Labour Law and Collective Labour Relations during the Period of Post-Communist Transformation." In Michal

Seweryński, ed., *Polish Labour Law and Collective Labour Relations in the Period of Transformation*. Warsaw: Ministry of Labour and Social Policy. Pp. 21–50.

Shapiro, L. B. 1977. *The Origin of the Communist Autocracy: Political Opposition in the Soviet State: First Phase 1917–1932*. Cambridge, Mass.: Harvard University Press.

Skilling, H. G. 1988. *Samizdat and an Independent Society in Central and Eastern Europe*. Basingstoke: Macmillan.

Slider, Darrell. 1985. "Reforming the Workplace: The 1983 Soviet Law on Labour Collectives." *Soviet Studies* 37, no. 2 (April): 173–83.

Slomp, Hans, Jacques van Hoof, and Hans Moerel. 1996. "The Transformation of Industrial Relations in Some Central and Eastern European Countries." In Joris Van Ruysseveldt and Jelle Visser, eds., *Industrial Relations in Europe: Traditions and Transitions*. London: Sage. Pp. 337–57.

Smillie, Ian, and Henny Helmich, eds. 1993. *Non-Governmental Organizations and Governments: Stakeholders for Development*. Paris: OECD, 1993.

Sobotka, Elzbieta. 1994. "'Social Dialogue': Assumptions, Realization, Prospects." In *Tripartism and Industrial Relations in Central and Eastern European Countries* (Current State and Prospects). Warsaw: Ministry of Labor and Social Policy. Pp. 13–21.

Sobotka, Elzbieta. 1995. "The Role of the Tripartite Commission for Social and Economic Affairs in the Development of Labour Relations in Poland." In Michal Sewerynski, ed., *Polish Labour Law and Collective Labour Relations in the Period of Transformation*. Warsaw: Ministry of Labour and Social Policy. Pp. 89–105.

Sorensen, Georg. 1998. *Democracy and Democratization: Processes and Prospects in a Changing World*. Boulder, Colo.: Westview Press.

Soskice, David. 1988. "Industrial Relations and Unemployment: The Case for Flexible Corporatism." In J. A. Kregel, E. Matzner, and A. Roncaglia, eds., *Barriers to Full Employment*. New York: St. Martin's Press. Pp. 212–226.

1999. "Divergent Production Regimes: Coordinated and Uncoordinated Market Economies in the 1980s and 1990s." In Herbert Kitschelt, Peter Lange, Gary Marks, and John D. Stephens, eds., *Continuity and Change in Contemporary Capitalism*. New York: Cambridge University Press. Pp. 101–34.

Sotirova, Maria, Elena Tseneva, and Ekaterina Ribarova. 1987. *Stopanskite rukovoditeli, rabotnitzite i profsajuznite dejtzi za predavaneto na sobstvenostta, stopanisvaneto i samoupravlenieto* (Attitudes of Economic Managers, Workers and Trade Union Leaders Toward the Transfer of Ownership, Management and Self-Management). Sofia: Georgi Dimitrov Trade Union Institute at the Central Council of the BTU.

Staniszkis, Jadwiga. 1984. *Poland's Self-Limiting Revolution*. Princeton: Princeton University Press.

1991. *The Dynamics of the Breakthrough in Eastern Europe: The Polish Experience*. Berkeley: University of California Press.

Stark, David. 1992. "Path Dependence and Privatization Strategies in East Central Europe." *East European Politics and Societies* 6, no. 1 (Winter): 17–54.

1996. "Recombinant Property in East European Capitalism." *American Journal of Sociology* 101, no. 4 (January): 993–1027.

Stark, David, and Laszlo Bruszt. 1998. *Postsocialist Pathways: Transforming Politics and Property in East Central Europe.* New York: Cambridge University Press.

Stark, David, and Victor Nee. 1989. "Toward an Institutional Analysis of State Socialism." In Victor Nee and David Stark, eds., *Remaking the Economic Institutions of Socialism: China and Eastern Europe.* Stanford: Stanford University Press. Pp. 1–31.

Stefan, Ioan. 1994. "Industrial Relations and Tripartism in Romania." Paper presented at the Roundtable Conference on Tripartism in Eastern Europe, Budapest, 26–27 May.

Stefancic, David R. 1992. *Robotnik: A Short History of the Struggle for Worker Self-Management and Free Trade Unions in Poland, 1944–1981.* Boulder, Colo.: East European Monographs; New York: Distributed by Columbia University Press.

Stomanjarski, Rumen. 1998. "Vyzmoznosti za investitzii v obshtina Vratza" (Investment Opportunities in the Vratza Municipality). Vratza, 25–26 September.

Streeck, Wolfgang. 1984. "Neo-Corporatist Industrial Relations and the Economic Crisis in West Germany, 1973–1982." In J. Goldthorpe, ed., *Order and Conflict in Contemporary Capitalism.* Oxford: Clarendon Press. Pp. 291–314.

Streeck, Wolfgang, and Philippe C. Schmitter. 1985. "Community, Market, State – and Associations? The Prospective Contribution of Interest Government to Social Order." In Streeck and Schmitter, eds., *Private Interest Government: Beyond Market and State.* Beverly Hills: Sage Publishers. Pp. 1–29.

Synak, Brunon. 1993. "The Polish Society: From Homogeneity to Diversity." In Jacques Coenen-Huther and Brunon Synak, eds., *Post-Communist Poland: From Totalitarianism to Democracy?* Commack, N.Y.: Nova Science Publishers.

Szelenyi, Ivan. 1978. "Social Inequalities in State Socialist Redistributive Economies: Dilemmas for Social Policy in Contemporary Socialist Societies of Eastern Europe." *International Journal of Comparative Sociology* 19, no. 1–2: 63–87.

1979. "Socialist Opposition in Eastern Europe: Dilemmas and Prospects." In Rudolf L. Tokes, ed., *Opposition in Eastern Europe.* Baltimore: Johns Hopkins University Press. Pp. 187–208.

1988. *Socialist Entrepreneurs: Embourgeoisement in Rural Hungary.* Madison: University of Wisconsin Press.

1989. "Eastern Europe in an Epoch of Transition: Toward a Socialist Mixed Economy?." In Victor Nee and David Stark, eds., *Remaking the Economic Institutions of Socialism: China and Eastern Europe.* Stanford, Calif.: Stanford University Press. Pp. 208–33.

Szelenyi, I., and R. Manchin. 1987. "Social Policy under State Socialism: Market Redistribution and Social Inequalities in East European Socialist Societies." In M. Rein, G. Esping-Andersen, and L. Rainwater, eds., *Stagnation and Renewal in Social Policy.* Armonk, N.J.: Sharpe. Pp. 102–39.

Tatur, Melanie. 1993. "Corporatism and Transformation." In Jerzy Hausner and Grzegorz Mosur, eds., *Transformation Processes in Eastern Europe: Western Perspectives and the Polish Experience.* Krakow: Institute of Political Studies, Polish Academy of Sciences. Pp. 255–64.

Thelen, Kathleen A. 1991. *Union of Parts: Labor Politics in Postwar Germany* (Ithaca and London: Cornell University Press).

Thelen, K., and S. Steinmo. 1992. "Historical Institutionalism in Comparative Politics." In S. Steinmo, K. Thelen, and F. Longstreth, eds., *Structuring Politics: Historical Institutionalism in Comparative Analysis*. Cambridge, Eng.: Cambridge University Press.

Thirkell, J.E.M., and Elena Atanassova Tseneva. 1992. "Bulgarian Labour Relations in Transition: Tripartism and Collective Bargaining." *International Labour Review* 131, no. 3: 355–66.

Thirkell, John, Richard Scase, and Sarah Vickerstaff. 1995. "Changing Models of Labour Relations in Eastern Europe and Russia." In John Thirkell, Richard Scase, and Sarah Vickerstaff, eds., *Labour Relations and Political Change in Eastern Europe*. London: UCL Press. Pp. 7–30.

Thompson, E. P. 1991. *Customs in Common*. New York: New Press.

Thompson, Paul, and Franz Traxler. 1997. "The Transformation of Industrial Relations in Postsocialist Economies." In Gerd Schienstock, Paul Thompson, and Franz Traxler, eds., *Industrial Relations between Command and Market: A Comparative Analysis of Eastern Europe and China*. New York: Nova Science Publishers. Pp. 291–314.

Tismaneanu, Vladimir, ed. 1999. *The Revolutions of 1989: Rewriting Histories*. London and New York: Routledge.

Tokes, R. L., ed. 1979. *Opposition in Eastern Europe*. Baltimore: Johns Hopkins University Press.

Tomandl, Theodor, and Karl Fuerboeck. 1986. *Social Partnership: The Austrian System of Industrial Relations and Social Insurance*. Ithaca, N.Y.: ILR Press and New York State School of Industrial and Labor Relations, Cornell University.

Tomaszewski, Jerzy. 1989. *The Socialist Regimes of East Central Europe: Their Establishment and Consolidation, 1944–67*. London and New York: Routledge.

Toskova, Vitka. 1995. "Bulgaria between the USSR and the USA (1944–1946)." *Bulgarian Historical Review* 1: 66–90.

Trebilcock, Anne, ed. 1994. *Towards Social Dialogue: Tripartite Cooperation in National Economic and Social Policy-Making*. Geneva: International Labor Office.

Treu, Tiziano, ed. 1992. *Participation in Public Policy-Making*. Berlin: de Gruyter.

Troxel, Luan. 1993. "Socialist Persistence in the Bulgarian Elections of 1990–1991." *East European Quarterly*, 26, no. 4 (January): 407–30.

Tseneva, Elena. 1988. *Sustojanie na profsajuznata rabota v uslovijata na samoupravlenie na trudovite kolektivi ot gorskoto stopanstvo: Analiz na rezultati ot kompleksno ekspertno izsledvane* (Trade Union Activity under the Conditions of Self-Management of Labor Collectives in the Timber Industry: Analysis of Results from an Expert Survey). Sofia: Federation of Trade Union Organizations from the Timber Industry.

1990. "Konfederatzijata na nezavisimite sindikati v Bulgaria v godinata na nejnoto razhdane: Hronologija na sabitijata" (The Confederation of Independent Trade Unions in Bulgaria in the Year of Its Birth: Chronology of Events). *Sindikalna praktika* 11: 5–40.

1991. *Kolektivnoto trudovo dogovarjane: Sindikalna strategija i taktika* (Collective Bargaining: Trade Union Strategy and Tactics). Sofia: Kak Zhiveem.

1992. "The Reconstruction of Industrial Relations in Bulgaria in a Transition Period to a Market Economy." In Jacques van Hoof et al., eds., *Westbound? Changing Industrial Relations in Eastern Europe.* Amsterdam: SISWO. Pp. 49–72.

Turner, Lowell. 1998. *Fighting for Partnership: Labor and Politics in United Germany.* Ithaca and London: Cornell University Press.

Vago, Bela. 1977. "Romania." In Martin McCauley, ed., *Communist Power in Europe, 1944–1949.* New York: Barnes and Noble Books. Pp. 111–30.

Vinton, Louisa. 1991. "Poland: Disparate Responses to Democracy and the Market." *RFE/RL Report on Eastern Europe* 2, no. 13 (March 29): 29–37.

Wade, Larry L., Alexander J. Groth, and Peter Lavelle, 1994. "Estimating Participation and Party Voting in Poland: The 1991 Parliamentary Elections." *East European Politics and Societies* 8, no. 1 (Winter): 94–121.

Walliamann, Isidor, and Christo Stojanov. 1989. "Social and Economic Reform in Bulgaria: Economic Democracy and Problems of Change in Industrial Relations." *Economic and Industrial Democracy* 10: 361–78.

Webber, Douglas. 1994. "The Decline and Resurgence of the 'German Model': The Treuhandanstalt and Privatization Politics in East Germany." *Journal of European Public Policy* 1, no. 2 (Autumn): 151–75.

Wedel, Janine R. 1998. *Collision and Collusion: The Strange Case of Western Aid to Eastern Europe 1989–1998.* New York: St. Martin's Press.

Williamson, Peter J. 1985. *Varieties of Corporatism.* Cambridge, Eng.: Cambridge University Press.

Williamson, Peter. 1989. *Corporatism in Perspective: An Introductory Guide to Corporatist Theory.* London, Newbury Park, and New Delhi: Sage Publications.

Wojtyla, Jan. 1995. "Social Dialogue in the Process of Regional Restructuring: The Example of Upper Silesia." In Michal Sewerynski, ed., *Polish Labour Law and Collective Labour Relations in the Period of Transformation.* Warsaw: Ministry of Labour and Social Policy. Pp. 107–24.

Wyzan, Michael. 1996. "Stabilization and Anti-Inflationary Policy." In Iliana Zloch-Christy, ed., *Bulgaria in a Time of Change: Economic and Political Dimensions.* Aldershot: Avebury. Pp. 77–106.

Wyzan, Michael L. 1998. "Bulgarian Economic Policy and Performance, 1991–97." In John D. Bell, ed., *Bulgaria in Transition: Politics, Economics, Society, and Culture after Communism.* Boulder, Colo.: Westview Press. Pp. 93–122.

Wyzan, Michael. 1999. "Bulgaria's Economy Anaemic under Currency Board." *RFE/RL Newsline*, 30 August.

Zaev, Z. 1964. "The Struggle of the Bulgarian Working Class against the Sabotage Efforts of the Factory Owners (1944–1947)." *Historical Review* 23: 124–50.

Zubek, Voytek. 1993. "The Fragmentation of Poland's Political Party System." *Communist and Post-Communist Studies* (March): 47–71.

Index

Lightning Source UK Ltd.
Milton Keynes UK
UKOW03n2328090914

238296UK00001B/28/P

9 780521 813143